Preface

The Second World War heralded a pace of change that none could have foreseen, even in 1939. In the space of six years, Great Britain had been catapulted headlong from the era of the biplane into that of the jet and missile. Sir Frank Whittle can lay claim to the birth and development of the turbojet; his company Power Jets Ltd, testing a running prototype as early as 1937. By 1945 the war was over, and the nation found itself dipping a toe into an ocean of new, promising and seemingly unlimitless technology. From this point on, technology moved apace rapidly. Much technology had been gleaned from development work carried out by Germany. Man was flying higher, faster and further than ever before, and had started to seriously look beyond the confines of this planet. The technology was there – the sky really was no longer the limit.

By 1950, Great Britain had tested the world's first jet airliner, the beautiful de Havilland Comet which entered service in 1952. The 1950s also saw the dawn of the 'V-Bomber Force'. These three designs really were the 'stuff of dreams' and captured many a young boy's imagination of the day.

Mention must also be made of the test pilots. The likes of John Derry, Jeffrey Quill, Peter Twiss, Geoffrey de Havilland and 'Bee' Beamont, who achieved an almost superstar status as they vied in competition at the prestigious Farnborough and Paris Air Shows. The Air Speed Record swung to and fro between Britain and the United States. No sooner had one nation broken a standing record, it was smashed by the other, only to be retaken again in as little as a month in some cases. The world's first fixed-wing jet-powered aircraft capable of vertical take off, hover and landing, the Hawker Siddeley Harrier entered service in the late 1960s. The world's first commercial supersonic passenger transport, the Anglo-French Concorde took to the skies in 1969, stunning crowds around the globe.

Sadly though, this rate of development was not to remain, at least not in the United Kingdom, as political interference got in the way. A number of now notorious White Papers on Defence, issued by successive Labour and Conservative governments, curtailed or cancelled so many promising projects. Notable among these was the cancellation in 1966 of TSR.2, which still rankles deeply in many British aviation enthusiasts' minds. Perhaps with more political foresight and less 'intervention', the story would only just be beginning!

We have purposely chosen the first 30 years, The Golden Years, 1945 to 1975, as this was arguably the most exciting period with many wonderful and new types rubbing shoulders with wartime and immediate post-war designs that were utilised for development purposes, making for an eclectic mix of shapes and colour schemes.

Differing from previous Flight Craft book formats, the thrust of this 'Special' is very much on the colour schemes and markings of the aircraft involved, and as such there are many more full colour illustrations included, superbly executed by Mark Rolfe, who has deliberately included many of the lesser types along with those that are perhaps better known, in order to make the coverage as complete as possible. Coupled with Malcolm Lowe's informative background text, we trust that you find our collective efforts of use and interest.

Neil Robinson and Martin Derry

Perhaps epitomising the post-war British Aviation era as much as any other type, the English Electric Lightning was one of the country's success stories. However, even before Lightning single-seat fighters entered service the need for a two-seat training variant was appreciated and so the design of a dual-seat machine commenced in summer 1957. Known as the P.11, it was almost identical to production F.1 Lightnings except that the forward fuselage was widened by 11½ins to accommodate side by side seats and, other than the deletion of the F.1's nose cannon, the P.11 was as operationally capable as the single-seater. Two prototype P.11s were constructed with XL628 flying for the first time on 6 May 1959, and the second, XL629, on 21 October. At some point both were redesignated T.4 in line with the twenty production airframes that followed. This photo shows P.11, XL628, which crashed into the Irish Sea on 1 October 1959 after its fin broke away. Fortunately its pilot managed to eject even though the aircraft was flying supersonically at the time.

British Military Test and Evaluation Aircraft
The Golden Years 1945 - 1975

Above: In 1946 and 1947, Radlett Airfield became the venue of the SBAC show (Society of British Aircraft Constructors – later changed to Society of British Aerospace Companies) prior to the event moving to Farnborough in 1948 where it continues today as a biennial event. Among the 'heavies' on display in this September 1946 photo is the rear of a Bristol Freighter; Avro Lancastrian 'Nene' engine test bed VH742; Handley Page Hastings prototype TE580; Avro Tudor 1 G-AGRE (displaying its new, impressively tall, fin and rudder), with a white Avro Lincoln lying beyond. Nearest the camera is the second De Havilland DH 108, TG/306, which, just days later, on 27 September, broke up during an attempt on the world airspeed record killing its pilot Geoffrey de Havilland Jr. Beyond the DH 108 is DH Vampire F.1 TG285, DH Hornet PX313 and an unidentified DH Mosquito.

The testing of military (and civil) aircraft prior to their introduction into service is a vital task. No aircraft can go to war until it has been thoroughly tested and passed as fully serviceable and safe for day-to-day operation. The systems, equipment, electronics, avionics, weapons (where applicable), and the hundred and one other aspects that make up modern aircraft, all need to be completely and rigorously tested and checked in order to ensure that an aircraft of any type can be safely operated. Similarly, new concepts in aircraft design, aerodynamics or equipment need to be proven before they can be applied to real aircraft designs and manufacture.

In Britain, there is a long and noble tradition in the vital roles of experimentation in to new concepts and products, and in the separate but closely related testing of aircraft, their equipment and weapons. This tradition goes right back to the earliest days of aviation and continues to this day – albeit in a much reduced environment compared to the era that was the heyday of British flight testing in the 1940s, and the decades that followed it during the Cold War years.

As aircraft became more sophisticated and were used for a growing range of activities, so the necessity to properly test and ensure the safety of these aircraft for their occupants and operators gained ever-increasing importance. Allied to this was the need to develop safe and workable new designs and equipment, leading to research and development playing an ever-growing role in the technology of aviation.

These processes matured gradually, and in the early days much of the testing and proving of aircraft designs, their engines and primitive systems, was performed by the pioneer designers and early pilots themselves. The real catalyst was the start of World War One. In Britain, the earliest proper military aviation structure had effectively been born with the organisation of the Royal

Flying Corps (RFC) in April 1912. At almost exactly the same time, a Royal Aircraft Factory was established at Farnborough in Hampshire, and this location subsequently became central to the development of military aviation in Britain.

The Royal Aircraft Factory initially undertook the design as well as the manufacture of aircraft types destined for British military service. However, in the middle of World War One a number of important developments took place that altered these early arrangements and set the scene for the decades that followed in several key areas. Significant amongst these was the official decision to allow the growing aircraft industry outside the military, to increasingly have the primary role of actually developing and building new aircraft types, with the established facilities at Farnborough henceforth increasingly concentrating on research and development (R&D) issues in support of the outside aircraft designers. This set the scene for Farnborough to become a centre of excellence in aviation-related research and development, for which it became world-renowned for many decades to come. In 1918 the Royal Aircraft Factory was renamed the Royal Aircraft Establishment (RAE), a name that was to become famous and synonymous with Farnborough in the following decades.

The first official aircraft specification in Britain arose from the 1916 Cabinet-level Air Board structure to formulate and co-ordinate requirements based upon the needs of the RFC and the Royal Naval Air Service (RNAS). Issued during 1917, the aircraft design that met this requirement, Type A.1(a), was the Sopwith Snipe, which first flew in November 1917, and thus became the first British military aircraft to be designed and manufactured under this new specifications arrangement. Each new specification henceforth defined the requirements for the intended new design, and its layout, expected performance, engine(s), armament and basic equipment.

In the years to come this structure underwent a number of refinements, not least in nomenclature. In 1920 a new numerical notation was introduced, starting with Specification 1/20, (the little-known Bristol Type 37 triplane), then in 1927, role prefix letters were introduced, (starting with Specifications such as R.4/27 for a large multi-engine maritime patrol flying-boat). By World War Two, the established and well-known military specification system was thus in force and included such famous types as the Fairey Swordfish (Specification S.15/33), the Supermarine Spitfire (Specification F.37/34), and the de Havilland Mosquito (Specification B.1/40).

Originally, experimental and evaluation work for the RFC was carried out as a part of the RFC's Central Flying School (CFS) at Upavon in Wiltshire. In December 1914 an Experimental Flight for these purposes was established within the CFS, which was renamed as a Test Flight in the mid-war period. At that time the testing of airborne armament was moved from this Flight to the rather less-populated and more remote Orfordness in Suffolk. In early 1917 the test flight organisation was moved from Upavon to a new airfield at Martlesham Heath near Ipswich. This became known as the Aeroplane Experimental Station, and gradually began to re-absorb the armament testing from Orfordness. The name changed to Aeroplane Experimental Establishment in 1920, and finally, in 1924, the well-known title, Aeroplane and Armament Experimental Establishment (A&AEE) was adopted.

The A&AEE remained at Martlesham Heath throughout the inter-war period, gradually refining and developing its methods and procedures until it too, like Farnborough, became a centre of excellence within the scope of its testing criteria. On the outbreak of World War Two, however, the A&AEE was immediately moved from Martlesham Heath to Boscombe Down in Wiltshire. There the A&AEE grew into a vitally important organisation, and its structure, workforce and flight test organisation expanded massively to cope with the enormous amount of test and evaluation work that it had to carry out in support of Britain's aerial war effort.

Often forgotten, but equally as important as the aircraft, equipment, weapons system or concept that needs to be tested, is the actual person who flies the aircraft that is being tested or is carrying the equipment that is under test. Test pilots are amongst the finest and most capable members of the flying profession. Just as manufacturers require highly skilled and capable test pilots to make the initial flights of their new products, and to test every production example of a particular

type before it is delivered, so the organisations such as the RAE and A&AEE needed equally capable military (or occasionally civilian) pilots to perform their many and diverse tests.

In fact the vast majority of test pilots are, and always have been, military or ex-military pilots, and in Britain a specific organisation was created to train and increase the capabilities of these particularly talented pilots. This was the Empire Test Pilots School (ETPS), which began life in 1943 at Boscombe Down to train eligible skilled pilots for test flying duties within the armed forces and for the wider aircraft industry.

Up to that time, test pilots had learned their trade in a 'hands on' fashion through practical experience. The ETPS at once set very high standards – its first course began in June 1943 – although the ETPS name came into general use in 1944. In subsequent years the school went through a number of relocations, but its high quality of teaching persisted and was subsequently much imitated in other countries. Indeed, in addition to British and Commonwealth pilots, the ETPS itself has also been the centre of excellence for many foreign trainee test pilots as well.

These institutions continued to operate with continuing professionalism as the difficult transition to peace was made in the weeks, months and years after the end of the war. Great impetus was placed in the immediate post-war years in the development of jet engines and the search for safe supersonic flight, which made those years some of the busiest of all. Indeed, with the dawn of the Cold War, flight testing continued to be vitally important in verifying new concepts and weapons, in addition to preparing new designs for frontline service, and it was only with the 'thawing' of the Cold War in the later 1980s and into the 1990s that this situation began to radically change, with down-sizing and 'rationalisation' (cost-cutting) taking its considerable toll of Britain's test establishments, resulting in the closing of some facilities and the commercialisation of others.

Today, aircraft in general, and front-line combat aircraft in particular, have become ever more costly and complex, leading to design and development periods becoming much longer for individual types. At the same time the size of Britain's military services has continued to shrink, leading to far fewer new aircraft types coming into service – and those that are in service being considerably smaller in quantity, while computerisation of some aspects of design and testing have all led to a very different environment in which testing takes place in our own times.

Malcolm V Lowe

Below: This image, centred on Avro York G-AGOA, provides an illustration of the plethora of British aircraft types available to view at Radlett in 1947. It also illustrates something of the sheer vitality of early post-war British aircraft designers and manufacturers.

Chapter 1: The 1945 to 1950 period

Above: Lancastrian 'Ghost' test-bed VM703 'R'. Following service with 231 Squadron and a period of storage at 20 MU, VM703 was delivered to De Havilland in October 1946 to be fitted with two Ghost jet engines with which it first flew on 24 June 1947. In early October 1947, this airframe had Walther rockets fitted in its belly and made its first rocket-assisted take-off on 6 October. VM703 was struck off charge (SOC) on 23 June 1950.

The enormous workload and highly successful test work that was performed by the RAE at Farnborough and by the A&AEE at Boscombe Down, in conjunction with their related units and out-stations, was an important, if often overlooked, contribution that helped significantly towards the Allied victory in 1945. Both organisations had seen a huge growth in their size and workload during the war, and many new concepts and innovations in addition to a large number of aircraft types and sub-types, had been tested and (to one extent or another) successfully put into service. The same was true in the wider sense for Britain's aircraft and component manufacturers themselves.

The wartime period for most aircraft companies had been a time of expansion and success, particularly when compared with the difficult times during the 1930s when many had struggled to survive before substantial orders had started to be placed. The coming of peace, however, brought about many swift changes. Although there were many challenges for the future – not least the myriad developments that jet engine technology promised – there was an inevitable down-sizing almost as soon as the war ended.

Nevertheless, the framework was in place at the end of the war for the creation and testing of new designs and concepts, together with the development and improvement of existing designs. Without doubt, at the end of World War Two Britain possessed one of the world's finest and most important aircraft industries, which was seemingly in good shape to meet the challenges of the post-war world. The industry was a significant

employer in terms of numbers, and several major companies, such as de Havilland and Gloster, were already forging ahead with designs that put them at the forefront of the new jet aircraft technology and manufacture. This happy situation continued to exist for a number of years, and the onset of the Cold War in the immediate post-war years gave considerable impetus to the need for future development. Indeed, these were exciting and forward-looking times for the British aircraft industry, and this was reflected by the large amount of research and development work, allied to a large amount of test flying, that took place in this and the following three decades.

A considerable expansion in the wartime facilities was planned at RAE Farnborough. The intention was to continue the excellent standard and breadth of research and development on a wide range of aviation-related subjects such as aerodynamics, aviation electronics (now simply called avionics), structures, and weapons, that had been so significant during the war. The workforce at Farnborough had peaked at some 6,000 at the height of the establishment's activities in the war years, this figure including technical and development staff in addition to ancillary personnel. In the run-down of some activities as the peace commenced in 1945, this figure was considerably reduced. Some activities, notably the development of piston engines, were closed down altogether not long after the end of the war. However, work on jet engines considerably expanded.

The National Gas Turbine Establishment (NGTE) was set up and located at Pyestock near to the RAE's facilities at Farnborough. This amalgamated some of the development work that had previously been carried out by the relevant engine departments at Farnborough, together with the famous Power Jets Ltd which had been so instrumental in the development of Britain's early jet engines. In April 1946 the overall responsibility for RAE Farnborough was taken on by the new Ministry of Supply, which replaced the wartime Ministry of Aircraft Production. A significant development in 1948 saw Britain's behind-the-scenes research and development centre gain a more open and public face, with the staging of the annual SBAC air display and trade exhibition at the airfield for the first time.

Left: Vickers Wellington II Z8570/G (for Guard) which was used to test the very earliest of British jet engines including the Whittle W2B. Its work done, Z8570/G was SOC on 30 October 1945.

Right: Handley Page Halifax A.9, RT814 'X', belonging to the Transport Command Development Unit. RT814 and RT816 arrived with this unit in December 1946 to replace earlier Halifax airframes with RT814 being used to test drop, among other items, a combined artillery piece and jeep as seen in this 1947 photograph. The drop in this instance was from a height of 8,000ft at 170mph. Ultimately replaced by other types, RT814 later served with the RAE and was eventually SOC on 28 March 1951. (Reportedly, the last active Halifax in RAF service was A.9 RT936 which was written off following an accident on 21 April 1953.)

This was the forerunner of the major biennial international aviation trade fair that takes place at Farnborough in our own times.

The A&AEE at Boscombe Down also saw its the wartime workforce run down due to the end of the war. At the peak of activities during the final months of the war, just over 2,300 military personnel were stationed at Boscombe Down, the majority of these being members of the RAF although forty-eight were Royal Navy personnel. There were over 100 civilians, these including scientists and support staff. In October 1944 there were 142 aircraft assigned to the various test units within the A&AEE. These significant numbers were reduced later in 1945, (only just over fifty aircraft were assigned by mid-1947), but the future of the site itself had been assured late in the war with the intended construction of a long runway and various extended facilities that established the precedent that Boscombe Down would eventually become Britain's chief experimental and testing airfield.

The specific organisation of departments within the A&AEE had already undergone a number of changes and reorganisations over the years. During 1944 three specific divisions were formalised within the A&AEE for the assessment and verification of performance, engineering, and armament. There were also sections for photography, navigation, radio and radar equipment. The actual flight testing was undertaken by four 'trials squadrons', these being A Squadron with specific responsibility for fighters, B Squadron with reference to four-engined aircraft, C Squadron which dealt with naval aircraft, and D Squadron which flew twin-engined and a variety of miscellaneous types. A separate Flight dealt with communications and 'special duties'. This organisational structure was carried into the post-war environment, although a number of changes were incorporated in subsequent years. One of the major changes took place in 1945, with the departure of the Empire Test Pilots School to Cranfield. The stay for the school was brief at this Bedfordshire airfield, however, and in 1947 the ETPS moved to Farnborough.

In addition to the official test work that took place within the particular terms of reference at Farnborough and Boscombe Down and their associated out-stations, much test and development work was also carried out in the wider aircraft

industry. Indeed, a tradition had built up of co-operation between some sections of the industry and the research and development facilities at RAE Farnborough, and this situation continued into the post-war era. In addition, manufacturers that specialised in particular aspects of aviation equipment also tended to perform some of their own flight-testing, often with reference to the personnel at Farnborough, prior to official flight testing at the RAE and A&AEE.

In the years immediately after World War Two, for example, a great deal of flight test work was undertaken by the industry into engine development. A variety of engine test-beds, often utilising large four-engined aircraft such as the Avro Lancaster, were important in the development of jet and turboprop engines during that period. Other companies, such as Martin-Baker with its famous line of ejection seats which were developed from 1944 onwards, also carried out some of their own flight testing. The development of ejection seats was, and still remains, an aspect of aviation technology where Britain literally leads the world. The onset of jet-powered aircraft which were faster than existing piston-engined combat aircraft necessitated the development of a safe and fast means of exiting an aircraft that was in difficulties.

This growing necessity was illustrated by the tragic death of an RAE test pilot in 1944 while flying an early Gloster Meteor. Martin-Baker subsequently started development work that led on to its successful and very widely-used series of ejection seats. Initial flight trials of an early dummy installation were performed by Martin-Baker in May 1945 using a specially-modified Boulton-Paul Defiant that had been loaned to the company through the MAP. The first live firing of a real human was made by one of Martin-Baker's employees who was successfully fired from a Gloster Meteor in July 1946. In subsequent years Martin-Baker continued to use Meteors for test work, flying from the company's immaculate Chalgrove airfield.

Without doubt the performance capabilities of combat aircraft moved ahead in leaps and bounds during the World War Two period, particularly with the development of the jet engine as a viable source of propulsion. By the end of the war the possibility of supersonic flight was starting to dawn. It was a barrier that some fast-flying propeller-driven and early jet aircraft had neared on a number of very dangerous occasions during and after the war, but the advances in aerodynamics and jet

Continued on page 8

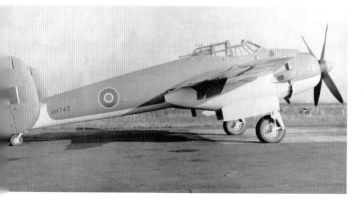

Left: Bristol Brigand TF.1 (Torpedo Fighter 1) RH742 seen on 9 July 1949 with its original heavily-framed cockpit complete with .5in mg. Readers familiar with the Beaufighter TF.10 will no doubt recognise the Brigand as an obvious replacement for its famous forebear. However, in 1946, the need for torpedo-armed aircraft quickly vanished once the Air Staff considered coastal strike aircraft to be obsolescent as post-war defence strategies were re-evaluated. Consequently, the only Brigands completed as TF.1s were RH742 to RH755, although the latter was converted to B.1 standard as indeed were the remainder of the initial order covering 80 airframes. None of the true TF.1s entered operational service, but most served with various establishments including the Air Torpedo Development Unit at some point. RH742 served with the latter as well as at the A&AEE and Empire Central Flying School; it was SOC on 17 June 1954.

Westland Welkin F.I, DX340, possibly based at Westlands aerodrome, Yeovil, Somerset, June 1945
Westland Welkins were designed for high altitude operations and as such were finished in the High Altitude Day Fighter Scheme of Medium Sea Grey upper surfaces to Pattern No 1 with PRU Blue undersides. Red/Blue National Marking Is were applied above wings and on fuselage sides with a matching Red/Blue fin flash. Serials were in black. DX340 was used by Westlands to test the installation of the Rolls Royce Merlin RM16SM engine. Note enlarged chin radiators. .

Reference: *An Industry of Prototypes – Britain's High Altitude Fighter Programme: Welkin and Type 432* by Bill Gunston, Wings of Fame Volume 6 pp 148-157.

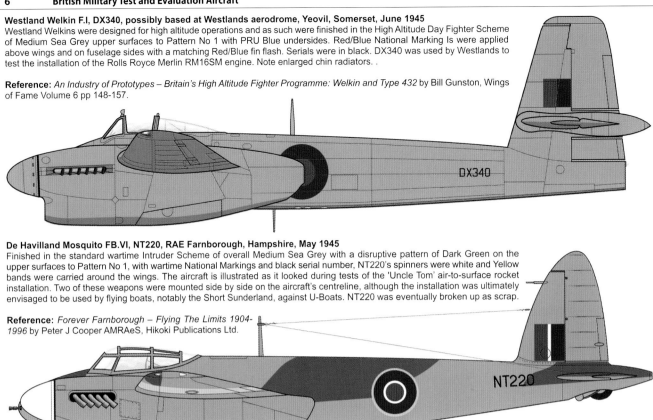

De Havilland Mosquito FB.VI, NT220, RAE Farnborough, Hampshire, May 1945
Finished in the standard wartime Intruder Scheme of overall Medium Sea Grey with a disruptive pattern of Dark Green on the upper surfaces to Pattern No 1, with wartime National Markings and black serial number, NT220's spinners were white and Yellow bands were carried around the wings. The aircraft is illustrated as it looked during tests of the 'Uncle Tom' air-to-surface rocket installation. Two of these weapons were mounted side by side on the aircraft's centreline, although the installation was ultimately envisaged to be used by flying boats, notably the Short Sunderland, against U-Boats. NT220 was eventually broken up as scrap.

Reference: *Forever Farnborough – Flying The Limits 1904-1996* by Peter J Cooper AMRAeS, Hikoki Publications Ltd.

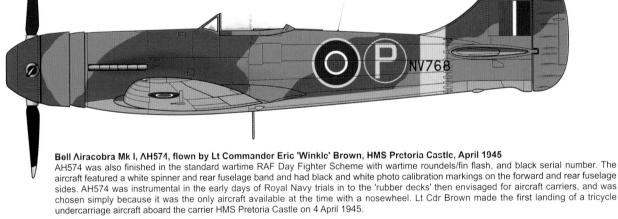

Hawker Tempest Mk V, NV768, flown by Chief Test Pilot Jack Oliver, Napier & Son, mid-1940s
NV768 was finished in the standard wartime RAF Day Fighter Scheme of Dark Green and Ocean Grey with Medium Sea Grey undersides with wartime roundels/fin flash, black serial number and Yellow 'P' marking. The so called 'Annular Tempest' was used by Napier's to test their design of an annular radiator fed through a ducted spinner to improve cooling to the Napier Sabre engine. Initially, Tempest Mk.V, EJ518 was converted to this configuration in 1944, but the aircraft crashed shortly afterwards. In October of the same year, NV768 was converted to the same standards as the previous aircraft. Although both designs proved successful and yielded much valuable information, the piston-engined fighter was in its twilight, and the design was not proceeded with.

References: *Flight* 7 October 1948 'Annular Tempest In The Air – Flying Behind a Napier Sabre with Annular Radiator and Ducted Spinner' by Wing Commander Maurice A Smith, DFC; *Hawker Tempest Mks I, V, II, VI and TT Marks*, by Michael Ovacik and Karel Susa, 4+ Publications.

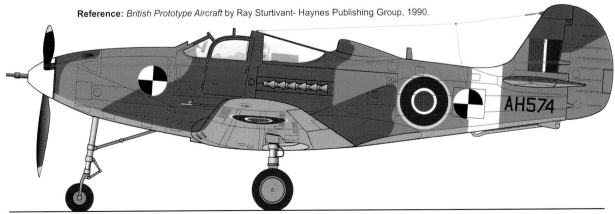

Bell Airacobra Mk I, AH574, flown by Lt Commander Eric 'Winkle' Brown, HMS Pretoria Castle, April 1945
AH574 was also finished in the standard wartime RAF Day Fighter Scheme with wartime roundels/fin flash, and black serial number. The aircraft featured a white spinner and rear fuselage band and had black and white photo calibration markings on the forward and rear fuselage sides. AH574 was instrumental in the early days of Royal Navy trials in to the 'rubber decks' then envisaged for aircraft carriers, and was chosen simply because it was the only aircraft available at the time with a nosewheel. Lt Cdr Brown made the first landing of a tricycle undercarriage aircraft aboard the carrier HMS Pretoria Castle on 4 April 1945.

Reference: *British Prototype Aircraft* by Ray Sturtivant- Haynes Publishing Group, 1990.

Handley Page Halifax C.VIII, PP285, Handley Page Aircraft Ltd, 1945
Finished in an overall highly polished natural metal scheme, something of a rarity on the Halifax, with what appear to be heat tarnished engine cowlings, it carried wartime RAF roundels and fin flashes, which were also applied on the inside faces of the fins, PP285 undertook various trials duties with Handley Page from 1945. The large fairing mounted in the bomb bay was a freight container and appears to have been finished in a medium grey (undercoat?). In all ninety-eight C.VIIIs were built by Handley Page, some later serving with BOAC.

Reference: *Wings of Fame* 'Handley Page Halifax Variants', Volume 8, Aerospace Publishing

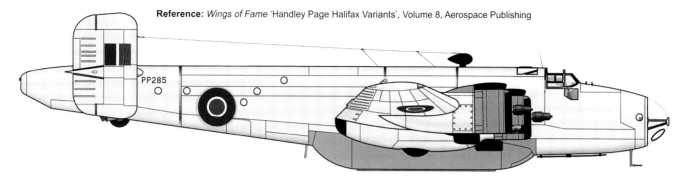

Boeing B-17G Fortress Mk III, HB778/Q, Structures & Mechanical Engineering Flight, Royal Aircraft Establishment, Farnborough, September 1946
HB778 was also in an overall natural metal finish with wartime RAF National Markings. The serials and individual aircraft code letter 'Q' were in red. This aircraft came onto RAE Farnborough's strength from USAAF stocks in March 1945, and was used for a variety of trials, initially with the Wireless Flight, before moving onto S&ME Flight. By this time, the aircraft was starting to look decidedly 'worn', and was sent back to the USAAF's 3rd Air Force in September 1952.

Reference: *Farnborough – 100 Years of British Aviation* by Peter J Cooper, Midland Publishing Ltd.

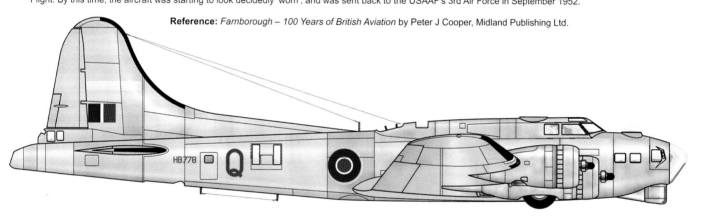

Bell P-63A-9-BE Kingcobra, FZ440 (42-69423), Aerodynamics Flight, Royal Aircraft Establishment, Farnborough, 1946
Two P-63A Kingcobras were used by the RAE, and were allocated the British MAP serials FR408 and FZ440. FR408 was finished in the standard US Olive Drab/Neutral Gray scheme, whereas FZ440, illustrated here, was in the overall natural metal finish, with Olive Drab anti-glare panel, wartime roundels/fin flashes and black serials. Both aircraft were used for high speed laminar flow research. The procedure consisted of coating the inner wing section with a chlorine-reactive chemical, the aircraft was then flown through a chlorine vapour trail dispersed by a second aircraft (initially, this was dispensed from a chimney!) FZ440 was struck off charge, then sold as scrap in 1949.

Reference: *Farnborough – 100 Years of British Aviation* by Peter J Cooper, Midland Publishing Ltd.

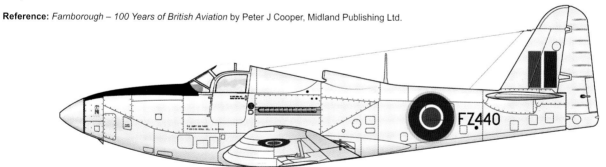

Bristol Brigand TF.1, RH754, A&AEE Boscombe Down, June 1947
Finished in an overall white scheme with wartime roundels/fin flashes, black serials and anti-glare panel, RH754 was used by the A&AEE to test various external weapons installations such as the RP VIII Type 6 rocket projectile as shown here coupled with the Mk IVC gunsight. It is also illustrated carrying a torpedo mounted on the fuselage centreline. RH754 ended its days on the Shoeburyness ranges as a gunnery target.

Reference: *Cold War Years- Flight Testing at Boscombe Down 1945-1975'* by Tim Mason, Hikoki Publications Ltd; *Aeromilitaria No 1*, 1979 'Brigands', Air Britain.

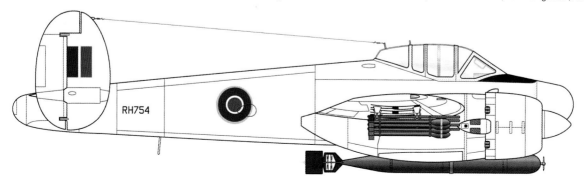

Continued from page 5

propulsion made supersonic flight a significant goal, towards which a number of countries, including Britain, started to work towards.

Eventually Specification E.24/43 was issued (this being one of a comparatively new but increasingly significant selection of 'E'-suffix experimental classification official Specifications) to cover the development of what would be the world's first manned supersonic aircraft, able to fly at some 1,000mph (1,609km/h) at 36,000ft (10,973m) – the Miles M.52.

The small but innovative Miles company was tasked with the development of a research aircraft to this requirement, and it created the M.52 design. With a configuration that partly drew from some aspects of ballistics, the M.52 was a straight wing, streamlined, projectile-like design, with its pilot positioned in the nosecone within a jettisonable container. Powered by an advanced turbojet with the then new concept of an afterburner

planned for the future, unfortunately, after much design work had been performed, the whole project was cancelled by the British government in February 1946. An air-dropped model of the M.52 was successfully launched several years after the M.52's cancellation and much of the M.52's ground-breaking technology was instead passed to the Americans, who used some of the advanced British ideas – such as the all-flying tailplane – on the Bell X-1, which became the first aircraft to 'officially' break the sound barrier in October 1947. This was a crippling blow to Britain's aircraft industry, and it ensured that in the post-war period the Americans would eventually take an unassailable lead in jet fighter design.

The M.52 was, in fact, one of a number of 'own-goals' in the post-war period, many caused by less than wise politicians, that led to an inevitable eventual decline in Britain's pre-eminent position in the aviation world – a reality that was to have very far-reaching effects not only on Britain's aircraft companies, but on the military and on the test establishments as well.

Left: Saunders-Roe SR.A1, TG263 – a twin-jet experimental flying-boat fighter – was the result of a concept brought about by the lack of permanent airfields across vast swathes of the Pacific Ocean while the war against Japan continued. Despite the war's conclusion the concept was pursued and the Saunders-Roe company produced their prototype SR.A1 jet fighters, the first of which, TG263, flew in July 1947 powered by two Metrovick Beryl jet engines. Two further 'boats' were also built, TG267 and TG271, and it was the latter which recorded a maximum speed of 516mph at 20,000ft using slightly more powerful Beryl engines of 3,850lb thrust each (as opposed to 3,500lb). Armament would have included 20mm Hispano cannon for which gun ports were provided in the nose although, reportedly, the guns themselves were never shipped. In this image one of the cannon ports is just visible above TG263's lowered wing float; once sufficient speed had been achieved the floats were retracted (inwards) into the wing to reduce drag. Needless to say, the jet flying-boat fighter concept remained purely experimental.

Left: Vickers Wellington T.10, LN715, which was used to develop the Rolls-Royce Dart engine in connection with Vickers Viscount trials. LN715 was SOC on 5 April 1951.

Below: Seen in March 1948, Gloster E.1/44, TX145, was the result of a 1942 proposal by Glosters for a jet fighter design. TX145 made its first flight in March 1948 and although its acceleration and rate of climb were deemed favourable its general handling characteristics were less so – a consequence of its low-set tailplane which is just visible in this image. This was corrected in the next E.1/44, TX148, but even so, despite both aircraft attaining speeds of 620mph at sea level, their limited development potential when compared to the Meteor meant the end of further development.

Saunders-Roe SR.A1, TG263, flown by Saunders-Roe Chief Test Pilot Geoffrey Tyson, 16 July 1947
With the war against Japan looking to continue beyond 1945, the feasibility of a fighter capable of taking off from, and landing back on water, seemed very attractive to Britain, with the possibility of an island hopping campaign against the Japanese mainland. As a result, Saunders-Roe submitted their design for a twin-jet flying-boat fighter, given the designation SR.44, but officially called called the SR.A1 – and unofficially dubbed 'The Squirt'. In the event, the war was over by August 1945, but the design showed much promise and development continued. Painted overall Aluminium/High Speed Silver finish, with wartime roundels/fin flashes with black serials and Yellow prototype 'P' markings, TG263 was powered by a pair of Metropolitan-Vickers F.2/4 Beryl MVB.1 axial-flow turbojets. The first flight of the SR.A1 took place on 16 July 1947 at the hands of Geoffrey Tyson. Initial tests were promising, despite encountering roll. This was overcome by design modifications to the rudder and tail area. Trials continued until 1951, when the aircraft [now given the Class B registration G-12-1] was sent to the Royal College of Aeronautics at Cranfield. It is interesting to note that one of the engines went on to be used in the late Donald Campbell's Bluebird K7.

Reference: *British Prototype Aircraft* by Ray Sturtivant- Haynes Publishing Group

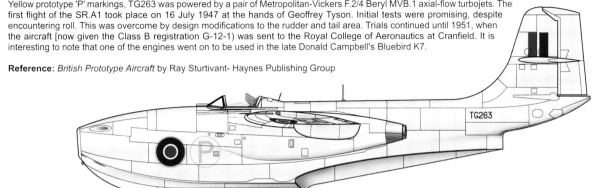

De Havilland Vampire F.3, VF317, A&AEE Boscombe Down, November 1947
Painted overall Aluminium/High Speed Silver finish with Red/Blue National markings and black serials, VF317 was added to the number of Vampires already on the strength of the A&AEE, and was used mainly for radio, IFF (Identification Friend or Foe) tests, arriving at Boscombe Down in November 1947. Note the non-standard presentation of the serial number with a slash between the letters and the numbers – a peculiarity seen on aircraft within this serial batch. Also of note is the non-standard cockpit canopy hood, possibly fitted for jettison test work. VF317's life at Boscombe Down was short though, leaving the establishment in February 1948.

Reference: *Cold War Years – Flight Testing at Boscombe Down 1945-1975'* by Tim Mason, Hikoki Publications Ltd

Vickers Wellington T.10, RP589, A&AEE Boscombe Down, 1948
One of the last Wellingtons in British use, RP589 was still on the strength of the A&AEE at Boscombe Down during 1948, as a navigation trainer. However, the aircraft was found to be wholly unsuitable for this role due to lack of internal space, poor field of view and the type's unsuitability as an astro-navigation trainer. Finish was overall painted Aluminium with post-war Red/White/Blue National Markings, black serial numbers and Yellow fuselage and wing 'trainer' bands.

Reference: *The Cold War Years – Flight Testing at Boscombe Down 1945-1975*, Hikoki Publications.

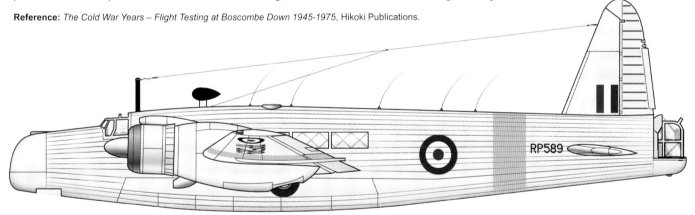

Gloster E.1/44, TX145, Gloster Aircraft Ltd, March 1948
In January 1942, Glosters put forward a proposal to the Ministry of Aircraft Production for a fighter design, gleaning experience learned from their famous E.28/39. A specification was drawn up and work commenced on development. However, it wasn't until July 1947 that SM809, the first flyable prototype, was ready for test. Unfortunately, during the aircraft's journey by road to Boscombe Down, the transporting vehicle was involved in an accident, the result of which SM809 was written off. Production had already begun on TX145, and this was accelerated to get the aircraft into the air as soon as was possible. Painted overall Aluminium/High Speed Silver finish with wartime National Markings, black serial number and Yellow prototype 'P' on the rear fuselage, TX145 made her first flight on 8 March 1948 with Chief Test Pilot Bill Waterton at the controls. Rate of climb and acceleration were favourable, but general handling left much to be desired and a number of modifications were made to the tail and fin (see p14).

Reference: *British Prototype Aircraft* by Ray Sturtivant, Haynes Publishing Group

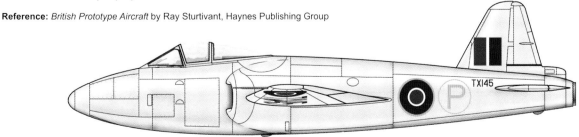

Gloster Meteor F.1, EE227/G, Royal Aircraft Establishment, Farnborough, January 1945
EE227/G was originally with 616 Squadron at Manston from 26 September 1944, coded YQ•Y, but when the unit began to replace its F.1s with F.3s, it was passed onto Farnborough in December 1944. Finished in Ocean Grey and Dark Green upper surfaces with Yellow undersides it had black serials and carried the Fighter Command Sky fuselage band. Fuselage roundels are the wartime style 36 inch diameter National marking IIIs with narrow Yellow surrounds, while those on the wings are the Red/White/Blue, 54 inch diameter National marking IAs (above) and 32 inch diameter National marking IIs (underneath). Of note is that the upper portion of the fin was removed for directional stability trials. It was replaced in February 1945 and the aircraft was sent to Rolls-Royce in March same year and fitted with Rolls-Royce RB.50 Trent turboprops.

Reference: *The Gloster Meteor* by Edward Shacklady, MacDonald Aircraft Monographs

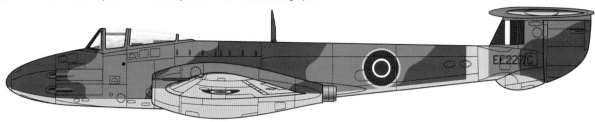

Gloster Meteor F.1, EE227/G, Rolls-Royce Ltd, Church Broughton, September 1945
The same aircraft as that illustrated above, with the fin reinstated and a Prototype 'P' added on the fuselage sides. In March 1945 the aircraft was fitted with two Rolls-Royce RB.50 Trent turboprops, actually modified Derwent turbojets. It was also fitted with lengthened undercarriage legs to clear the propeller arcs. EE227 made its first flight under Trent turboprop power from Church Broughton on 20 September 1945. The pilot was Gloster chief test pilot, Eric Greenwood. Maximum level speed attained was 470mph. It initially flew without endplates fitted to the tailplanes, but directional stability problems led to these being fitted. Flight problems continued and aircraft was subsequently fitted with propellers of reduced diameter (4ft 101/2in). EE227 went to the A&AEE at Boscombe Down for simulated deck landing trials on 18 April 1948. It was converted back to standard F.1 form in May 1948 and ended up at Farnborough, used for fire destruction tests, until being scrapped at end of 1948.

References: *Wings of Fame, Volume 14: Variant Briefing - 'Gloster Meteor Part One:*
Wartime development F.9/40 to F. Mk 4; *The Gloster Meteor* by Edward Shacklady, MacDonald Aircraft Monographs

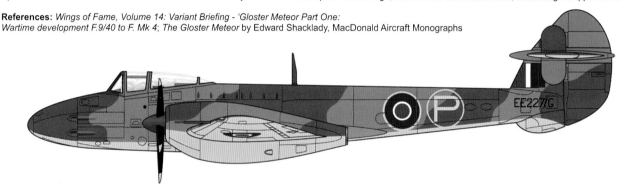

Gloster Meteor F.3, EE348, ZQ•J, Central Fighter Establishment, August 1946
This aircraft was fitted with AI radar (as used on NF.11) by the Central Radar Establishment and tested by the Central Fighter Establishment (CFE). It was finished in the standard wartime RAF Day Fighter Scheme of Dark Green and Ocean Grey with Medium Sea Grey undersides and 18 inch wide Sky rear fuselage band. Wartime National markings were carried, those above the wings being the 54 inch diameter Red/White/Blue National marking IAs, with 32 inch diameter National marking IIs under the wings and National marking IIIs on fuselage sides. The black serial number was positioned in the usual place on the rear fuselage and the CFE's Sky codes (ZQ) and individual aircraft letter (J) were approximately 18 inches high.

References: *Wings of Fame Volume 14 Variant Briefing- 'Gloster Meteor Part One:*
Wartime development F.9/40 to F. Mk 4; *The Gloster Meteor* by Edward Shacklady, MacDonald Aircraft Monographs

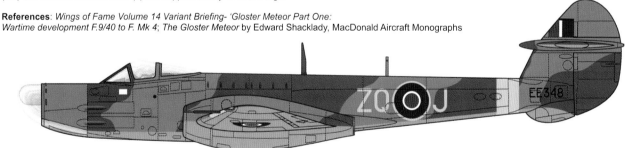

Gloster Meteor F.4, RA490, Gloster Aircraft Ltd, September 1947
RA490 was painted overall Aluminium/High Speed Silver finish with wartime National markings (IAs above, and IIs below, the wings and IIIs on fuselage sides, with matching fin flashes) and black serials. This aircraft was fitted with two Metropolitan-Vickers (MetroVick) F.2/4 Beryl axial-flow turbojets, delivering 3,850lb static thrust. These were the same type as used on Saunders-Roe SR.A1 flying boat fighter (see p9). RA490 only flew with these engines twice. On the second flight it suffered hydraulic failure forcing Gloster test pilot William 'Bill' Waterton to make a wheels-up landing. The aircraft was severely damaged, but was repaired and refitted with two Rolls-Royce Nene turbojets (see next chapter).

Reference: *Wings of Fame Volume 14: Variant Briefing- Gloster Meteor Part One:*
Wartime development F.9/40 to F. Mk 4; *The Gloster Meteor* by Edward Shacklady, MacDonald Aircraft Monographs

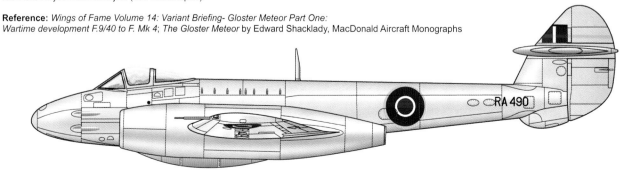

De Havilland 108 Swallow, VW120, flown by De Havilland Chief Test pilot John Derry, Royal Aircraft Establishment Farnborough, April 1948
The De Havilland DH 108 'Swallow' (although 'Swallow' was not officially recognised as the aircraft's name), was developed at the end of World War Two as a response to the growing realisation that the swept wing was the way forward if higher speeds were to be achieved. Three machines were built powered by the Rolls Royce Goblin 2 turbojet, serialled TG283, TG306 and VW120 – illustrated here. This particular aircraft established a new world air speed record of 605.23mph in the hands of Chief Test Pilot John Derry on 12 April 1948, with a further 'first' for Derry on 9 September of the same year, when he became the first British pilot to exceed Mach 1 in a dive from 30,000ft.

Finish was overall natural metal, with Red/White/Blue wartime roundels (National marking IIIs), Red/Blue fin flash, and a Yellow prototype 'P' marking on the rear fuselage.

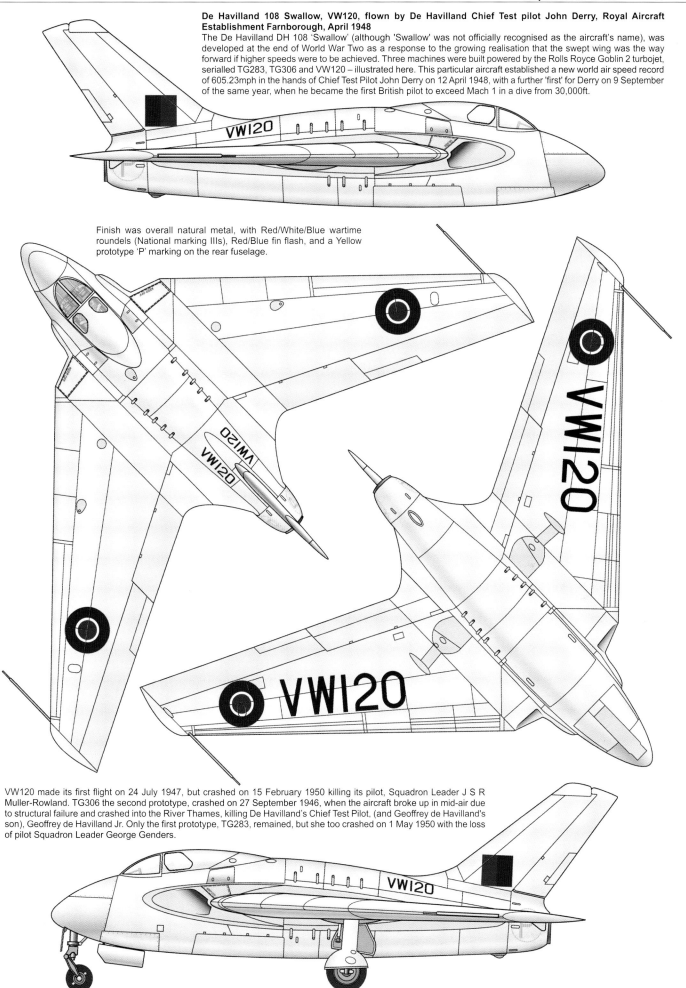

VW120 made its first flight on 24 July 1947, but crashed on 15 February 1950 killing its pilot, Squadron Leader J S R Muller-Rowland. TG306 the second prototype, crashed on 27 September 1946, when the aircraft broke up in mid-air due to structural failure and crashed into the River Thames, killing De Havilland's Chief Test Pilot, (and Geoffrey de Havilland's son), Geoffrey de Havilland Jr. Only the first prototype, TG283, remained, but she too crashed on 1 May 1950 with the loss of pilot Squadron Leader George Genders.

Reference: *British Prototype Aircraft* by Ray Sturtivant, Haynes Publishing Group, 1990 and *Scale Models* magazine November 1981 issue, 'DH 108 Swallow' by Arthur L Bentley.

Above: Handley Page Hastings C.1 prototype TE580 reveals its temporary anhedral tailplane during a series of experiments intended to cure longitudinal instability issues. Tested with a dihedral tailplane too, both configurations ultimately proved unsuccessful and TE580 was restored to its original form. However, C.1 TG502 was used to trial a new horizontal tailplane fitted 16ins lower on the fuselage which did help to improve the instability issues. The modification was applied to later Marks of Hastings but was never applied retrospectively to the C.1s, but TG502 did retain the mod and thus became something of a hybrid.

Left: Of the 300 Lancaster B.IIs built, LL735 was amongst the very last of its Mark to continue flying, that it did so was because it was used to help develop the Metropolitan-Vickers (Metrovick) F.2/4 Beryl jet engine seen extending from the rear fuselage with its distinctive intake above.

Below: First flown on 23 March 1944, LL735 was delivered to the RAE five days later and subsequently fitted with the F.2/4 jet engine. In 1949 a more powerful Metrovick F.2/4 replaced the earlier one, albeit this time mounted in the bomb bay – thus dating these two images to the period 1946 to 1948. LL735 was withdrawn on 31 March 1950 and scrapped.

Armstrong Whitworth AW.52, TS368, Royal Aircraft Establishment, September 1948
TS368 first flew on 1 September 1948 and was placed on static display at that year's SBAC Show at Farnborough, painted in an overall white scheme with black photo-calibration panels. Black serials were carried on the outer faces of the fins and a Yellow prototype 'P' marking on both sides of the nose. This was the second prototype built, the first being TS363, which crashed on 30 May 1949 when it developed uncontrollable flutter at high speed. immediately prior to which test pilot John Lancaster made the first successful ejection seat exit from a British aircraft. TS368 continued with the programme, although its speed was limited to 250 knots. It ended its days on the Shoeburyness ranges as a target.

References: *British Prototype Aircraft* by Ray Sturtivant, Haynes Publishing Group; *Farnborough 100 Years of British Aviation* by Peter J Cooper

Gloster E.1/44, TX148, Gloster Aircraft Ltd, Boscombe Down, January 1949
A second E.1/44 aircraft, serialled TX148, took to the skies in early 1949, again from Boscombe Down, also finished in overall painted Aluminium/High Speed Silver finish with post-war National markings, black serial number, and Yellow prototype 'P' on the rear fuselage. Handling was much improved, and although the design didn't got into series production, the revised tailplane design adopted for TX148 was used on the Meteor F.8. TX145 (see p9) and TX148 carried on test work, with both aircraft eventually being sent to the Proof and Experimental Establishment at Shoeburyness.

Reference: *British Prototype Aircraft* by Ray Sturtivant, Haynes Publishing Group

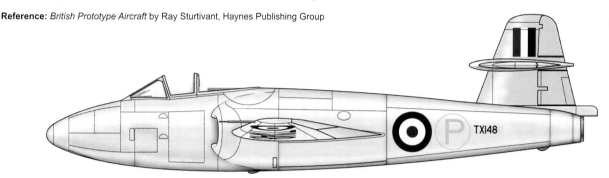

Gloster Meteor F.4, RA435, Rolls-Royce Ltd, April 1949
RA435 was used to test and develop the Derwent 5 engine by Rolls-Royce Ltd, from August 1947. Finished in overall painted Aluminium/High Speed Silver with wartime National markings – IAs above and IIs below the wings and National marking IIIs on the fuselage sides with matching fin flashes – and black serial number on the rear fuselage. From 1 April 1949, the engines were fitted with afterburners, as illustrated. Many test flights included flying only with the starboard afterburner lit. RA435 was passed to Nos 215 and 209 AFSs (Advanced Flying Schools), then to No 2 STT (School of Technical Training) and finally to No 4 STT in June 1955.

References: *The Gloster Meteor* by Edward Shacklady, MacDonald Aircraft Monographs; Meteor – Gloster's First Jet Fighter by Steven J Bond, Midland Counties Publications Ltd

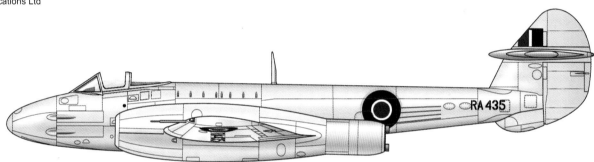

De Havilland Vampire F.2, TG276, A&AEE, Boscombe Down, May 1949
Three Vampires, TG276 (illustrated), TG280 and TX807 were experimentally fitted with the Rolls-Royce Nene turbojet. Because of the engine's larger size and need for increased airflow, two external 'Elephant Ear' intakes were built into the upper fuselage. For obvious reasons, the aircraft was referred to as 'Vampire- Elephant Ears', even in official documentation of the time. Finished in overall painted Aluminium/High Speed Silver, the aircraft carried wartime roundels and fin flashes and black serials on the outer faces of the booms and under the wings.

Reference: *Cold War Years – Flight Testing at Boscombe Down 1945-1975* by Tim Mason, Hikoki Publications Ltd

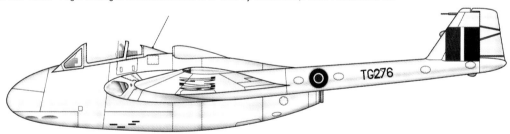

Avro Lincoln B.2, RF561, A&AEE Boscombe Down, 1949
Heavily modified, RF561 was used for radar tests by the A&AEE during the latter half of the 1940s, mainly on behalf of the Telecommunications Research Establishment. Finished in the standard Bomber Command scheme of Dark Green and Dark Earth to Pattern No 2, with the remaining areas in Glossy Anti-Searchlight Black, post-war Red/White/Blue National markings were carried above the wings, on the fuselage sides and all four faces of the the twin fins. The serial numbers on the rear fuselage sides were red, while those under the wings were white. Propeller spinners were red.

Reference: *'Cold War Years – Flight Testing at Boscombe Down 1945-1975'* by Tim Mason, Hikoki Publications Ltd.

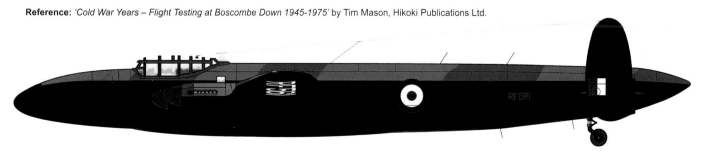

De Havilland Mosquito TT.39, PF606, Boscombe Down, late-1940s
PF606 was used for general radio test and trials work at Boscombe Down. Finished in the post-war Target-Towing Aircraft scheme of painted Aluminium/High Speed Silver upper surfaces, with Yellow under surfaces with black diagonal bands, post-war Red/White/Blue roundels were carried in six positions. No fin flashes were applied. Serials and 'ROYAL NAVY' titles were in black, those under the wing were not compromised by the black diagonal bands which were truncated around the serials. A broad Yellow band was applied around the upper surfaces of the rear fuselage. Note the external IFF and VHF antennae.

Reference: *Cold War Years – Flight Testing at Boscombe Down 1945-1975* by Tim Mason, Hikoki Publications Ltd.

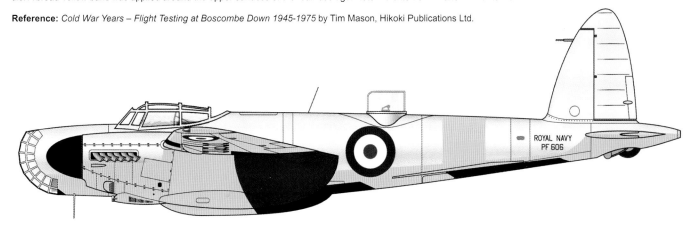

De Havilland Sea Vampire F.21, VG701, used in flexible (rubber) deck trials aboard HMS Warrior, February 1949
VG701 was one of several Vampires used in these trials from December 1947 onwards, although this particular aircraft became affiliated to the programme in July 1948. Finished in Extra Dark Sea Grey upper surfaces with Sky undersides to Pattern No 2, it carried post-war Red/White/Blue roundels in six positions with 'ROYAL NAVY' titles and serials in black on the outer faces of the rear booms, The black 'I' on a white rectangle on the nose is thought to be a photo-calibration marking. VG701 made a series of successful belly landings from 15 February 1948 despite being involved in a minor crash resulting in flap damage. The rubber deck programme continued until at least 1952, when the idea was dropped completely.

Reference: *British Prototype Aircraft* by Ray Sturtivant, HaynesPublishing Group

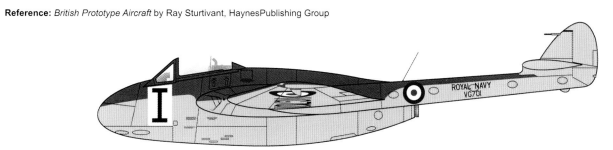

Above: Seen on 9 July 1949, Vampire F.1 TG285, was in the charge of Controller of Supplies (Air) or CS(A). TG285, from the first production batch of Vampire F.1s for the RAF, made its first flight in October 1945 but was almost immediately handed over to RAE Farnborough. In the event, it never served with the RAF and by the time this photo was taken TG285 was undertaking carrier barrier trials. (For RN carriers, a jet-barrier was developed consisting of two horizontal wires stretched across the deck with lengths of flexible fabric stretched vertically between them. This allowed the clean lines of a jet's nose and cockpit to part them before the strips engaged the wings etc., thereby arresting the runaway.) By 23 February 1950, TG285 was involved with unmanned barrier trials which were probably quite destructive as it was SOC in July and later scrapped.

Above: This image illustrates the very first occasion on which the hose and drogue method of refuelling was used to transfer fuel, in flight, between Meteor F.3 EE397 and Lancaster G-33-2 (ex-PB972) on 24th April 1949, in which the Meteor pilot made three link-ups without apparent problems. Four months later the same pilot achieved a record endurance for a Meteor by remaining airborne for a little over 12 hours to prove that this method of in-flight refuelling was viable. The Lancaster's markings 'G-33-2' was a 'B condition' identification rather than a registration with 'G-33' being allocated to Flight Refuelling Ltd on 1 January 1948. (G-33-1 was allocated to Lancaster B.III, ND648.)

Left: With the introduction of jet-powered fighters to the RAF, particularly the Meteor, with their insatiable appetite for fuel, Flight Refuelling Ltd (FRL) continued their pioneering work in testing various methods of in-flight refuelling. Ultimately, in Britain, the probe and drogue method of refuelling became permanently established. This image is believed to have been taken at Staverton, Gloucestershire, where Lancaster B.I, PB972, had arrived in March 1945 presumably as a standard Lancaster which was later extensively modified to help explore the various methods of in-flight refuelling then being trialled.

Above: First flown on 17 March 1944, LZ551, the second DH Vampire prototype (after TG274) became the subject of much interest from the Royal Navy for whom several modifications were made to the airframe. The most obvious in this image is the presence of an arrester hook, less obvious is the 40 per cent increase in flap area and new, long-travel, oleo legs – all necessary for the deck landing trials that commenced aboard HMS Ocean on 3 December 1945, the first occasion on which a solely jet-powered aircraft landed on a carried at sea. Obviously missing is the nose wheel – either it had been retracted or removed entirely – while weights on each tail boom support the airframe. Was this because a lowered nose wheel might foul Ocean's arrester wires before the arrestor hook itself engaged one; or was it to do with the crash barrier given that the barriers then in service were intended to stop propeller-driven runaways and might easily decapitate the pilot of a jet? LZ551 continued to be used for numerous carrier-related trials with many units until, on 15 September 1947, it was sold back to the manufacturers and subsequently preserved.

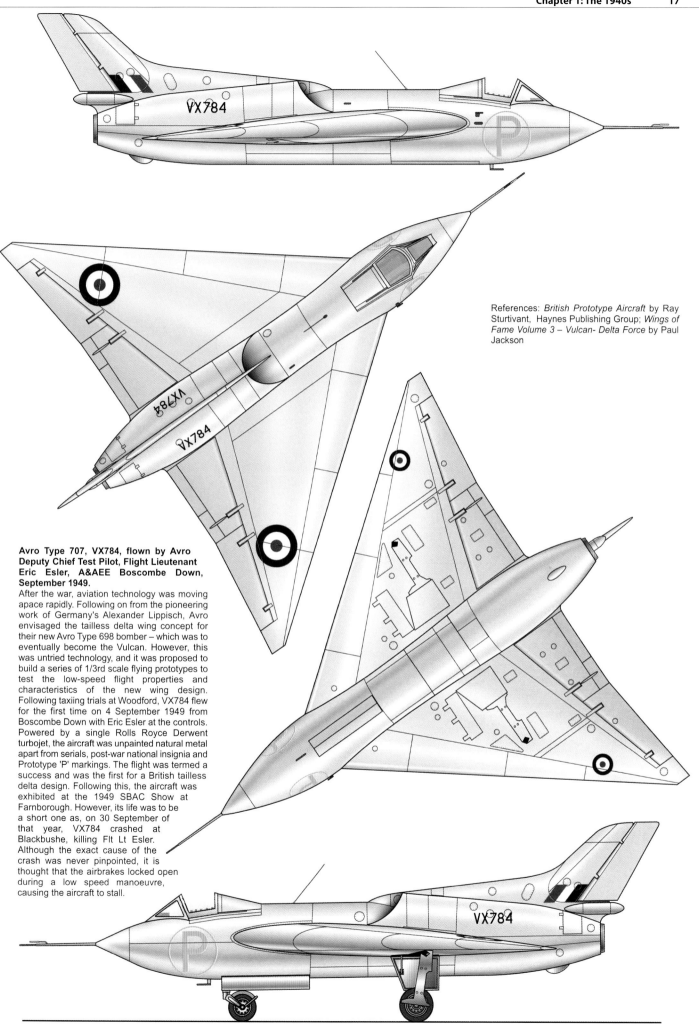

References: *British Prototype Aircraft* by Ray Sturtivant, Haynes Publishing Group; *Wings of Fame Volume 3 – Vulcan- Delta Force* by Paul Jackson

Avro Type 707, VX784, flown by Avro Deputy Chief Test Pilot, Flight Lieutenant Eric Esler, A&AEE Boscombe Down, September 1949.

After the war, aviation technology was moving apace rapidly. Following on from the pioneering work of Germany's Alexander Lippisch, Avro envisaged the tailless delta wing concept for their new Avro Type 698 bomber – which was to eventually become the Vulcan. However, this was untried technology, and it was proposed to build a series of 1/3rd scale flying prototypes to test the low-speed flight properties and characteristics of the new wing design. Following taxiing trials at Woodford, VX784 flew for the first time on 4 September 1949 from Boscombe Down with Eric Esler at the controls. Powered by a single Rolls Royce Derwent turbojet, the aircraft was unpainted natural metal apart from serials, post-war national insignia and Prototype 'P' markings. The flight was termed a success and was the first for a British tailless delta design. Following this, the aircraft was exhibited at the 1949 SBAC Show at Farnborough. However, its life was to be a short one as, on 30 September of that year, VX784 crashed at Blackbushe, killing Flt Lt Esler. Although the exact cause of the crash was never pinpointed, it is thought that the airbrakes locked open during a low speed manoeuvre, causing the aircraft to stall.

Chapter 2: The 1950s

Above: Built to test the tailless delta wing arrangement later to be used by the Avro Vulcan, Avro 707B, VX790, displays the later dorsal intake for its single R-R Derwent jet engine that replaced the original split intakes with which it was equipped for its first flight on 6 September 1950. Initially painted bright blue as seen here, VX790 was later painted overall silver which it retained until withdrawn from use in 1960. VX790 was either scrapped or burnt at Bedford shortly afterwards. (Please see the extensive illustration captions which accompany VX790 and others within the Avro 707 experimental jet series.)

Events such as the Berlin Airlift of 1948 to 1949 and the Korean War of 1950 to 1953, illustrated how 'hot' the Cold War between East and West had rapidly become in the immediate post-war years. The decade of the 1950s was one of significant work in aircraft design and technology in Britain, and this was reflected by the considerable demands of flight testing during that time. Principally involved was much diverse test work by both Farnborough and Boscombe Down and their related test establishments, in addition to considerable work by the wider aircraft industry itself.

A significant related development saw the opening of a new RAE at Bedford, (actually at Thurleigh airfield), as Britain's third but no less vital major official aviation test establishment alongside Farnborough and Boscombe Down. A considerable amount of work that had commenced following the end of World War Two, particularly in response to Allied investigations into German technology, came to fruition in the early 1950s with the increasing readiness of the new and increasingly extensive facilities at Thurleigh. Located just outside Bedford, it had been a USAAF bomber airfield, and it was completely transformed into a major new test establishment in the late 1940s and early 1950s.

As the war in Europe had neared its conclusion, it had become increasingly obvious to Allied scientists and designers that Germany was well ahead of the Allies in many areas of aviation research and development. The Germans had successfully introduced at least two jet-powered aircraft into front-line service by the end of the war – the Messerschmitt Me 262 and the Arado Ar 234 – together with one rocket-powered interceptor – the Messerschmitt Me 163. Many examples of these advanced aircraft and their powerplants were captured by the Allies. A significant number of German aircraft of various types were moved to Farnborough for evaluation, and important test work was carried out on some of them in the immediate post-war period.

A major task for the Allies at the end of the war was the tracking down of organisations and institutions where very advanced research and development had been carried out in Germany during the Nazi era. It was also necessary to locate the scientists and designers who had been associated with the many important and exceptional projects of the German aviation industry. One of the most significant of the German research centres was the *Luftfahrt Forschungsanstalt Hermann Göring* (LFA, Aeronautical Research Institute, also known as the Hermann Göring Research Institute), near Braunschweig (Brunswick). This was a significant research and development organisation, that had carried out a wide range of advanced research and was very well equipped with test facilities. These included wind tunnels, and important sections of the research centre were located underground.

This area of Germany came under British control after the war, and a major effort was duly made to transfer data, scientists, and eventually actual equipment, to Britain. Some of this equipment was eventually set up at the new RAE Bedford site, which was built on a grand scale at considerable expense to the British taxpayer. Indeed there had been a plan at one stage to develop the Bedford location into a 'super airfield', featuring an extremely long runway with the amalgamation of the sites of three former wartime airfields of Thurleigh, Twinwood Farm, and Little Staughton. The resulting research institution would have been named the National Aeronautical Establishment (NAE), but in the event this grand plan was not realised, and RAE Bedford operated as a highly significant out-station to RAE Farnborough during its existence as a flight test centre. Nevertheless it became a major organisation in its own right, and performed important research and development into high-speed flight and allied aerodynamic examination as well as many other related issues.

Originally stationed at Farnborough, its flight test department (Aero Flight) came to operate a number of highly important flight test aircraft from the 1950s onwards, and several specific research departments moved from Farnborough to Bedford during the existence of the latter site. Amongst these was the naval air department.

At Boscombe Down, a number of significant developments took place during the decade. Much of the post-war expansion of the airfield's facilities was completed in the late 1940s and early 1950s, this including the construction of two further runways to go with the original hard runway of the mid-1940s – the access to which was also improved. In 1950 a major organisation moved onto the site with the arrival from RAF Beaulieu in Hampshire of the Airborne Forces Experimental Establishment (AFEE). This unit had originally been formed in 1941 at Ringway, and over the years had become involved in the development of the aerial delivery of all types of airborne cargo. This included paratroops, supplies, and even large loads such as field guns. A great deal of the establishment's work had additionally and vitally been centred on glider development work, with glider-towing by converted four-engined bomber types being particularly important.

On joining the A&AEE from September 1950 onwards, it became one of the establishment's test divisions, and formed a new D Squadron at Boscombe Down. The AFEE was not the only major organisation that came to Boscombe Down during that period, for in July 1956 the final part of the Marine Aircraft Experimental Establishment was absorbed into the A&AEE. This organisation had been associated for many years with Felixstowe, having originally been formed in 1915 as the

Seaplane Experimental Station, and subsequently re-named as the Marine Aircraft Experimental Establishment in April 1924. It had been highly important in the development of military flying-boats and many related marine aircraft functions, but its work finally ran down as Boscombe Down continued its work as the pre-eminent centre for services-related flight testing, evaluation and release for front-line service.

The disastrous decision to cancel the Miles M.52 programme was finally seen, even at the highest levels of government, to have been extremely unwise. Britain eventually embarked during the 1950s, albeit well behind her competitors, on the research necessary to create a viable supersonic front-line combat aircraft. Much of the data obtained from Germany at the end of World War Two proved to be very useful in this quest, and a considerable amount of activity ensued in R&D, design, and the construction of research aircraft to explore possible configurations. This included research into suitable wing planforms, all of which needed to be flight tested. Swept-back wings, crescent-shaped wings and delta shapes became highly significant in subsequent research.

The development of nuclear weapons also created its own requirements for the establishment of a viable airborne nuclear deterrent, resulting in considerable design work and flight testing to find a suitable airborne platform to deliver nuclear weapons. An Advanced Bomber Project Group was formed to aid in the creation of a suitable manned nuclear bomber force, which received much input from RAE Farnborough into possible designs. This eventually led to the successful adoption into front-line RAF service of the Avro Vulcan, Handley-Page Victor, and Vickers Valiant, each one of which dated from official Specifications of the late-1940s after the end of World War Two.

Left: The Supermarine Type 535, VV119, had first flown in March 1950, only at that time it was the Type 528 with a tailwheel undercarriage. Two months later it was grounded prior to receiving a host of changes of which the most obvious was the addition of a nosewheel (while retaining the original twin tailwheel as a 'tail bumper') and, much less obviously, a four foot increase in length plus an afterburner for its Nene engine. VV119, now the Type 535, first flew in its revised form on 23 August 1950 and lit its afterburner for the first time eight days later. Effectively VV119 became the lead-in prototype to the two Avon-powered Supermarine Swift prototypes WJ960 and WJ965, but it's worth noting that some sources insist VV119 was the Swift prototype whilst referring to WJ960 and WJ965 as 'pre-production' Swifts! Historical ambiguities aside, the essential truth for readers 'of a certain age' is that VV119 was, and always will be, Prometheus – the star performer in the 1950's British movie Sound Barrier. VV119's actual fate was less dramatic than that of Prometheus as it became maintenance airframe 7285M at Halton on 23 September 1955 and was later scrapped.

Left: The prototype Venom NF.2 night fighter was first flown as a private venture by the De Havilland company in August 1950 by test pilot John Derry – hence the B condition identification G-5-3. Standard Venom wings and tail booms as fitted to single seat Venoms were married to a new, wider, fuselage accommodating two crewmen side by side for better crew efficiency than that achieved in a tandem seat arrangement. The venture was successful and production orders for the RAF followed. G-5-3 later received the serial WP227 and was sent to the A&AEE for evaluation on behalf of the RN which led to the development of the Sea Venom FAW.20 for the Fleet Air Arm. Its work done, WP227 was grounded and became maintenance airframe 7098M in July (or September) 1953 and was SOC in December 1956.

The decade of the 1950s saw the general adoption of a new system of official Specifications. The procedures that had been put in place with the specifications system of the 1920s finally came to an end during 1949. The last-ever official Specification under that particular system, that led to a production front-line type, was Specification F.23/49. This resulted in the English Electric P.1 series, better known in its production form as the Lightning. The new system that was generally adopted from the early 1950s onwards retained an initial prefix letter, or letters, to denote role or category, but was followed by a simple numbering system that started at 100.

The very first Specification under this new system was Specification ER.100 for a swept-wing research aircraft, which led to the Short SB.5. A suffix letter could also be added to the end of the Specification's designation, to show the progress of the Specification - either at the industry tendering stage ('T'), or the development stage ('D'), or when the manufacture of a prototype had been reached ('P'). By that period the creation of a Specification had become dependant on the issuing of an initial Operational Requirement (OR), or an Air Staff Target (AST), Naval Air Staff Target (NAST), or later a Staff Requirement/Air (SR/A). In fact the whole system of the initial raising of an official requirement by the military had been overhauled in the early 1940s with the inception of Air Publication (AP) 970, which intended to form the guidelines within a single source of all the stages that were required in the creation of a new design – from the initial recognition of the need for a particular type, right through to the service introduction of the ensuing design. This aimed, and partly succeeded, in eliminating time delays and considerable unnecessary paperwork.

The quest for supersonic speed had a number of spin-offs, the most visible of which was the capturing for Britain of the prestigious world air speed record. On 10 March 1956 a Fairey Delta 2 research and trials aircraft (WG774) was flown by Peter Twiss to a new world record speed of just over 1,132mph (1,822km/h) on two runs over a timed course above southern England. This bettered the previous record, achieved by a North American F-100C Super Sabre, by some 310mph (499km/h) – the largest single margin by which the world speed record for aircraft had ever been increased. Although Britain had held speed records before in the post-war period, this particular achievement was a genuine and very positive milestone for Britain's still-great aircraft industry, and it was the first air speed record to exceed the 1,000mph (1,609km/h) barrier.

Unfortunately, in the same way that the Miles M.52 cancellation had been a major disaster in the immediate post-war era, so the 1950s also suffered a milestone catastrophe for the aircraft industry in Britain. In the spring of 1957, the Conservative government's Minister of Defence, Duncan Sandys, proclaimed that all work on future fighter projects would stop after the supersonic English Electric P.1 (Lightning) programme so that ground-to-air missile systems would henceforth provide Britain's air defence – and that manned bombers would no longer be needed in the future.

His plans formed a part of what was to become a notorious White Paper, issued in April 1957, which was one of the most significant in the history of Britain's aviation industry. In effect this unbelievable piece of policy-making by the government of the day spelled complete disaster for important sections of Britain's aircraft industry, as well as for many research and development programmes, and their associated flight testing.

Although fortunately none of Sandys' predictions came true, the damage had been done. It is possible to chart the decline of significant aspects of Britain's aviation infrastructure from the 1960s onwards due to this and subsequent inexplicable official reasoning, as reflected in various subsequent Defence Reviews, which were in effect nothing but significant defence cuts. In the short-term it meant the death of several promising projects, including possible front-line developments of the Fairey Delta 2 design that had successfully gained the world air speed record for Britain in 1956.

Below: Boulton Paul's Nene-powered P.111 was an experimental aircraft designed to explore the characteristics of tailless delta-winged flight. VT935 first flew on 10 October 1950 from Boscombe Down for which flight reports were good although the aircraft was described by one test pilot as '...touchy'! Following a landing accident VT935 was repaired and received various improvements, while a nose probe and a coat of overall gloss yellow paint with a black fuselage cheatline was also applied. Following the accident and subsequent modifications, VT935 was redesignated the P.111A and first flew as such from Boscombe Down on 2 July 1953. VT935, its flying life over, went to the Cranfield College of Aeronautics for use as an instructional airframe in 1958. This photo was taken there some time later, at which time the (removeable) fin tip extension was in situ although the equivalent wing tip extensions, and the nose probe, had been removed.

Boulton-Paul P.111, VT935, RAE Boscombe Down, October 1950
Boulton-Paul's P.111, VT935, first flew on 10 October 1950 from RAE Boscombe Down, with chief test pilot, Squadron Leader Bob Smythe at the controls. Finished in overall High Speed Silver with post-war roundels, black serials on the rear fuselage, black fin tip and anti-glare panel and a Yellow prototype 'P' marking on the nose, it was powered by a single Rolls-Royce Nene RN.2, developing over 5,000lb thrust. Flight reports were generally good, but the aircraft could be taxing to fly. VT935 was involved in a landing accident when the landing gear failed to extend. It was repaired and modified to improve its flight characteristics. These included a redesigned windscreen, undercarriage doors and airbrake configuration, plus the addition of a nose probe. The aircraft was also repainted in overall gloss bright yellow with a black fuselage cheatline – see below. Interestingly, the aircraft had detachable wingtips of three differing designs to allow for comparison between 'square' and 'pointed delta' wingtips – this illustration shows the shorter 'square' version attached.

Reference: *British Prototype Aircraft* by Ray Sturtivant, Haynes Publishing Group

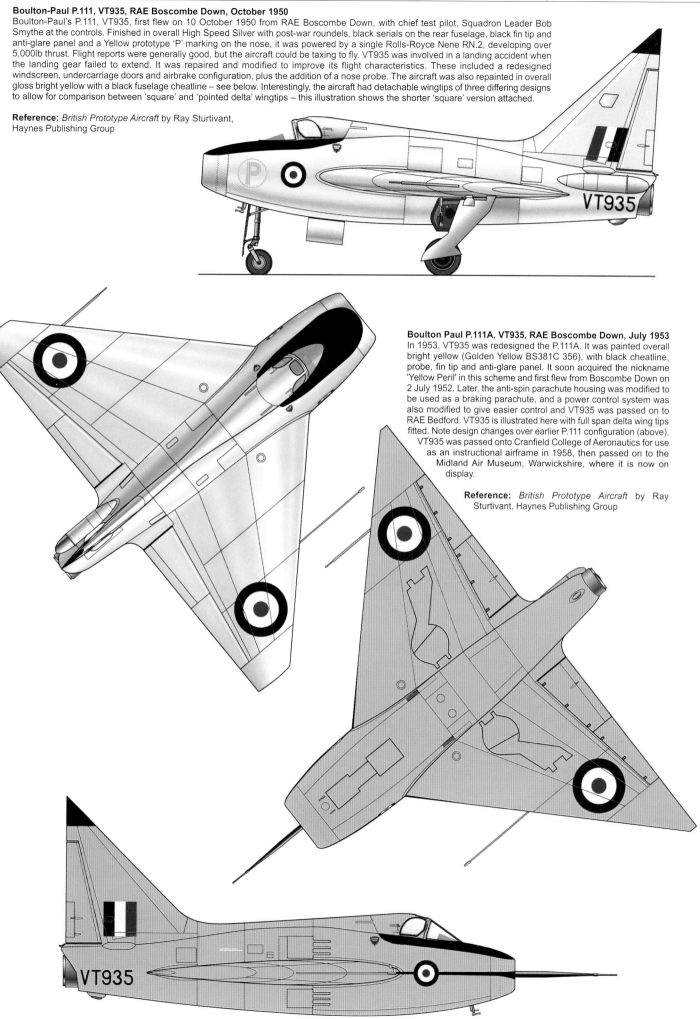

Boulton Paul P.111A, VT935, RAE Boscombe Down, July 1953
In 1953, VT935 was redesigned the P.111A. It was painted overall bright yellow (Golden Yellow BS381C 356), with black cheatline, probe, fin tip and anti-glare panel. It soon acquired the nickname 'Yellow Peril' in this scheme and first flew from Boscombe Down on 2 July 1952. Later, the anti-spin parachute housing was modified to be used as a braking parachute, and a power control system was also modified to give easier control and VT935 was passed on to RAE Bedford. VT935 is illustrated here with full span delta wing tips fitted. Note design changes over earlier P.111 configuration (above). VT935 was passed onto Cranfield College of Aeronautics for use as an instructional airframe in 1958, then passed on to the Midland Air Museum, Warwickshire, where it is now on display.

Reference: *British Prototype Aircraft* by Ray Sturtivant, Haynes Publishing Group

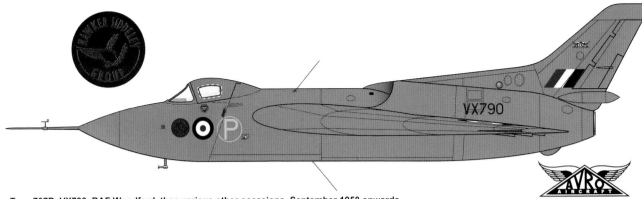

Avro Type 707B, VX790, RAF Woodford, then various other occasions, September 1950 onwards
VX790 was actually the second Avro 707 to fly, taking to the skies on its first flight from RAE Boscombe Down on 6 September 1950 with Avro Chief Test Pilot, Roland 'Roly' Falk at the controls. VX790, which received the 707B designation was some twelve feet longer than first 707, VX784, and incorporated the nose section intended for the still under development Avro 707A (see opposite). Power was again courtesy of a single Rolls Royce Derwent 5, but the new aircraft incorporated a number of changes and improvements. Chief amongst these was a new wing layout with redesigned leading edge sweep, and airbrakes moved from the fuselage to new positions above and below the wings. Initially, the bifurcated engine intake of the original design was retained as can be seen in the top profile, although this gave way to a single NACA-type in February 1951. Problems encountered with airflow disruption caused by the canopy led Avro to re-evaluate the intake design for the 707A. Flight testing from Dunsfold continued until a landing accident on 21 September 1951 forced a return to Woodford for repair. The aircraft spent the rest of its career at Boscombe Down where it was again damaged in a landing accident during September 1956. Thereafter it served at RAE Bedford, where it ended its days as a spares source for Avro 707A WZ736 and the sole Avro 707C WZ744 (see below). Following the British aviation industry's penchant at the time for bright prototype schemes, VX790 was finished overall in a light blue. This gave way to an overall High Speed Silver finish which it retained to its final days. As can be seen, a variety of marking positions and permutations were carried throughout its life, although it is hard to ascertain the precise time periods involved.

References: *British Prototype Aircraft* by Ray Sturtivant, Haynes Publishing Group, 1990; *Avro Aircraft since 1908* by A J Jackson, Putnam Aeronautical Books, 2000 (third edition); *A Short Illustrated History of the Royal Aerospace Establishment Bedford* by Arthur Pearcy, Airlife Publishing 1999; Aeroflight.co.uk.

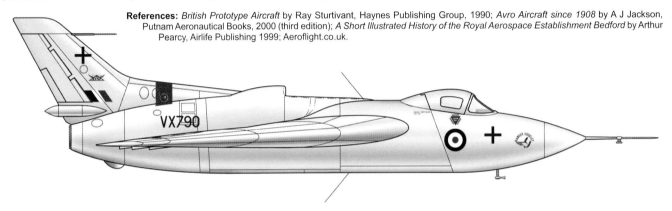

Avro Type 707A, WZ736, Royal Aircraft Establishment, mid-1950s
The second Avro 707A, WZ736, was originally finished in an overall bright orange scheme, and flew from RAF Waddington on 20 February 1953. Although she was never actually involved in the Vulcan programme, she did serve with the Royal Aircraft Establishment undertaking throttle development research. Towards the twilight of its RAE career, WZ736 was painted overall Yellow (BS381C: 356) with black nose cheatline as illustrated here. WZ734 was struck off charge on 19 May 1962 and used as a spares aircraft for Avro 707C, WZ744 (see below).

Avro Type 707C WZ744, Royal Aircraft Establishment, July 1953
This fourth profile shows WZ744, the sole Avro 707C built. Finished in overall natural metal with post-war National markings and black serials and anti-glare panel, it was conceived as a dual-seat conversion trainer, and made its initial flight on 1 July 1953 with Squadron Leader T B Wales at the controls. Two Avro 707Cs were contracted, the other being WZ739, but as the Vulcan proved to be an easy aircraft to convert to, WZ739 was cancelled leaving WZ744 to carry on general test-work with the RAE. Fundamentally, the aircraft was similar to the 707A, the obvious difference being provision for two crew, seated side-by-side, under a Vulcan-esque canopy. WZ744 was passed to RAF Finningley in 1966, and is now on display at the RAF Museum, Cosford.

Reference: *British Prototype Aircraft* by Ray Sturtivant, Haynes Publishing Group

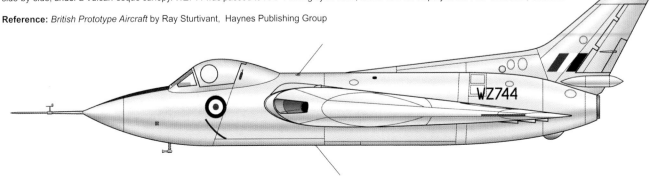

Avro Type 707A WD280, Royal Aircraft Establishment, June 1951 - February 1953
The first Avro 707A, WD280, first flew from Boscombe Down on 14 June 1951. Despite the aircraft's 'A' Type designation, it actually followed the Avro 707B (opposite); that aircraft Type making its maiden flight in September the previous year. However, unlike the Avro 707B, the Avro 707A was designed to explore the high subsonic end of the speed envelope. Studies with the 707B had shown that airflow to the dorsal-mounted engine intake became inefficient at higher speeds due to disruption caused by the canopy. A redesign was undertaken, and the intakes moved to the wing root leading edges as with the Type 698 (Vulcan) prototype.

Initially, WD280 was finished in an overall colour unofficially termed 'Salmon Pink', but this scheme gave way to an overall gloss red as illustrated. On 13 November 1951 an order was placed for three more aircraft; a second 707A, and two side-by-side trainers to be designated 707C, although as related opposite, one of these was later cancelled.

WD280 was fitted with a kinked delta wing as introduced in the later 'Phase Two' Vulcan wing modifications – see ghosted areas at wing leading edges on the plan views.

In 1956, WD280 was passed over to the Australian Aeronautical Research Council (AARC), and transported from Renfrew to Fisherman's Bend, Melbourne, aboard HMAS Melbourne, arriving at RAAF Laverton where she was repainted overall silver and operated by the Aircraft Research and Development Unit (ARDU). WD280 stayed there until she was struck off charge on 10 February 1967 and was sold for £400 to an Australian private collector, Mr Geoffrey Mallett who kept the aircraft in his garden! She was finally bought by the RAAF Museum in 1999, where she is now being restored with the help of Mr Mallett.

Summary of Avro 707 colours
Avro 707: Single aircraft – VX784. Overall unpainted finish.

Avro 707A: Two aircraft – WD280 and WZ736. WD280 was initially painted overall 'Salmon Pink'. Later repainted overall red, followed by overall silver after shipping to Australia.

WZ736 was painted overall orange followed by overall Golden Yellow (BS381C: 356) with black nose flashes. Followed Avro 707B into use.

Avro 707B: One aircraft (built as a replacement for VX784)- VX790 was finished in a bright blue scheme and carried a variety of markings. Later, the aircraft was painted overall silver. Preceded Avro 707A into use.

Avro 707C: Two aircraft commissioned- WZ739 and WZ744. Only WZ744 was built and was finished in overall silver.

References: *British Prototype Aircraft* by Ray Sturtivant, Haynes Publishing Group; *Wings of Fame Volume 3*: 'Vulcan- Delta Force' by Paul Jackson; The RAAF Museum; Aeroflight www.aeroflight.co.uk

Left and below: Powered by a single Rolls Royce Derwent jet engine, these two images show Short SB.5, WG768, which was built to explore the low speed performance of the wing and tail designs proposed by English Electric for use on their P.1 prototype. Initially, WG768 was painted overall High Speed Silver with black undersides until it was repainted overall gloss blue in 1960. The first photo shows WG768 circa 1954 after the tailplane had been relocated from atop the fin to the position shown here, while the second shows the same aircraft circa 1968, possibly just before or soon after its retirement from the Empire Test Pilots School (ETPS) with which it had arrived in 1967 and acquired the code '28'.

Short SB.5, WG768, A&AEE Boscombe Down and ETPS, RAE Farnborough, December 1952 to October 1960

Initially painted overall High Speed Silver with black under surfaces, (see top profile), WG768 was repainted in 1960 in overall gloss blue (bottom profile). Serials for the silver and black scheme were black, whilst those for blue scheme were white. Latterly, the blue scheme carried small RAE crest on nose. The Short SB.5 was constructed to explore the low speed performance of the wing and tail design proposed by English Electric for use on their P.1 prototype. Powered by a single Rolls Royce Derwent turbojet, the aircraft featured a unique characteristic, in that the wing and tailplanes were interchangeable.

Three different wing sweep configurations were available – 50°, 60° and 69°. The tailplane could be high or low-set. The undercarriage was fixed as the aircraft was only intended for low-speed flight. Resplendent in its original silver and black finish, WG768 first flew from A&AEE Boscombe Down on 2 December 1952 with Short's Chief Test Pilot, Tom Brooke-Smith, at the controls. On this occasion, the aircraft flew with 50° wing sweep and a high set tailplane. In the summer of 1953, the wing sweep angle was increased to the 60° option, however the tailplane was left in the 'high' position. The aircraft was then reconfigured to the low-set tailplane position (still with 60° wing sweep) in January 1954, and it carried on flying in this layout until October 1960. WG768 was then fitted with a Martin Baker ejection seat, re-engined with a Bristol Siddeley Orpheus turbojet and repainted in overall gloss blue. By then, she had been relocated to RAE Bedford, and flew with the maximum 69° wing sweep on 18 October 1960. Once the tests were over, WG768 was passed onto the Empire Test Pilots School at RAE Farnborough in 1967, where, coded '28', she carried on flying with the ETPS until 1968. She was placed in storage at Topcliffe, and is now on display at the RAF Museum, Cosford.

Reference: Air Enthusiast 48 'A Tale of Two Tails' by Daniel Ford; Wings of Fame Volume 7 'English Electric Lightning' by Jon Lake; *British Prototype Aircraft* by Ray Sturtivant, Haynes Publishing Group

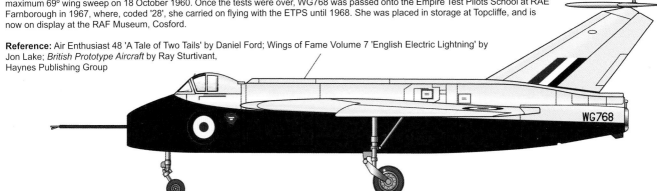

Short SB.5, WG768, A&AEE Boscombe Down and ETPS, RAE Farnborough, December 1952 to October 1960

Initially painted overall High Speed Silver with black under surfaces, (see top profile), WG768 was repainted in 1960 in overall gloss blue (bottom profile). Serials for the silver and black scheme were black, whilst those for blue scheme were white. Latterly, the blue scheme carried small RAE crest on nose. The Short SB.5 was constructed to explore the low speed performance of the wing and tail design proposed by English Electric for use on their P.1 prototype. Powered by a single Rolls Royce Derwent turbojet, the aircraft featured a unique characteristic, in that the wing and tailplanes were interchangeable. Three different wing sweep configurations were available – 50°, 60° and 69°. The tailplane could be high or low-set. The undercarriage was fixed as the aircraft was only intended for low-speed flight. Resplendent in its original silver and black finish, WG768 first flew from A&AEE Boscombe Down on 2 December 1952 with Short's Chief Test Pilot, Tom Brooke-Smith, at the controls. On this occasion, the aircraft flew with 50° wing sweep and a high set tailplane. In the summer of 1953, the wing sweep angle was increased to the 60° option, however the tailplane was left in the 'high' position. The aircraft was then reconfigured to the low-set tailplane position (still with 60° wing sweep) in January 1954, and it carried on flying in this layout until October 1960. WG768 was then fitted with a Martin Baker ejection seat, re-engined with a Bristol Siddeley Orpheus turbojet and repainted in overall gloss blue. By then, she had been relocated to RAE Bedford, and flew with the maximum 69° wing sweep on 18 October 1960. Once the tests were over, WG768 was passed onto the Empire Test Pilots School at RAE Farnborough in 1967, where, coded '28', she carried on flying with the ETPS until 1968. She was placed in storage at Topcliffe, and is now on display at the RAF Museum, Cosford.

Reference: Air Enthusiast 48 'A Tale of Two Tails' by Daniel Ford; Wings of Fame Volume 7 'English Electric Lightning' by Jon Lake; *British Prototype Aircraft* by Ray Sturtivant, Haynes Publishing Group

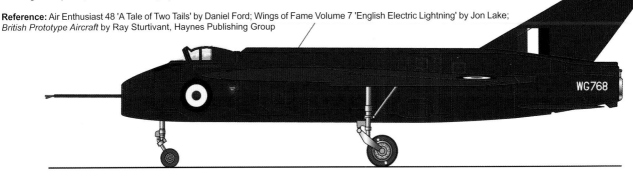

Handley Page HP.88, VX330, RAF Carnaby, June 1951

During World War Two, a crescent wing layout had been proposed for use on the Arado Ar 234 jet bomber, but this never really progressed beyond a single semi-built example. Although the idea generated some interest with the Allies, the concept was not given any further consideration as a viable idea. However, over the course of the initial development stages of the Handley Page Victor bomber, much debate arose concerning the design of the horizontal flight and control surfaces. The crescent wing idea was resurrected, but as it was untested technology, it became necessary to design and build a scale prototype to ascertain the flying qualities of the new wing. In order to save time and money, the Supermarine Attacker was used as a platform with certain aspects of the Swift incorporated, notably the fuel system and wing roots. A flying prototype was built to Air Ministry Specification E.6/48, by General Aircraft Ltd, by then owned by Blackburn Aircraft Ltd. Serialled VX330, the aircraft was finally ready for taxiing tests at Blackburn's Brough factory in February 1950. However, this date was pushed back to June the following year, due to the aircraft being damaged during transportation. Upon successful completion of these trials, VX330 took to the air for the first time on 21 June 1951 with Blackburn chief test pilot Gartrell Richard Ian 'Sailor' Parker at the controls. From the outset, the aircraft displayed longitudinal stability problems, although these were gradually overcome by the time of the seventeenth flight, on 5 August. VX330 was due to make an appearance at that year's SBAC show, but during a calibration flight test, she broke up killing Handley Page test pilot Duggie Broomfield. In spite of this, the design was found to be basically sound. The crash did little to hamper the Victor programme, with much useful information gained from the HP.88 tests. VX330 is shown here at the time of her first flight, resplendent in her attractive overall Royal Blue scheme with post-war National markings and white serials.

Reference: *British Prototype Aircraft* by Ray Sturtivant, Haynes Publishing Group, 1990. Flight International 19 June, 1969

Supermarine Type 508, VX133, A&AEE Boscombe Down, August 1951

The Supermarine Type 508 was developed from the Supermarine Type 505, which was planned for the 'flexible deck' theory, (of belly landing on the deck of a standard carrier on to a mat of thick rubber which was found to be impractical), and never flew. The 505 was redesigned with a standard tricycle undercarriage layout and re-designated Type 508. Finished in overall natural metal, with 32 inch diameter roundels on the fuselage and wing upper and lower surfaces, 4 inch high black serial number on the rear fuselage and 24 inch high under the wings, VX133 was powered by two AJ.65 turbojets and first flew from Boscombe Down on 31 August 1951 with Vickers Supermarine Chief Test Pilot Michael John 'Mike' Lithgow at the controls. The most radical aspect of the aircraft was the use of a V-tail arrangement to allow a more rigid construction, and to ensure that the horizontal tail surfaces were out of the way of the exhausts. Initially, the aircraft experienced a number of problems although these were gradually overcome and VX133 continued to conduct tests from not only Boscombe Down, but Chilbolton, Thurleigh (Bedford) and aboard the carriers HMS Eagle and HMS Bulwark for deck landing trials, and aboard HMS Centaur for hangar door tests. VX133 ended her days at RNAS Culdrose and was later sent to the Predannack fire dump.

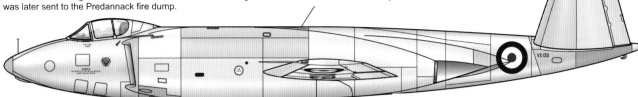

Inset: Supermarine Type 529 VX136 rear fuselage section showing dorsal strakes

Essentially similar to VX133, VX136 was able to accept armament, (VX133 only had the gun ports), although in the event, guns were never fitted. The main changes to this aircraft were in the tail area, with provision for rearward facing radar (again, never fitted) and fin strakes. Making its first flight on 29 September 1952, VX136 undertook a series of tests until it was damaged beyond repair in a landing accident in December 1953. The airframe ended its days as a gunnery target at the Proof & Experimental Establishment (P&EE) at Shoeburyness.

Reference: 'Scimitar- Supermarine's Last Fighter' by Richard A. Franks; Dalrymple & Verdun Publishing.

Armstrong Whitworth Meteor NF.11, WD604, A&AEE Boscombe Down, February 1952

WD604 was used in trials of jettisonable wingtip tanks, which were found to be a better design for jettisoning than the underwing type. Finished in the standard Night Fighter scheme of Medium Sea Grey overall with Dark Green disruptive pattern on the upper surfaces, with post-war National markings and and black serials, the lower portion of nose appears to be a slightly lighter shade. Each tank was fitted with a vertical dorsal fin towards the front, the rear section of which appears to be white. Of note is the camera mounted behind cockpit, positioned to photograph each tank as it flew past the other. In the event, the layout was not proceeded with as jettisoning affected the aircraft's yaw angle. WD604 was later passed onto de Havilland Propellers for missile test trials.

References: 'The Gloster Meteor' by Edward Shacklady, MacDonald Aircraft Monographs; Wings of Fame 'Variant Briefing: Gloster Meteor Part Two: Post-war development PR.5 to U.21A'; 'Cold War Years – Flight Testing at Boscombe Down 1945-1975' by Tim Mason, Hikoki Publications

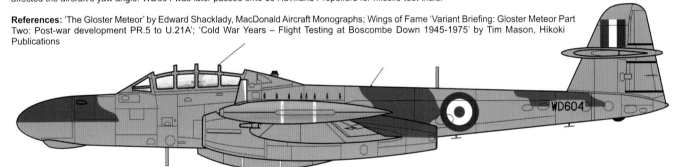

Gloster Meteor F.8, VZ442, operated by Gloster Aircraft Ltd and then the Royal Aircraft Establishment, Boscombe Down, circa 1950s

Overall silver/aluminium, with post-war National markings and black serials. VZ442 was used in canopy jettison tests in the blower tunnel, and later airborne tests where it was flown minus the hood (as illustrated). VZ442 was later used for rocket projectile firing tests, and ended up on Sandhurst scrapheap.

Reference: 'The Gloster Meteor' by Edward Shacklady, MacDonald Aircraft Monographs

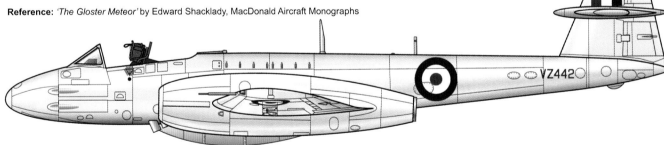

Left: Flying shot of the Gloster 'Prone' Meteor F.8, WK935, from the Royal Aircraft Establishment and Institute of Aviation Medicine at Farnborough, seen in February 1954. It would appear that the extended nose portion was of a slightly darker (fresher?) natural metal shade than the rest of the fuselage. (see illustration opposite)

Gloster Meteor F.8, WA982, Royal Aircraft Establishment, Farnborough, prior to Boscombe Down delivery for handling trials, November 1951
Finished in overall Aluminium/High Speed Silver, with post-war national markings and black serials, WA982 was fitted with a Red Hawk missile mock-up mounted on each wing tip to test the aerodynamic properties of this weapon. Red Hawk was later downgraded to Pink Hawk, then to Blue Jay. WA982 went on to Rolls-Royce Ltd, to test Soar turbojet engines.

Reference: *'Farnborough -100 Years of British Aviation'* by Peter J Cooper, Midland Publishing

Gloster Meteor F.4, RA490, Royal Aircraft Establishment, Farnborough, August 1954
RA490 was fitted with two Rolls-Royce Nene turbojets mounted ahead of the wing, thought to be by the National Gas Turbine Establishment, then further modified with an F.8 type fin and jet deflectors on the tailplanes, by Westland Aircraft Ltd. Finished in overall Aluminium/High Speed Silver with black serials and post-war national markings, the aircraft was used to investigate lowering stalling speeds by jet deflection. RA490 first flew in this configuration at Westland's in May 1954 in the hands of Westland chief test pilot, Sqn Ldr Leo de Vigne, then went onto Farnborough in August of the same year for test flights. The idea was not proceeded with due to increased weight penalties.

References: 'Meteor - *'Gloster's First Jet Fighter'* by Steven J Bond, Midland Counties Publications Ltd; *'The Gloster Meteor'* by Edward Shacklady, MacDonald Aircraft Monographs; Wings of Fame Volume 14 - Variant Briefing 'Gloster Meteor - Part One: Wartime development F.9/40 to F Mk 4'

Gloster Meteor F.8, WK935, Royal Aircraft Establishment and Institute of Aviation Medicine, Farnborough, February 1954
WK935 was modified by Armstrong-Whitworth Aircraft Ltd and made its first flight on 10 February 1954. Finished in overall Aluminium/High Speed Silver with standard post-war markings, the extended nose portion had a slightly darker shade to the rest of the fuselage. The aircraft was designed to test theory that incurred 'g' was lower on the body if in a prone position. A second pilot lay on padded couch in the extended nose with arm and chin rests. Control was by means of hanging pedals and a short control column. The main cockpit was occupied by a 'safety' pilot. In the event of ejection, the prone pilot slid backwards off his couch and through jettisonable hatch in the floor. The programme was abandoned as it was found that the prone position caused discomfort after a period of time, plus concerns over safety in the event of a bail out. The development of pressure 'g' suits began to address the problem. WK935 is now on display in the RAF Museum Cosford.

Reference: Wings of Fame Volume 15 Variant Briefing - 'Gloster Meteor Part Two: Post-war development PR Mk 5 to U Mk 21A; *'The Gloster Meteor'* by Edward Shacklady, MacDonald Aircraft Monographs

Gloster Meteor T.7, VW443, Royal Aircraft Establishment, Farnborough, September 1957
VW443's modified nose held camera equipment behind a circular panel and was used in the U Mk.15 experimental drone flying programme in this configuration. Prior to its RAE service, VW443 was operated by the National Gas Turbine Establishment (NGTE) Flight, and then, de Havilland Propellers at Hatfield where it was used in trials of the Firestreak (Blue Jay) air-to-air missile programme. The aircraft was finished in the overall silver/aluminium scheme with post-war national markings and black serials. Of note is the modified canopy.

References: Air Britain Photo Archives; *'The Gloster Meteor'* by Edward Shacklady, MacDonald Aircraft Monographs

Armstrong Whitworth Meteor NF.11, WD790, (upgraded to NF.12 standard), Ferranti Flying Unit, Turnhouse, 1958
At this time, WD790 was involved in development of the AI Mk 23 AIRPASS radar as used in the English Electric Lightning, and also Red Brick/Indigo Corkscrew radar systems for Bloodhound and Thunderbird surface-to-air missile systems. Finished in the standard Night Fighter scheme of Medium Sea Grey overall with Dark Green disruptive pattern on the upper surfaces, post-war National markings were carried with black serials on the rear fuselage and under the wings. The leading edges of nacelles are believed to have been red. It was later fitted with nose cone from Canberra B(I).8 WT327.

References: Wings of Fame Volume 15: Variant Briefing: Gloster Meteor Part Two: Post-war development- PR.5 to U. 21A; 'Gloster Aircraft since 1917' by Derek N James; *'The Gloster Meteor'* by Edward Shacklady, MacDonald Aircraft Monographs

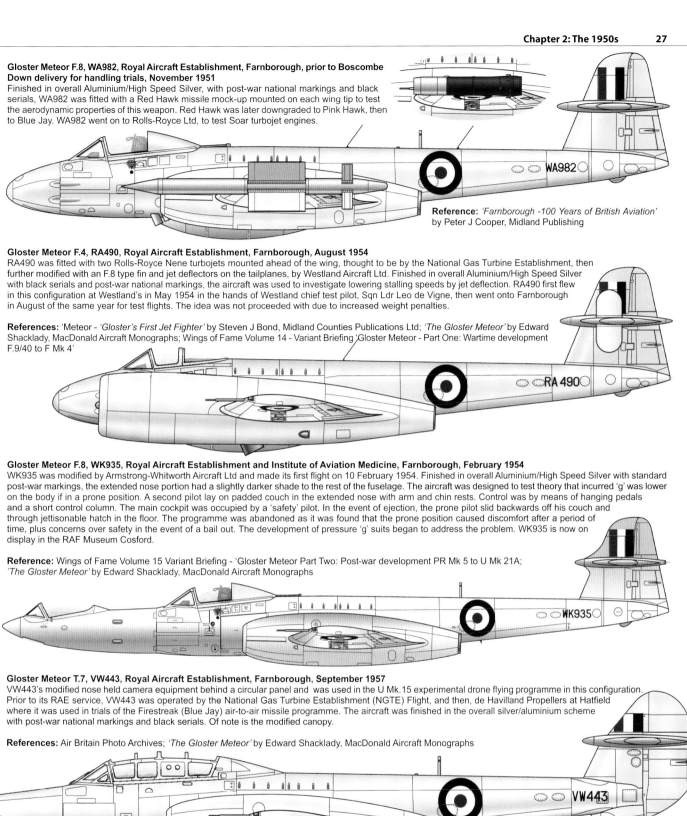

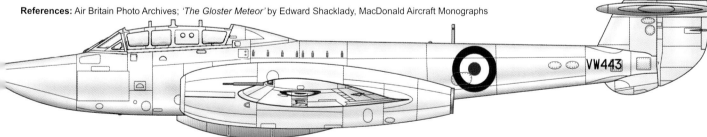

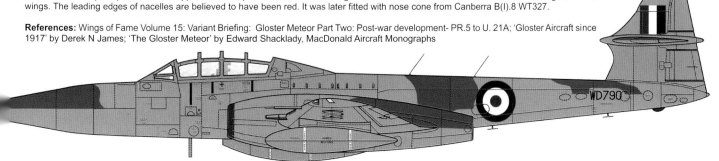

Douglas Dakota IV, KJ829, operated by Rolls Royce during the development of Rolls Royce Dart turboprop, March 1950
KJ829 was operated by Rolls Royce during the early months of 1950 for the development of the Rolls Royce
Dart turboprop. The aircraft later became G-37-2 and then temporarily G-AOXI, under
operation with British European Airways. Finished in overall natural
metal with post-war National markings and
black serials in black, it featured
a black anti-glare panel
and de-icing boots.

Reference:
*Airfix
Magazine*
November
1980

Douglas Dakota III, TS423, on loan to Ferranti Ltd, circa 1955-59
TS423 was used by Ferranti Ltd in development of the AI.23 AIRPASS (Airborne Interception Radar and Pilot Attack Sight
System), as used on the English Electric Lightning – note the Lightning nose cone. Overall natural metal
finish with white fuselage spine, fin and rudder and blue cheatline, post-war roundels
were carried in six positions (no fin flashes) with black serials on
the rear fuselage and under the wings. Again,
black de-icing boots were fitted.

Reference: Air Britain
Photo Archives

Above left: Douglas Dakota 4, KJ839, in use as an Armstrong Siddeley Mamba turboprop test bed. KJ839 was acquired for use by the company on 1 June 1949 and continued to serve in the role until at least June 1954 when this photo was taken. KJ839 should not be confused with Dakota 4, KJ829, (see illustration above), which was used in the development of the Roll-Royce Dart engine.

Above: A close-up of KJ839's Mamba engine test bed installation.

Left: English Electric Canberra PR.3, VX181, seen at Finningley in September 1965. First flown in March 1951, this Canberra spent its entire active career as a test aircraft, principally with the A&AEE, the motif of which is displayed on the fin. VX181 last flew in June 1969 when it was flown to RAF Pershore, Worcestershire, for use as a ground training machine and was subsequently scrapped. Apart from its impressive colour scheme, the white lettering on the side of the nose is believed to have commemorated the two record flights set by this aircraft in January 1953 when it flew from London to Darwin in 22 hours and 21 seconds, completing en route a record time to Karachi of 8 hours 52 minutes and 28 seconds!

Bottom left: English Electric Canberra U.10 target drone, WJ987, was converted from a B.2 by Short Brothers & Harland in 1957, and is seen here in 1958 displaying black and white calibration bands. U.10s were operated by remote control from the ground via a VHF radio link, although the cockpit was occupied. WJ987 was used in trials of guided surface-to-air and air-to-air missile systems for which it acted as a target. On 5 March 1959, this aircraft was handed over to the Royal Australian Air Force. (see third illustration from the top, opposite)

English Electric Canberra B.2, WH912, Armament Flight, Royal Aircraft Establishment, Farnborough, October 1955
This aircraft was used for research into VT bomb fuses and featured a modified nose with extended cone. Finished in the overall High Speed Silver scheme with black serials, WH912 suffered a wheels-up landing on 23 November 1959. After repair it was sent to Hunting Engineering, Luton on 1 December 1960.

Reference: 'Farnborough – 100 Years of British Aviation' by Peter J Cooper, Midland Publishing Ltd

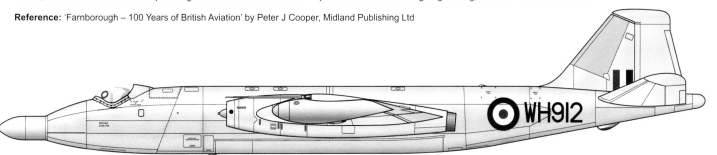

English Electric Canberra B.2, WJ582, Meteorological Research Flight, Royal Aircraft Establishment, Farnborough, September 1956
WJ582 took part in various high-altitude research tasks, including radioactive particle sampling from US and Soviet nuclear tests and ozone sampling. It is thought to have been finished in PRU Blue overall rather than the High Altitude Photo Reconnaissance Scheme of PRU Blue and Medium Sea Grey, as a definite colour demarcation line cannot be seen on the upper fuselage or engine nacelle on the reference photos. Fuselage and underwing serials are white. An RAE crest appears to have been carried on the nose – see inset. WJ582 crashed, hitting the sea on approach to RAF Leuchars, on return from a stratospheric test mission over the Arctic on 20 February 1962.

Reference: 'Farnborough – 100 Years of British Aviation' by Peter J Cooper, Midland Publishing Ltd

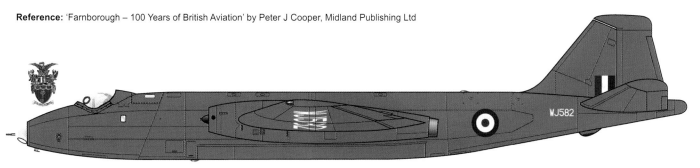

English Electric Canberra U.10, WJ987, Royal Aircraft Establishment, Bedford, 1958
WJ987 was converted from a B.2 by Short Brothers & Harland and originally served with 76 Squadron. Finished in overall High Speed Silver with black serials, it had black and white band calibration markings around the front and the rear fuselage, and black and white wing leading edges and tips. As a U.10, WJ987 was operated under remote control from ground by VHF radio link, although cockpit was occupied. It was also used in trials of guided surface-to-air and air-to-air missile systems, whereby it would act as a target, and would track incoming missiles; recording and transmitting back to the ground data of flight characteristics and miss distance.

Reference: 'A Short Illustrated History of the Royal Aerospace Establishment Bedford' by Arthur Pearcy

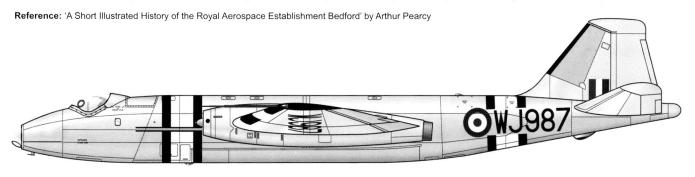

English Electric Canberra T.4, WJ992, Blind Landing Experimental Unit, RAE Bedford, October 1958
WJ992 originally started life as a B.2 and was converted to T.4 specification, being transferred to the RAE at Pershore in September 1962. Finished in overall High Speed Silver, with white fuselage upper decking, it is thought that the cheatline was red, (as illustrated), but it might possibly have been blue. Note fairings on nose area housing blind landing equipment.

References: www.byway.co.uk and 'A Short Illustrated History of the Royal Aerospace Establishment Bedford' by Arthur Pearcy

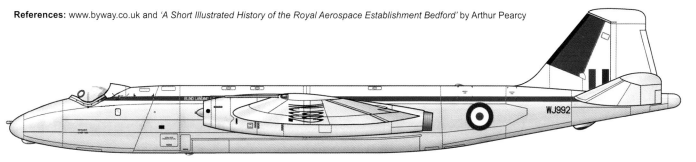

Avro Lancaster B.I (Special), PD119, Royal Aircraft Establishment. Shoeburyness, May 1951
PD119 was flown by the Royal Aircraft Establishment from 1951 on research duties. The aircraft formally served with Nos 617 (the famed 'Dambuster' unit), 156 and 15 Squadrons before being passed over to the RAE. Its fate is unknown. Finish was overall painted Aluminium/High Speed Silver to Pattern No 1 with yellow and black diagonal bands on the under surfaces and post-war National Markings. Serial number was black.

References: *Avro Lancaster The Definitive Record*, Airlife; *Aircraft of World War Two*, Octopus Books

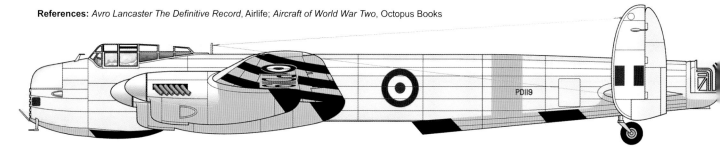

Fairey Gannet T.Mk.2, XA515/24, Empire Test Pilots School, RAE Farnborough, late 1955
XA515 was delivered to RAE Farnborough in November 1955, after previously serving with Fairey Aviation at White Waltham and then the A&AEE at Boscombe Down. During service with these former two operators. it was used in trials of the GGS Mk.4 gunsight. After delivery to Farnborough, it acquired its '24' numeral coding, and served until September 1960 when it was used for fire fighting practice. The aircraft was scrapped in 1962. Finish was overall Aluminium with Yellow 'Trainer' bands around the wings and rear fuselage. The walkways, anti-glare panel and spinner were in black.

Reference: *Scale Aircraft Modelling* Vol 8 No 10 July 1986; '*The Cold War Years - Flight Testing at Boscombe Down 1945-1975*' Hikoki Publications; '*Fleet Air Arm Fixed Wing Aircraft since 1946*' Air Britain

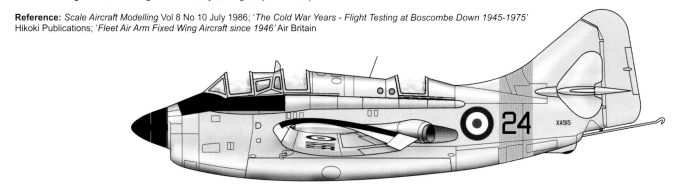

Armstrong Whitworth Meteor NF.11, WD765/5, Empire Test Pilots School, Farnborough, mid-1957
WD765 arrived at the ETPS in February 1957, having come from 29 MU although it may have served with 228 OCU previously, and was one of a number of NF.11s operated by the ETPS. Finished in the standard Night Fighter scheme of Medium Sea Grey overall with Dark Green disruptive pattern on the upper surfaces, it had post-war national markings and black serials and nose code '5'. 'Empire Test Pilots School' titles were also painted on nose in black. Of note is the angled edge to the radome. Unfortunately, WD765 crashed at Mapledurwell, Basingstoke on 20 October 1958 when the fuselage broke up and it was Struck Off Charge in December 1958.

References: '*Meteor- Gloster's First Jet Fighter*' by Steven J Bond, Midland Counties Publications; '*Farnborough – 100 Years of British Aviation*' by Peter J Cooper, Midland Publishing

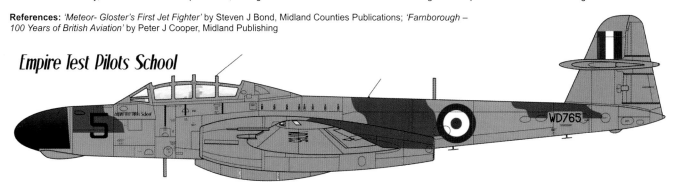

Westland Dragonfly HR.1, VX595/29, Empire Test Pilots School, RAE Farnborough, 1958
VX595 was the first Dragonfly production prototype, and was delivered to Farnborough in September 1957. Finished in Extra Dark Sea Grey upper surfaces to Pattern No 2 with remainder of the fuselage in Sky, it carried the ETPS crest on cabin door. Serials and code '29' were in black. VX595 was struck off charge in October 1964, and remains in storage at the Fleet Air Arm Museum at Yeovilton.

Reference: '*Farnborough – 100 Years of British Aviation*' by Peter J Cooper, Midland Publishing

Fairey FD.2, WG774, RAE Farnborough, September 1956
WG774 made its first flight on 6 October 1954 with Fairey's test pilot, Peter Twiss at the controls, after his involvement in the Fairey FD.1 programme. Finished in overall highly polished natural metal finish, with yellow-orange flashes to the nose area and serials and anti-glare panel in black, the aircraft crash-landed at Boscombe Down, due to a fuel feed problem on 17 November 1954. Due to Twiss's skill as a pilot, the aircraft only suffered minor damage in the forced landing. After this incident, the aircraft was modified by the fitment of a ram-driven fuel pump. This was also fitted to WG777.

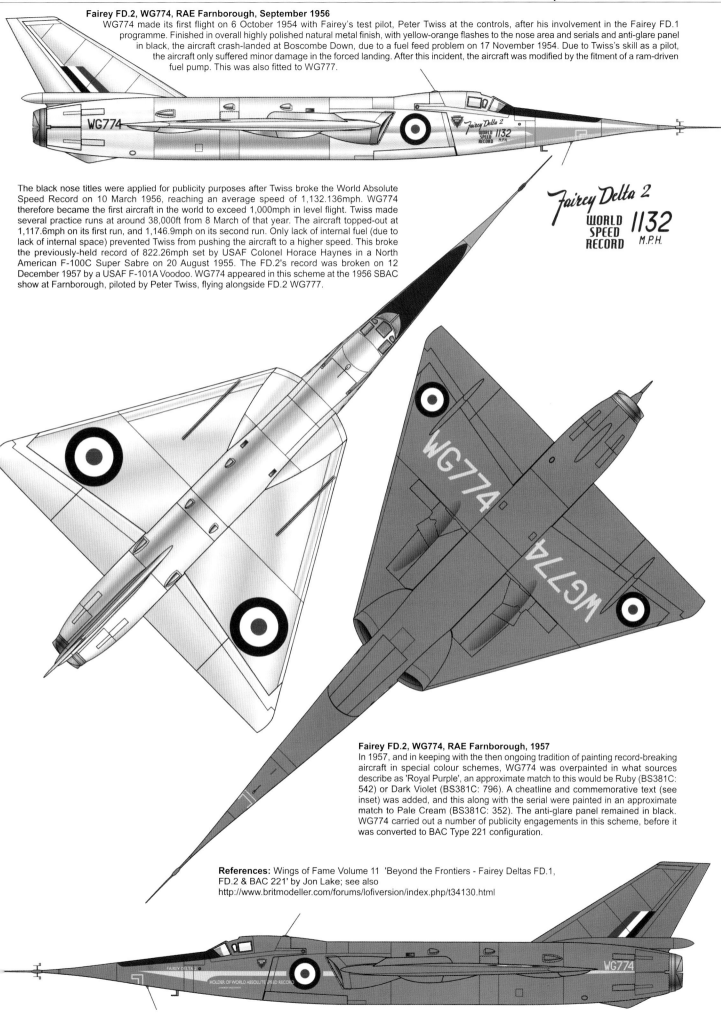

The black nose titles were applied for publicity purposes after Twiss broke the World Absolute Speed Record on 10 March 1956, reaching an average speed of 1,132.136mph. WG774 therefore became the first aircraft in the world to exceed 1,000mph in level flight. Twiss made several practice runs at around 38,000ft from 8 March of that year. The aircraft topped-out at 1,117.6mph on its first run, and 1,146.9mph on its second run. Only lack of internal fuel (due to lack of internal space) prevented Twiss from pushing the aircraft to a higher speed. This broke the previously-held record of 822.26mph set by USAF Colonel Horace Haynes in a North American F-100C Super Sabre on 20 August 1955. The FD.2's record was broken on 12 December 1957 by a USAF F-101A Voodoo. WG774 appeared in this scheme at the 1956 SBAC show at Farnborough, piloted by Peter Twiss, flying alongside FD.2 WG777.

Fairey FD.2, WG774, RAE Farnborough, 1957
In 1957, and in keeping with the then ongoing tradition of painting record-breaking aircraft in special colour schemes, WG774 was overpainted in what sources describe as 'Royal Purple', an approximate match to this would be Ruby (BS381C: 542) or Dark Violet (BS381C: 796). A cheatline and commemorative text (see inset) was added, and this along with the serial were painted in an approximate match to Pale Cream (BS381C: 352). The anti-glare panel remained in black. WG774 carried out a number of publicity engagements in this scheme, before it was converted to BAC Type 221 configuration.

References: Wings of Fame Volume 11 'Beyond the Frontiers - Fairey Deltas FD.1, FD.2 & BAC 221' by Jon Lake; see also http://www.britmodeller.com/forums/lofiversion/index.php/t34130.html

Westland Wyvern S.4, VZ790, A&AEE Boscombe Down, during 'Red Angel' rocket trials, July 1954
'Red Angel' was the code name given to the warhead that was intended to be used on the cancelled Armstrong Whitworth 'Blue Slug' anti-shipping missile; itself an offshoot of the Sea Slug surface-to-air missile. Wyvern S.4, VZ790, was modified by Westlands in May 1954 for the carriage of two of these weapons, before being passed on to the A&AEE at Boscombe Down in July of the same year, where it undertook handling and flight limitations trials. The aircraft was then passed on for holding before being issued to No.827 Squadron at RNAS Ford. Finish was standard Fleet Air Arm Extra Dark Sea Grey upper surfaces to Pattern No 2 with Sky under surfaces and post-war National Markings.

References: *Scale Aircraft Modelling* Vol 14 No 2 November 1991; *'The Cold War Years – Flight Testing at Boscombe Down 1945-1975'* Hikoki Publications; *'Fleet Air Arm Fixed Wing Aircraft since 1946'* Air Britain

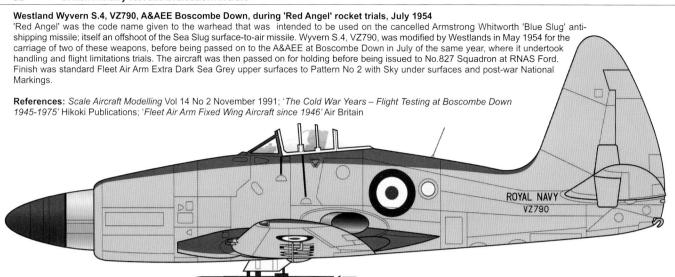

Hawker Sea Hawk FB.3, WM983, 1,000lb air-to-surface rocket tests, A&AEE Boscombe Down, May 1955
Initially delivered to 'C' Squadron at A&AEE Boscombe Down in June 1954, Sea Hawk WM983 is shown as it appeared during rocket handling tests in mid-1955. Two of these formidable 1,000lb weapons could be carried, and just about approached the aircraft's load-carrying limit. WM983 spent around a year with the A&AEE before being passed on to 811 Naval Air Squadron at RNAS Ford. The black and white checkerboard markings on the missiles were for photographic calibration purposes. Finish was standard FAA Extra Dark Sea Grey upper surfaces to Pattern No 2 with Sky undersides, post-war National Markings and black serials.

Reference: *The Cold War Years – Flight Testing at Boscombe Down 1945-1975'*, Hikoki Publications; *'Fleet Air Arm Fixed Wing Aircraft since 1946'*, Air Britain

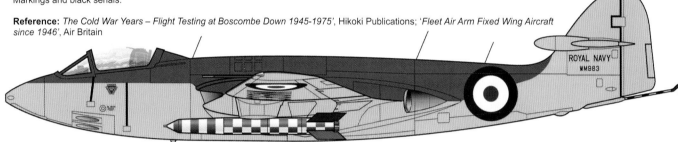

De Havilland Sea Venom FAW.21, XG607/467, 893 Naval Air Squadron during 'Project Blue Jay' air-to-air missile trials aboard HMS Victorious, January 1959
Initially codenamed Blue Jay, the de Havilland Firestreak was Great Britain's first fully operational air-to-air missile. Sea Venom XG607 was one of three aircraft modified in 1957 at de Havilland Christchurch to carry Blue Jay, the others being XG612 and XG662. All guns were removed, and the gun camera was moved to a new position in the port outer cannon bay. Flight trials with dummy rounds began with 700 NAS at RNAS Ford, in the summer of 1958, XG607 being coded '522'. The three aircraft were then passed to 893 NAS for operational service trials of the missile in 1958, aboard the carrier HMS Victorious. 893 NAS would become the only unit to operate Firestreak equipped Sea Venoms in the Royal Navy. XG607 was finally 'Struck Off Charge' in December 1962. Finish was standard Extra Dark Sea Grey upper surfaces with Sky undersides. It is believed that the tail cone acorns were red.

References: *'De Havilland Venom and Sea Venom The Complete History'* Sutton Publishing; *'De Havilland Venom'* by Roger Lindsay; *'Fleet Air Arm Fixed Wing Aircraft since 1946'* Air Britain; *'Rockets and Missiles'* Salamander Publishing.

Supermarine E.10/44 Attacker, TS416, Royal Aircraft Establishment, Farnborough, September 1950
TS416 was the third Attacker prototype, and arrived at Farnborough on 27 May 1950. It was used by the RAE Naval Air Department, principally as an arrester trials aircraft, and was, from 5 May 1950, fitted with Rocket Assisted Take Off Gear (RATOG). Finished in the standard FAA Extra Dark Sea Grey upper surfaces with Sky undersides to Pattern No 2, with post-war Red/White/Blue roundels and black 'ROYAL NAVY' titles and serials, TS416 was latterly involved in jet deflection trials and served at Farnborough until 12 August 1954, when it was sent to St Merryn for use as a ground instructional airframe.

Reference: *'Farnborough – 100 Years of British Aviation'* by Peter J Cooper, Midland Publishing Ltd

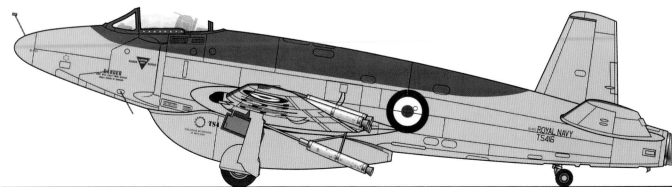

Fairey FD.1, VX350, RAE Boscombe Down, 6 February, 1956
Specification E.10/47 was issued on 19 September 1947 and called for a feasibility study into an interceptor capable of being launched from a ramp, and to be able to climb to height in as short a time as possible. Borrowing loosely from Germany's ill-fated wartime Bachem Ba 349 'Natter' rocket-powered interceptor, Fairey's stubby FD.1 was cleared for taxiing trials in 1950. After commencement of these tests on 12 May 1950, piloted by Fairey test pilot, Group Captain Gordon Slade, and serialled VX350, the aircraft to the skies for the first time exactly a year later. Powered by a single Rolls Royce Derwent 5 RD7 turbojet, the FD.1 only reached a maximum speed of 345mph due to structural constraints being placed upon the tailplane. Plans to remove the horizontal tail surfaces came to naught. Had this change been made, it was claimed that the aircraft was capable of attaining over 600mph – in theory at least. Group Captain Slade commented that it was probably one of the most difficult aircraft he'd had to fly, although rate of roll was particularly fast. The aircraft was grounded for a period whilst measures were taken to make it more controllable. VX350 was effectively written off in a landing accident on 6 February 1956 when she lost her main undercarriage, and ended her days as a gunnery target on the Shoeburyness ranges. The aircraft is shown here, at the time of its last flight, in its highly polished natural metal finish, with post-war national markings and black serials on the rear fuselage and under the wings.

Reference: Wings of Fame- Volume 11 'Beyond the Frontiers: Fairey Deltas FD.1, FD.2 & BAC 221', Aerospace Publishing Ltd, 1998; 'British Prototype Aircraft 'by Ray Sturtivant, Haynes Publishing Group, 1990.

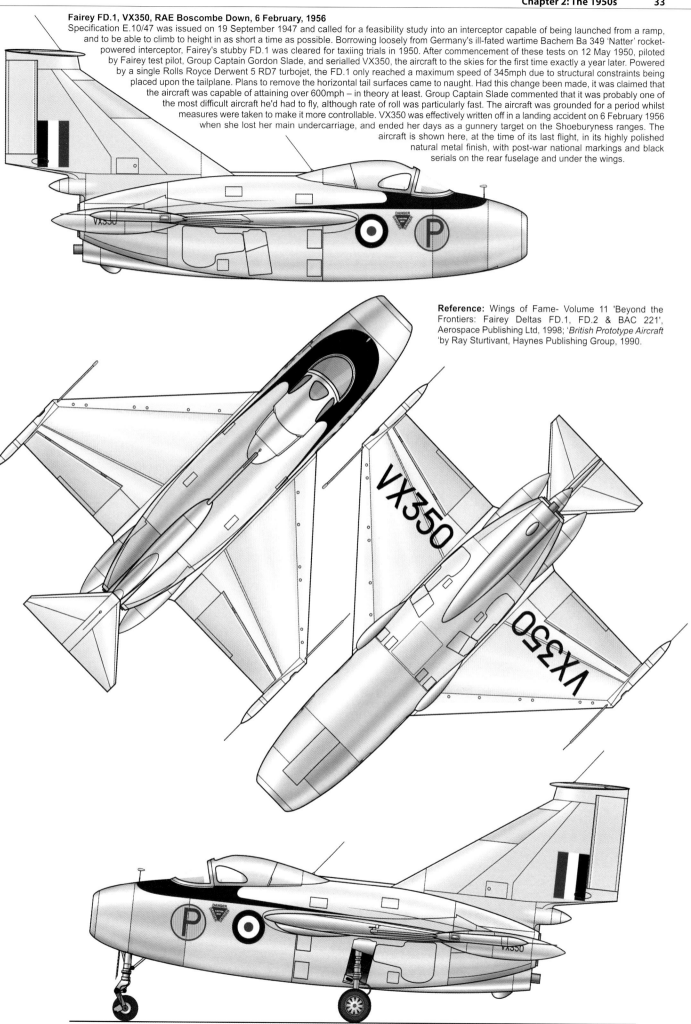

Above and left: Hawker Hunter F.6, WW598, first flew at the end of 1955 and was never allocated to the RAF. It later joined the 'Aero Flight' at RAE Bedford having at some point received the overall blue colour scheme seen here. Later, WW598 would participate in the TSR2 programme (for which it was painted white) and was ultimately operated by the RAE at Llanbedr. In May 1974, it was sold to Hawker Siddeley, refurbished, and later delivered to the Lebanese Air Force. The words AERO FLIGHT appear in white on the aircraft's nose, below which, within the white cheat line, the words RAE BEDFORD have been applied in red. (see illustration opposite)

Armstrong Whitworth Meteor NF.11, WM373, Fairey Guided Weapons Division, Fairey Aviation Ltd, early/mid-1950s
WM373 was used by Fairey in the development of the Fireflash (Blue Sky) air-to-air missile system and is shown carrying one of these weapons on each wingtip – (AW Meteor NF.11 WM374 was also used in the same programme), Painted in an overall gloss white scheme with Post Office Red (BS381C: 537) fuselage and fin trim, standard post-war national markings were carried with black serials and anti-glare panel. The modified nose housed a camera and measuring equipment. WM373 went on to serve with the Royal Radar Establishment (RRE) before being sent to Woomera, Australia on 13 April 1955.

References: 'The Gloster Meteor' by Edward Shacklady, MacDonald Aircraft Monographs; Gloster Aircraft since 1917 by Derek N James, Putnam's; 'Trials & Testbed Meteors' by Barry Jones; Australian War Memorial photo; 'Missile Age Meteors'; Mark Rolfe's personal archives

Avro Lincoln B.2, RF533, RAE Farnborough, April 1955
RF533 was one of the more famous of the test Lincolns, being sent to Telecommunications Flying Unit (TFU) Defford in 1948 as a radar test aircraft. A number of air-intercept radar units were fitted into the specially modified nose. Finished in the standard post-war Bomber Scheme of Medium Sea Grey upper surfaces to Pattern No 2 with Anti-Searchlight Glossy Black under surfaces, fuselage serials were in red, while the underwing serials were white. The nose cone was red and yellow. RF533 also undertook various engine trials including tests of the Napier Naiad and Rolls Royce Tyne turboprop; the aircraft being able to fly on the power of this single engine alone. This profile depicts RF533 as it looked while undergoing missile/turbojet development work.

Reference: 'Farnborough – 100 Years of British Aviation' by Peter J Cooper, Midland Publishing Ltd

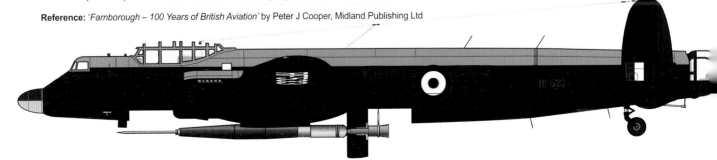

Hawker Hunter F.6, WW598, (converted to P.1109A configuration), Aero Flight Systems, RAE Bedford, circa mid-late 1950s
WW598 first flew on 31 December 1955 and was used for various trials at Dunsfold before being passed onto RAE Farnborough, and then to RAE Bedford (High Speed Flight), where it was converted to P.1109A configuration and used for de Havilland Firestreak air-to-air missile system tests. WW598 was finished in overall Roundel Blue (BS381C:110) with cheatline, serials and 'AERO FLIGHT' titles in white. (see also pp46 and 58)

Reference: 'A Short Illustrated History of the Royal Aerospace Establishment Bedford' by Arthur Pearcy, Airlife; plus online discussion groups

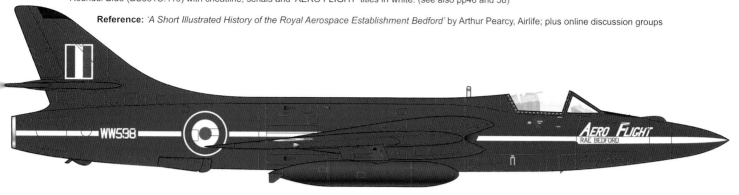

Hawker Hunter F.4, XF310, Hawker Aircraft Company, RAE Llanbedr, circa 1957
XF310 was originally modified by Fairey Aviation Ltd to test the Fairey 'Blue Sky' (Fireflash) air-to-air missile system, two of which were carried. Finished in the standard RAF Day Fighter scheme of gloss Dark Green and Dark Sea Grey upper surfaces with what appears to be Aluminium/High Speed Silver undersides (as illustrated), but may have been white or Light Aircraft Grey, no national markings were carried initially, although serials were applied, in the standard black. The nose carried the associated radar system, with pitot/instrumentation probes on both wings. The Hawker Siddeley Group logo was applied to both sides of the nose. At some stage in 1957, XF310 was further modified to house a camera in the nose, and post-war national markings were applied, as illustrated. XF310 was operated from RAE Llanbedr, and made a number of successful test firings. In the event, the RAF opted to proceed with the de Havilland 'Blue Jay' (Firestreak). XF310 was later converted to T.7 standard, then to T.8C, and ended up in Australia.

Reference: 'Wings of Fame' Volume 20 'Hawker Hunter' by Jon Lake Aerospace Publishing Ltd

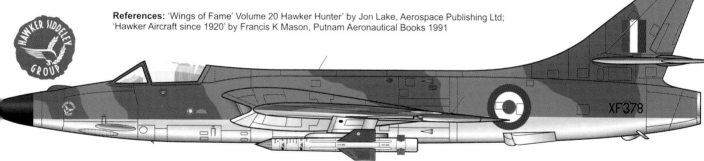

Hawker Hunter F.6 (P.1109B), XF378, de Havilland Aircraft Company/Hawker Aircraft Company, RAE Llanbedr, 1957
XF378 carried the full AI Mk 20 radar/Blue Jay (Firestreak) kit in a modified nose fairing, and was active over the Aberporth ranges during 1957. It was based at RAE Llanbedr at the time and carried two Blue Jays, the colouring for which appears to have been white with red fins, which also carried RAF roundels. Finished in the standard RAF Day Fighter scheme of gloss Dark Green and Dark Sea Grey upper surfaces with Aluminium/High Speed Silver undersides, post-war national markings were carried in all standard positions with black serials on the rear fuselage and under the wings. The Hawker Siddeley Group logo was also applied to both sides of the nose.

References: 'Wings of Fame' Volume 20 Hawker Hunter by Jon Lake, Aerospace Publishing Ltd; 'Hawker Aircraft since 1920' by Francis K Mason, Putnam Aeronautical Books 1991

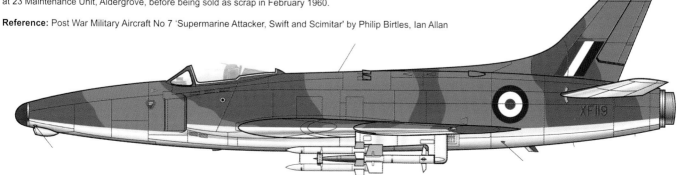

Supermarine Swift FR.7, XF119, No 1 Guided Weapons Missile Development Squadron, RAF Valley, circa 1958
XF119 was one of the twelve first production batch Swift FR.7s, and No 1 Guided Weapons Development Squadron, based at RAF Valley operated ten of these aircraft – serials XF115 to XF124. XF119 is illustrated here carrying two Fairey 'Blue Sky' (Fireflash) beam-riding, air-to-air missiles. Finished in the standard RAF Day Fighter scheme of gloss Dark Green/Dark Sea Grey upper surfaces and Aluminium/High Speed Silver undersides with post-war national markings and black serials, the Swifts operated by this unit were the first fighters in UK service to carry guided missiles operationally. XF119 ended its days at 23 Maintenance Unit, Aldergrove, before being sold as scrap in February 1960.

Reference: Post War Military Aircraft No 7 'Supermarine Attacker, Swift and Scimitar' by Philip Birtles, Ian Allan

Avro Ashton Mk.2, WB491, National Gas Turbine Establishment Pyestock, Fleet, Hampshire, 1956
The National Gas Turbine Establishment (NGTE) was established in 1946 from the merger of Power Jets Ltd and the Royal Aircraft Establishment's own jet turbine research institution. Based on the Avro Tudor piston airliner, the Avro Ashton Mk.1, WB490, first flew on 1 September 1950. The Mk.2, WB491, arrived at Farnborough on 4 September 1955 and undertook various turbine trials, including the Rolls Royce Avon and Conway, housed in a fairing underneath the fuselage. Painted Aluminium/High Speed Silver finish overall with post-war national markings, black serials and anti-glare panel, a total of six Ashton's were built – one Mk.1 WB490, one Mk.2 WB491, two Mk.3s WB493 and WB494 and two Mk.4s WB492 and WE670. Despite never entering series production, they mainly served as general test, navigation aids and bomb release systems trials aircraft. WB493 was operated by Bristol Siddeley as a testbed for the Olympus and Orpheus turbojets. Only the forward fuselage of WB491, illustrated here, survives to this day, at the Newark Air Museum, Nottinghamshire.

Reference: *Farnborough 100 Years of British Aviation* by Peter J Cooper, Midland Publishing Ltd

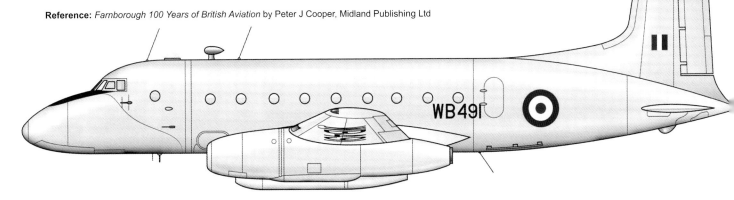

Left: Based on the Avro Tudor piston airliner, six Avro Ashtons were constructed and although the type never entered series production the airframes provided an invaluable service in helping to develop many new aircraft and jet engine technologies. Avro Ashton 3, WB493, first flew on 18 December 1951 and subsequently joined the RAE's fleet of aircraft. In 1955 it went to the Bristol Engine Division at Filton as a testbed for Olympus and Orpheus turbojets. In this image, WB493 is seen at Filton in May 1963, and while at first glance it appears to be a twin-jet aeroplane, it was in fact four engined. WB493 was scrapped a month later, on 29 June 1963 – although one source suggests 30 September 1963.

Note FYI: Mark describes WB493 as a Mk.4, however, the three sources I've found say Mk.3!

Above and left: The Saunders-Roe (Saro) SR.53 was a composite rocket and jet-powered single-seat fighter research aircraft powered by a 1,750lb thrust Viper jet engine for 'normal cruising' purposes in the upper section of the fuselage with an 8,000lb thrust DH Spectre liquid-fuel rocket loitering below. The concept came about following a 1951 Air Ministry request to consider the viability of a high-performance point-defence fighter capable of dealing with the possible threat of high flying Soviet bombers attacking the UK. Saro's first SR.53, XD145, flew on 16 May 1957 from Boscombe Down and quickly displayed a notable capability by reaching 50,000ft in just two minutes. A second SR.53, XD151, was also built but it crashed on 5 June 1958 killing the pilot. RAF interest in the type was muted almost from the beginning for several practical reasons, while Ministry of Supply support was withdrawn in anticipation of the looming 1957 Defence White Paper and no further SR.53s were built. (see 4-view opposite)

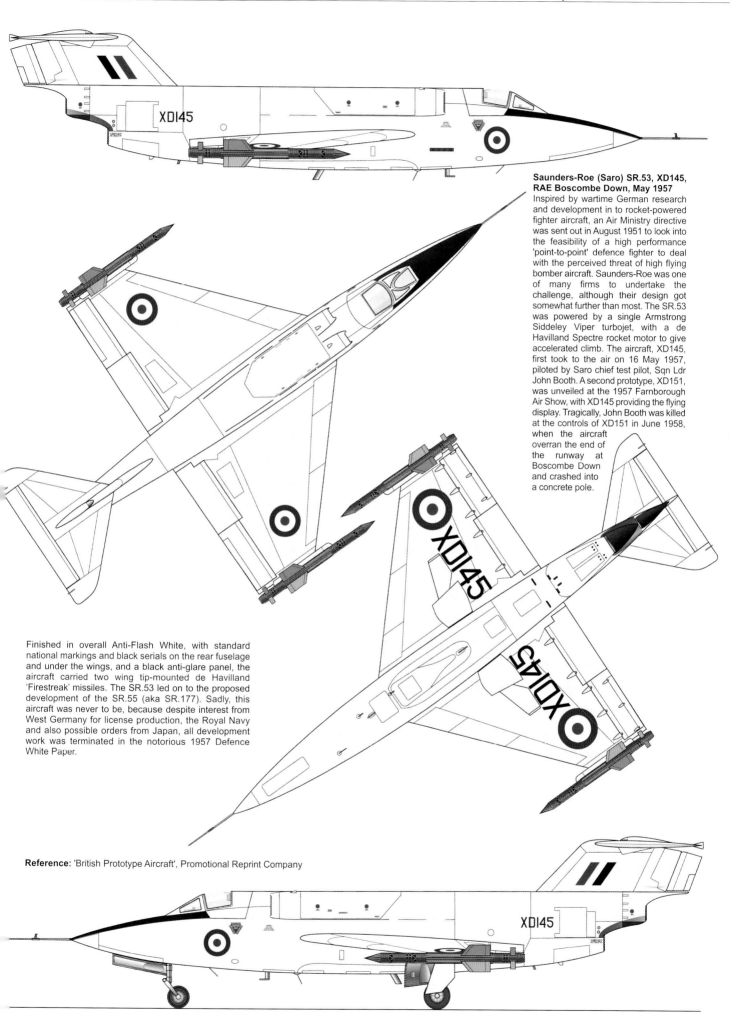

Saunders-Roe (Saro) SR.53, XD145, RAE Boscombe Down, May 1957
Inspired by wartime German research and development in to rocket-powered fighter aircraft, an Air Ministry directive was sent out in August 1951 to look into the feasibility of a high performance 'point-to-point' defence fighter to deal with the perceived threat of high flying bomber aircraft. Saunders-Roe was one of many firms to undertake the challenge, although their design got somewhat further than most. The SR.53 was powered by a single Armstrong Siddeley Viper turbojet, with a de Havilland Spectre rocket motor to give accelerated climb. The aircraft, XD145, first took to the air on 16 May 1957, piloted by Saro chief test pilot, Sqn Ldr John Booth. A second prototype, XD151, was unveiled at the 1957 Farnborough Air Show, with XD145 providing the flying display. Tragically, John Booth was killed at the controls of XD151 in June 1958, when the aircraft overran the end of the runway at Boscombe Down and crashed into a concrete pole.

Finished in overall Anti-Flash White, with standard national markings and black serials on the rear fuselage and under the wings, and a black anti-glare panel, the aircraft carried two wing tip-mounted de Havilland 'Firestreak' missiles. The SR.53 led on to the proposed development of the SR.55 (aka SR.177). Sadly, this aircraft was never to be, because despite interest from West Germany for license production, the Royal Navy and also possible orders from Japan, all development work was terminated in the notorious 1957 Defence White Paper.

Reference: 'British Prototype Aircraft', Promotional Reprint Company

Chapter 3: The 1960s

Above: Nine Blackburn Buccaneer NA.39 prototypes were ordered in June 1955 of which XK489 (nearest to the camera) was the fourth although, importantly, it was the first fully navalised NA.39 – XK486, 487 and 488 being rather more basic airframes. First flown on 31 January 1959, XK489 served with many establishments in preparation for the introduction of the Buccaneer S.1 into naval service including carrier landing trials aboard HMS Victorious, Centaur and Ark Royal at various times, as well as trialling modified flight controls and other systems. Used extensively, XK489 was withdrawn from use on 24 December 1963 and SOC on 22 September 1964 and dismantled.

The decade of the 1960s was one of considerable change within Britain's aircraft industry. The significant pace of post-war R&D, the success of developing a viable supersonic fighter in the shape of the English Electric Lightning, the many other achievements including the introduction in to service of the powerful V-Bomber fleet, should all have heralded continuing expansion and an onward trend in Britain's aviation industry and infrastructure. Instead, although much important work continued to take place, the 1960s saw the start of a significant and long-term contraction in the aircraft industry, and the growing necessity to find international partners in major programmes as the cost of developing new aircraft designs and technology began to ominously spiral. There were many factors that contributed to this unfortunate trend, but the overall effect was to lead to far fewer British designs being developed, with the obvious contraction in the necessity for R&D and flight testing in Britain.

Muddled government priorities, sometimes confused official specifications, the increasing dominance in the civil as well as the military sector of American designs, all contributed to the contraction of Britain's aircraft industry in the years and decades that followed the disastrous Sandys pronouncements of 1957. The most obvious manifestation of the future contraction of the aircraft industry at its highest levels was the creation in 1960 of the British Aircraft Corporation Ltd (BAC), which brought together several of Britain's major companies in the programme that led to the TSR.2 strike aircraft. This merger within the new BAC organisation of the significant parts of several companies including English Electric, Bristol and Vickers, was a pointer towards the eventual disappearance of several of the long-standing names in British aviation, and was an ominous foretaste of the eventual massive contraction in aircraft design and manufacture in Britain. Although in the short-term it appeared to be expedient for several companies to work together on future projects and requirements, particularly to meet the ever-spiralling costs of creating new designs and the ability to pool resources and talents, in the long-term (and of

course with the benefit of hindsight) this strategy has proven to be of no obvious benefit to Britain's aircraft industry.

Unfortunately, just as the 1950s had seen the spectacular 'own-goal' of the Sandys White Paper, so the 1960s witnessed a further reason why Britain's aircraft industry was eventually reduced to a shadow of its former self, with associated implications for R&D and flight testing. The TSR.2 project, that had become such a focal point for the future of Britain's military aircraft prowess, was cancelled in 1965. This event was a calamity for the British aircraft industry, and resulted in many talented engineers and designers leaving the industry altogether, or going abroad where their talents would be appreciated and used properly.

The main purpose of creating the BAC conglomeration had been to develop and put into service the TSR.2, and its cancellation left the aircraft industry considerably weakened and

Continued on page 44

Left: Although of poor-quality, this colour photo of Bristol Type 188, XF926, is none-the-less significant as it probably dates from around the time the aircraft was put in to storage at Filton in the autumn of 1963. (See 4-view opposite)

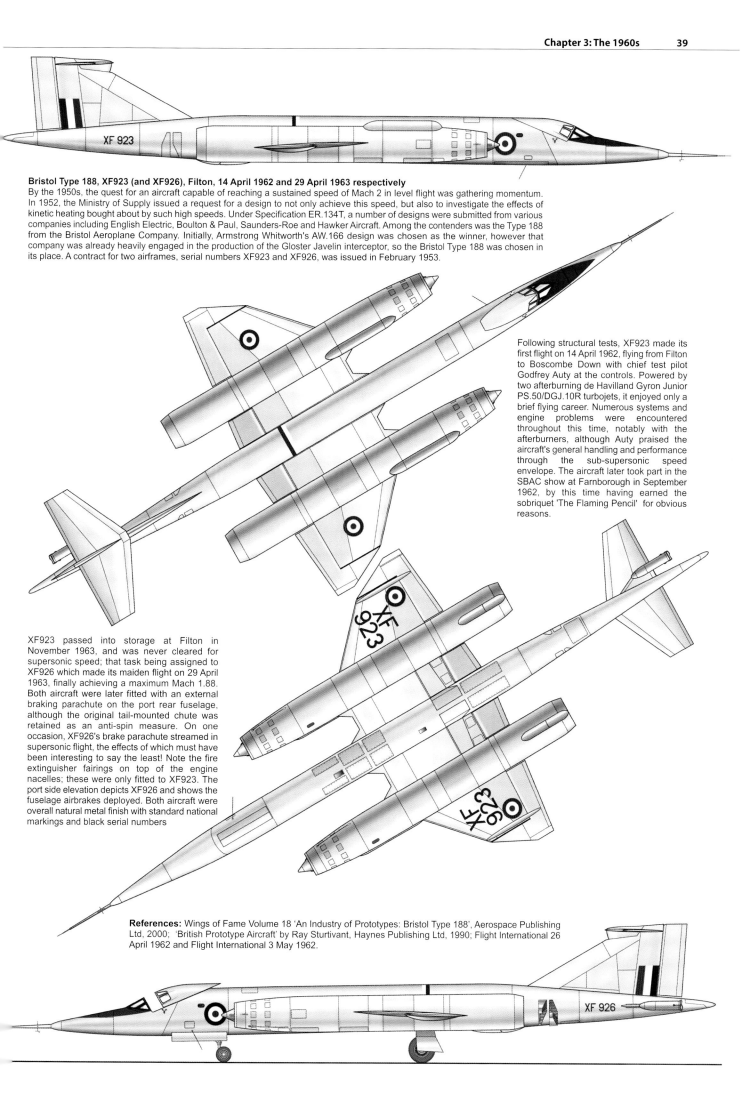

Bristol Type 188, XF923 (and XF926), Filton, 14 April 1962 and 29 April 1963 respectively
By the 1950s, the quest for an aircraft capable of reaching a sustained speed of Mach 2 in level flight was gathering momentum. In 1952, the Ministry of Supply issued a request for a design to not only achieve this speed, but also to investigate the effects of kinetic heating bought about by such high speeds. Under Specification ER.134T, a number of designs were submitted from various companies including English Electric, Boulton & Paul, Saunders-Roe and Hawker Aircraft. Among the contenders was the Type 188 from the Bristol Aeroplane Company. Initially, Armstrong Whitworth's AW.166 design was chosen as the winner, however that company was already heavily engaged in the production of the Gloster Javelin interceptor, so the Bristol Type 188 was chosen in its place. A contract for two airframes, serial numbers XF923 and XF926, was issued in February 1953.

Following structural tests, XF923 made its first flight on 14 April 1962, flying from Filton to Boscombe Down with chief test pilot Godfrey Auty at the controls. Powered by two afterburning de Havilland Gyron Junior PS.50/DGJ.10R turbojets, it enjoyed only a brief flying career. Numerous systems and engine problems were encountered throughout this time, notably with the afterburners, although Auty praised the aircraft's general handling and performance through the sub-supersonic speed envelope. The aircraft later took part in the SBAC show at Farnborough in September 1962, by this time having earned the sobriquet 'The Flaming Pencil' for obvious reasons.

XF923 passed into storage at Filton in November 1963, and was never cleared for supersonic speed; that task being assigned to XF926 which made its maiden flight on 29 April 1963, finally achieving a maximum Mach 1.88. Both aircraft were later fitted with an external braking parachute on the port rear fuselage, although the original tail-mounted chute was retained as an anti-spin measure. On one occasion, XF926's brake parachute streamed in supersonic flight, the effects of which must have been interesting to say the least! Note the fire extinguisher fairings on top of the engine nacelles; these were only fitted to XF923. The port side elevation depicts XF926 and shows the fuselage airbrakes deployed. Both aircraft were overall natural metal finish with standard national markings and black serial numbers

References: Wings of Fame Volume 18 'An Industry of Prototypes: Bristol Type 188', Aerospace Publishing Ltd, 2000; 'British Prototype Aircraft' by Ray Sturtivant, Haynes Publishing Ltd, 1990; Flight International 26 April 1962 and Flight International 3 May 1962.

Short SC.1, XG900, at A&AEE Boscombe Down and RAE Bedford, circa early 1960s
The SC.1 can lay claim to being the first British fixed-wing VTOL (Vertical Take Off and Landing) aircraft, although the story goes back earlier, to the early 1950s. The Royal Aircraft Establishment and Roll-Royce came together to work on an aerial vehicle to test this theory, the result being the Thrust Measuring Rigs, (commonly known as the 'Flying Bedsteads').

Although the measuring rigs were to provide much useful data, the design of a fixed wing vertical take-off and landing aircraft was already underway and a contract was awarded to

Short Brothers & Harland of Belfast for two aircraft capable of VTOL. These were allocated the serials XG900 and XG905.

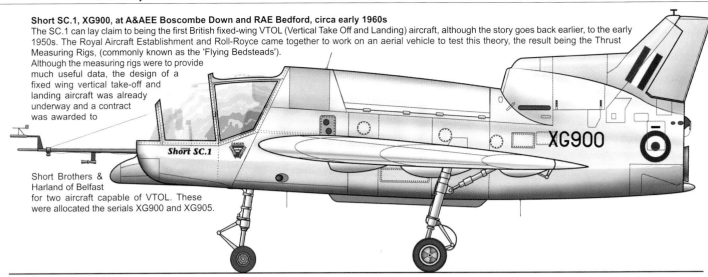

An odd beetle-like aircraft, the SC.1 was to be powered by five Rolls-Royce RB.108 turbojets (four of which were to be mounted vertically), with XG900 making its initial taxi-trials at Boscombe Down on 17 December 1956. Only the forward propulsion unit was installed, and on 7 April 1957 the first conventional take-off and landing was made with Short's Chief Test Pilot, Tom Brooke-Smith, at the controls. By this time, the externally identical XG905 had been constructed and this aircraft was fitted with all five engines. The vertical lift motors were able to tilt through 35° to give better transition to forward flight. XG905 made the first tethered vertical hover for the SC.1 on 26 May 1958 and the first free flight took place on October 25 the same year. The first transitional flight from hover to forward to hover was made on 6 April.

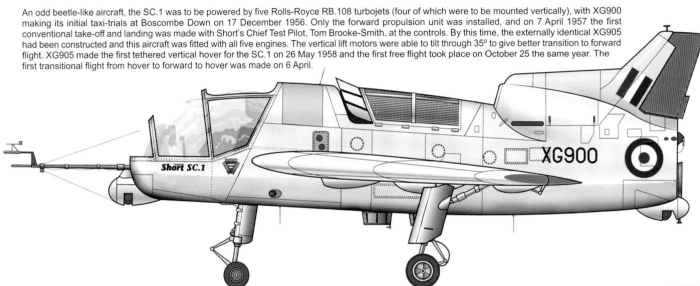

Tragedy struck however, when on 2 October 1963, XG905 experienced a severe control loss, and crashed, the pilot J R Green being killed, although the aircraft was rebuilt. A redesign was undertaken at this stage mainly to the cockpit area. By the mid-1960s, the VTOL concept had moved on apace with the introduction into the test circuit of the Hawker P.1127, and later Kestrel, with the unique rotating nozzle engine, and the mounted lift-jet concept employed on the SC.1 became redundant. XG900 was demoted to ground running test work only. Both aircraft were retired in 1971 – XG900 was sent to the Science Museum and other locations for display, whilst XG905 went back to Shorts.

XG900 was painted in an overall silver finish with black serials and national markings initially (upper profile) – with the Day-Glo areas (lower profile) added later.

Reference: 'British Prototype Aircraft' by Ray Sturtivant, Haynes Publishing Group

Above: The first British production De Havilland Chipmunk was T.10, WB549, which, following delivery on 17 November 1949 was subsequently used by the A&AEE and later the ETPS as seen in this image taken at Cranfield in 1962 with the Empire Test Pilots School's crest on the engine cowling. WB549 was probably used as a hack with this unit until sold to the civil market on 26 February 1973 to become G-BAPB. (See profile illustration of WD321 opposite)

Left: Built in 1943, North American Harvard IIb, FT375, was one of three Harvards used by the A&AEE alongside KF183 (see profile illustration opposite) and KF314. FT375 was sold in the 1990s and registered as G-BWUL. It has changed hands several times since, but as of February 2015 was still flying with the Italian-registered 'G-BWUL Flying Group'.

Hunting Percival Provost T.1, XF685/20, Empire Test Pilots School, RAE Farnborough, early 1960s
This Hunting Percival Provost was one of several piston-engined types that served in 'second role' duties with the ETPS in the early 1960s. Finished in the overall painted aluminium scheme with standard national markings and Day-Glo cowling, rear fuselage, wing tips, flaps and tailplane banding, serial number and numeral '20' were in black, as was the spinner and the anti-glare panel. The ETPS crest and titles were carried on the cowling sides (see inset).

Reference: Scale Aircraft Modelling Vol 10/5 February 1988

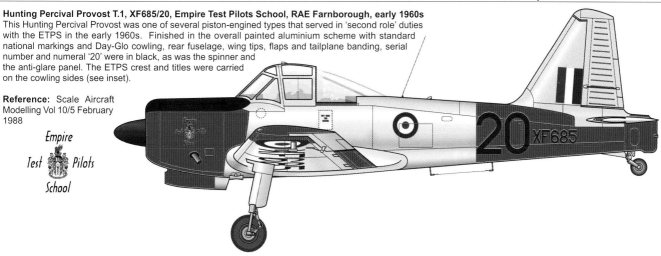

De Havilland Chipmunk T.10, WD321/3, Empire Test Pilots School, RAE Farnborough, circa 1962
WD321 arrived at Farnborough in early 1956 and was subsequently used as a communications 'hack' between RAE Aberporth and Llanbedr. WD321 returned to Farnborough in 1958, where it was allocated to the ETPS. Painted overall silver/aluminium with standard national markings and black serials. Yellow 'Trainer bands' were carried around the rear fuselage and around the wings and the anti-glare panel and numeral '3' were in black. The ETPS crest and titling were also carried on the cowling sides with the crest on white rectangular background. WD321 went to Boscombe Down in February 1968 and was put on to the civil circuit in 1975 as G-BDCC.

References: 'Farnborough - 100 Years of British Aviation' by Peter J Cooper, Midland Publishing; Scale Aircraft Modelling Vol 13/9 June 1991: 'Aircraft in Detail: de Havilland Canada DHC-1 Chipmunk' by Alan W Hall with Mike Keep

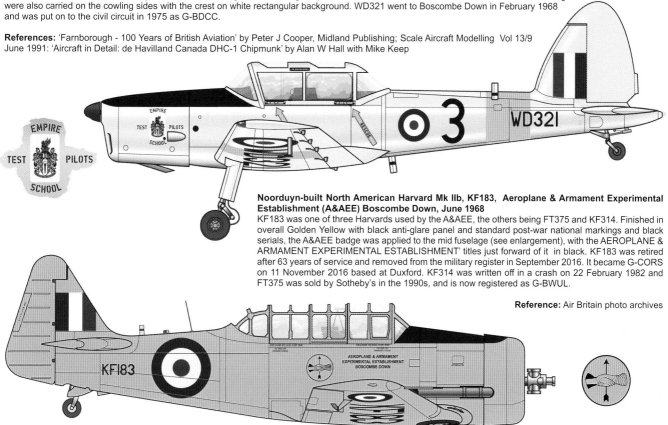

Noorduyn-built North American Harvard Mk IIb, KF183, Aeroplane & Armament Experimental Establishment (A&AEE) Boscombe Down, June 1968
KF183 was one of three Harvards used by the A&AEE, the others being FT375 and KF314. Finished in overall Golden Yellow with black anti-glare panel and standard post-war national markings and black serials, the A&AEE badge was applied to the mid fuselage (see enlargement), with the AEROPLANE & ARMAMENT EXPERIMENTAL ESTABLISHMENT' titles just forward of it in black. KF183 was retired after 63 years of service and removed from the military register in September 2016. It became G-CORS on 11 November 2016 based at Duxford. KF314 was written off in a crash on 22 February 1982 and FT375 was sold by Sotheby's in the 1990s, and is now registered as G-BWUL.

Reference: Air Britain photo archives

Auster AOP.9, XP277, Radio Flight, RAE Farnborough, March 1969
Finished in an overall white scheme with standard national markings and a dark blue (possibly Roundel Blue as illustrated) cheatline, XP277 was one of several Auster AOP.9s serving with various Flights within the RAE, another one being WZ672, also in the overall white scheme with blue cheatline, in the Aero Flight at RAE Bedford. In XP277's instance, the fuselage serials and 'ROYAL AIRCRAFT ESTABLISHMENT' titles were in white; with the serials under wing in and the 'RADIO FLIGHT' titles on fin fillet in black. The black propeller had a red spinner cap and there was a black anti-glare panel. Note the underwing radome pod.

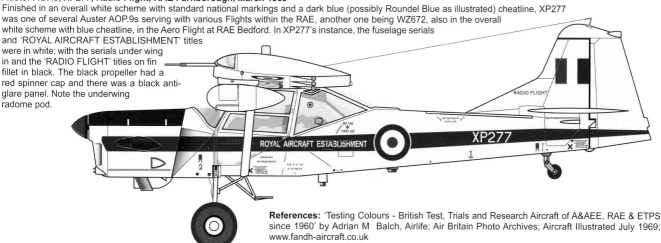

References: 'Testing Colours - British Test, Trials and Research Aircraft of A&AEE, RAE & ETPS since 1960' by Adrian M Balch, Airlife; Air Britain Photo Archives; Aircraft Illustrated July 1969; www.fandh-aircraft.co.uk

Hawker P.1127, XP831, Hawker Aircraft Company, February 1963
XP831 was the first airframe to be involved in the tethered flights in October/November 1960, flown by Hawker Siddeley Chief Test Pilot Alfred William 'Bill' Bedford at the controls. XP831 then went on to perform a vertical take-off followed by a circuit and then a short landing. It then performed a short take-off and flew a circuit followed by a vertical landing, proving the VSTOL concept and cementing the Harrier's future. XP831 is illustrated here at the time of the trials aboard HMS Ark Royal in the English Channel, in its overall natural metal scheme with national markings and serial number applied and Hawker logos and titles applied to the nose in dark blue and photo calibration markings. Note the black rubber intake lips. The aircraft crashed during a demonstration at the Paris Salon in June 1963, but was repaired, and flew from Dunsfold on 13 October 1964. It was passed onto RAE Bedford's Aerodynamic Flight on 2 February 1965 (the inset above right shows the nose markings applied during this time). XP831 made its final flight from RAF Northolt on 10 October 1972 when it flew to the RAF Museum at Hendon, where it is now an exhibit.

References: 'Hawker P.1127/Hawker Siddeley Kestrel & Harrier Mks 1-4' by Tony Buttler, Warpaint 74; World Air Power Journal Vol 6/Summer 1991 'British Aerospace/McDonnell Douglas Harrier' by Paul Jackson, Aerospace Publishing Ltd; On Target Special 'HMS Ark Royal - Fifty Years of Flight 1955-2005' by Denis J Calvert, The Aviation Workshop Publications Ltd.

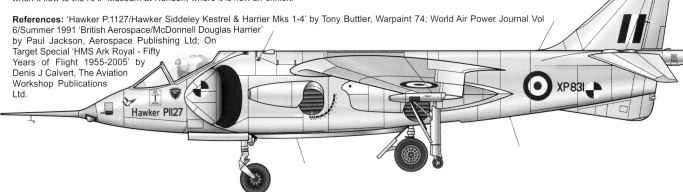

Hawker P.1127, XP972, Hawker Aircraft Company, as displayed at Farnborough on 7 September 1962
Carrying the markings of the Tripartite Evaluation Squadron on the wing upper surfaces (see insets), formed by the UK, United States of America and West Germany, XP972 was fitted with the Pegasus 2 engine, and made its first flight on 5 April 1962. It was the third P.1127 built, and the first of a four-aircraft development batch comprising XP972, XP976, XP980 and XP984. It was used for wing development testing and is shown here with the wing planform that would eventually be used on the Kestrel. In an overall natural aluminium finish with black serials, while at Farnborough the dark blue 'Hawker P1127' titles and Hawker logo on nose were carried. The aircraft crashed at Tangmere on 30 October 1962 while being flown by Hugh Merewether when the engine main bearing failed.

Reference: Warpaint Series 74 'Hawker P.1127/Hawker Siddeley Kestrel & Harrier Mks 1-4'- by Tony Buttler, Warpaint Books Ltd; Air-Britain Digest November/ December 1985 '25 Years of Practical V/STOL' by John Cook

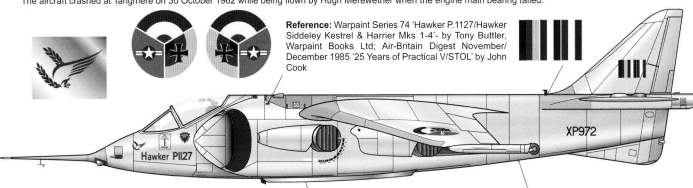

Above left: Hawker Siddeley Kestrel FGA.1, XS688, photographed at Farnborough in September 1964, represented the next stage of VTOL development between the P1127 and Harrier GR.1. XS688 clearly displays the markings of the Tri-partite Evaluation Squadron consisting of the UK, USA and West Germany, as well as its black inflatable rubber intake lips.

Above: Hawker Siddeley P1127, XP831, seen here quite late on in its life in September 1966, was used to develop the concept of jet-powered vertical take off and landing, or VTOL, which led to the eventual development and production of the Harrier GR.1 which entered RAF service in 1969.

Left: Designed to explore the concept of blown flaps, the Hunting H.126, XN714, first flew on 26 March 1963 and went to Boscombe Down in October 1964. This photo is believed to have been taken at the 1965 Paris Airshow, although it is not certain.
(See 4-view opposite)

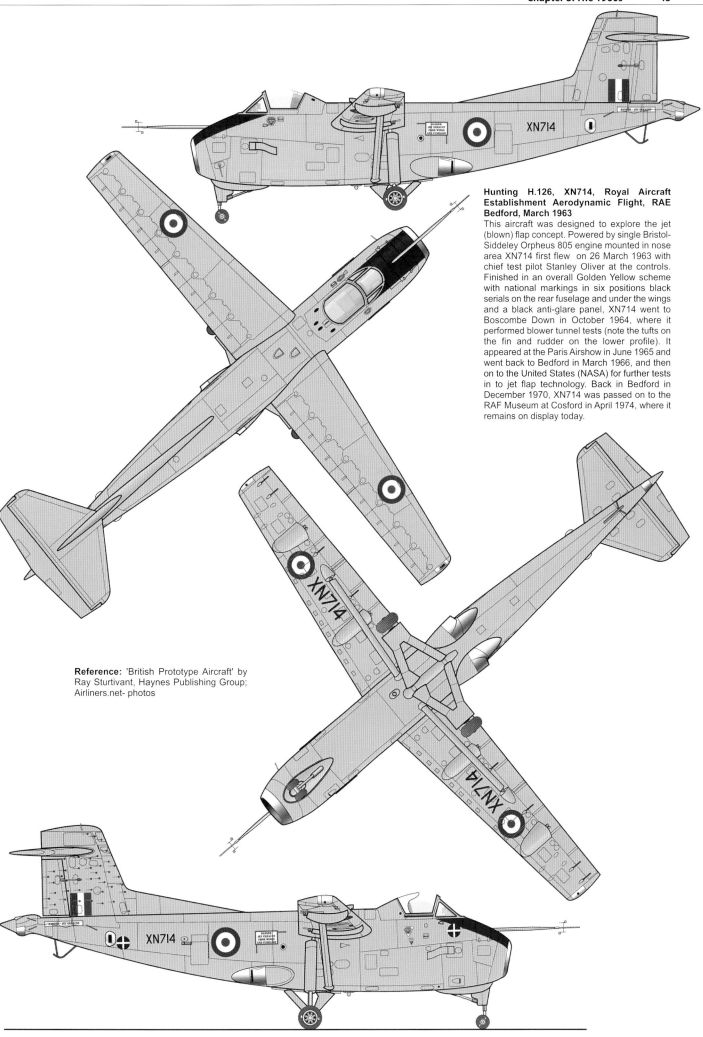

Hunting H.126, XN714, Royal Aircraft Establishment Aerodynamic Flight, RAE Bedford, March 1963

This aircraft was designed to explore the jet (blown) flap concept. Powered by single Bristol-Siddeley Orpheus 805 engine mounted in nose area XN714 first flew on 26 March 1963 with chief test pilot Stanley Oliver at the controls. Finished in an overall Golden Yellow scheme with national markings in six positions black serials on the rear fuselage and under the wings and a black anti-glare panel, XN714 went to Boscombe Down in October 1964, where it performed blower tunnel tests (note the tufts on the fin and rudder on the lower profile). It appeared at the Paris Airshow in June 1965 and went back to Bedford in March 1966, and then on to the United States (NASA) for further tests in to jet flap technology. Back in Bedford in December 1970, XN714 was passed on to the RAF Museum at Cosford in April 1974, where it remains on display today.

Reference: 'British Prototype Aircraft' by Ray Sturtivant, Haynes Publishing Group; Airliners.net- photos

Continued from page 38

without a recognisable sense of direction as far as military aircraft programmes were concerned. Subsequent efforts to purchase the American General Dynamics F-111 swing-wing strike aircraft also eventually collapsed. A considerable amount of design and research work for the TSR.2 had been undertaken at the time of the ending of the programme, and a considerable amount of taxpayers' money had been spent on a project that eventually went nowhere. Nevertheless, some benefits did eventually arise from the ashes of the TSR.2 programme, including development work on terrain-following capability that was later to gain great importance for other projects.

On a more positive note, the 1960s also witnessed the developing importance of international co-operation in aircraft programmes. The most obvious example of this was the Anglo-French Concorde civil airliner project, which developed into a highly successful collaborative venture that placed the British and French aircraft industries ahead of the rest of the world in this high-profile programme. A considerable amount of design work and flight testing was carried out in Britain as well as in France in support of what grew into the Concorde story, and it became one of the highlights of the 1960s for the British aircraft industry.

Considerable work was performed by the RAE into the many advanced aspects of the Concorde design. At Bedford, much flight testing took place into wing shapes and the handling qualities of wing designs that were tried out for the Concorde layout. A number of aircraft, such as the Bedford Aero Flight's Handley-Page HP.115, became significant participants in the programme. Also included was the world record-breaking Fairey Delta 2, WG774, which was extensively re-built as the BAC 221 as a part of the Concorde research project.

Although the Concorde was a civil airliner project, it had nevertheless required the close involvement of the considerable expertise of the RAE. This illustrated the significant point that the important relationship between the RAE and the wider aircraft industry had continued to exist despite the cut-backs and uncertainties of the era. It is important to point out that in addition to the considerable and vital work that the RAE and the A&AEE performed for the British military, there was also a long and necessary tradition of similar collaboration over civil projects. This had existed since British civil aviation was commenced again as a properly independent entity as World War Two was ending and in the immediate post-war period.

Continued on page 48

Avro Vulcan B.1, XA894, Bristol Siddeley Engines Ltd, February 1962

XA894 was delivered to Filton in July 1960, and the fuselage was modified to accommodate a Bristol Siddeley Olympus 22R turbojet in a central fairing as part of the test programme for the TSR.2 strike aircraft. To allow for clearance of the aircraft's nosewheel, the intake was bifurcated. Finished in overall high speed silver, with radome, serials and fin tip in black, the starboard mainwheel door was in Anti-flash White, and was probably a replacement unit and there was heavy staining around lower nacelles. After ground runs commenced in January 1962, XA894 first took to the skies on 23 February. In June that year, the Olympus was upgraded to 22R-1 standard with full reheat. On 3 December 1962, XA894 was performing a ground run up, when the aircraft broke up without warning. The resultant fuel spill caused a massive fire, which completely destroyed the aircraft. Fortunately, the crew managed to escape. XA894 was replaced in 1964 by XA903 – see below.

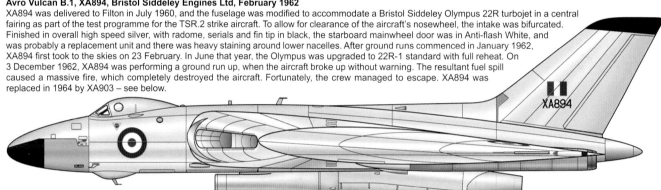

Reference: Wings of Fame Vol 3 'Vulcan- Delta Force' by Paul Jackson, Aerospace Publishing Ltd; see also
http://www.aviationarchive.org.uk/stories/pages.php?enum=GE131&pnum=1&maxp=3 and
http://www.avrovulcan.org.uk/other_photographers/894_farnborough_1.htm

Avro Vulcan B.1, XA903, Bristol Siddeley Engines Ltd, September 1966

XA903 was originally delivered to the A&AEE on 31 May 1957 and was instrumental in the trials of the Avro Blue Steel air-launched nuclear stand-off missile, but following the destruction of Vulcan XA894, it was transferred to Bristol Patchway in January 1964 to continue development work of Bristol Siddeley/SNECMA Olympus 593 turbojet engine for the Concorde programme. The engine was housed in a modified Concorde engine nacelle and mounted in the bomb bay. Finished in overall Anti-flash White with black serials, radome and fin tip, the tail cone was aluminium and again there was heavy staining around the lower nacelles. Much of the aircraft's interior was stripped out to make way for extra equipment and a seven-man crew. It was also fitted with a 27mm cannon and later in its career, served as a test bed for the Turbo Union RB.199 turbofan used in the Panavia Tornado.

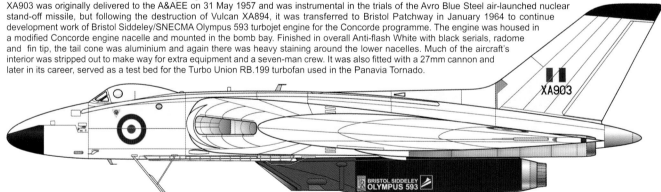

References: Wings of Fame Vol 3 'Vulcan - Delta Force' by Paul Jackson, Aerospace Publishing Ltd; 'Vulcan - Last of the V-Bombers' by Duncan Cubitt, Osprey Aerospace; Air Britain photo archives; On Target Special 'V-Bombers - Britain's Cold War Nuclear Deterrent' by Glenn Sands & Gary Madgwick, The Aviation Workshop Publications Ltd; Mark Rolfe private archives

Left: Avro Vulcan B.1, XA903, seen testing the Bristol Siddeley/SNECMA Olympus 593 jet engine in connection with the Concorde programme, the test engine can be seen mounted in the bomb bay.

Above and left: Two images of Supermarine Swift F.7, XF114, from the Royal College of Aeronautics, Cranfield, in June 1966 displaying its distinctive overall black paint scheme with white Union Flag marking on its upper fuselage and a sliding 'Donald Duck' cartoon on its nose. Presumably the latter was indicative of the fact that this airframe spent its entire life on aquaplaning duties at various establishments until retired in April 1967, ten years after XF114 had been delivered to Boscombe Down.

Supermarine Scimitar F.1, XD229, Armament Flight, Royal Aircraft Establishment Farnborough, September 1963

XD229 arrived at Farnborough on 26 June 1958 and was used to develop the weapons systems for the Scimitar. Used jointly by Farnborough and also operational at West Freugh, it was finished in a special colour scheme described as overall 'Powder Blue' with white fin and dorsal fin strake. Anti-glare panel, nose cone, wing, tailplane and fin leading edges were in black with the 'Royal Aircraft Establishment' titles on nose in white see inset).
XD229 was scrapped and used as a spares aircraft from 10 October 1966. The aircraft was fitted with the original blunt nose-cone.

Reference: 'Farnborough - 100 Years of British Aviation' by Peter J. Cooper, Midland Publishing Ltd

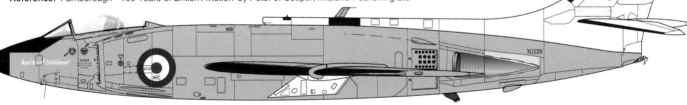

Supermarine Swift F.7, XF114, Royal College of Aeronautics, Cranfield, June 1966

XF114 first arrived at A&AEE Boscombe Down on 14 March 1957. Initially in standard RAF Day Fighter camouflage, XF114 acquired the overall gloss black scheme with white serials and Union Flag-style marking on upper fuselage in the late 1950s/early 1960s and spent its entire life on aquaplaning test runs at Boscombe Down and other establishments up until her retirement from Cranfield in April 1967. Over time, the overall gloss black scheme became quite weathered, and a 'Donald Duck' cartoon figure was painted on nose. Placed into storage at Aston Down, XF114 went onto Flintshire Technical College to be used as an instructional airframe and is now the only Swift in existence that could feasibly be made flyable.

References: Air Enthusiast 70 July-August 1997 'Supermarine Extremes – Contrasting Survivors' by Ken Ellis; Postwar Military Aircraft No 7 Supermarine Attacker, Swift and Scimitar' by Philip Birtles, Ian Allan Ltd

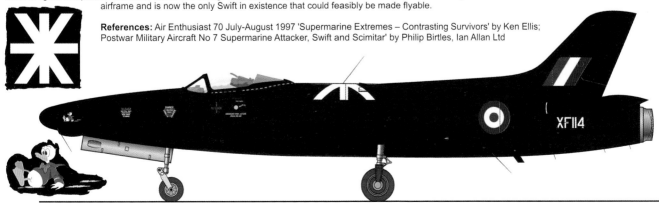

Hawker Hunter F.6 (converted to P.1109A spec), WW598, Royal Aerospace Establishment, Bedford, August 1960
In the summer of 1960, WW598 was used for TSR.2 cockpit visibility trials – note the tape applied to the inside of the canopy, representing a similar area of the TSR.2's front cockpit, although various layouts were experimented with. WW598 was painted in an overall 'white' scheme, which was in effect an 'off-white' finish which may have been the effects of overpainting the overall blue scheme illustrated on p35 (Chapter 2), in a thin coat of white. Note the weathering on the underwing drop tank. Serials were repainted in black and a black anti-glare panel was applied. It would also appear that the aircraft only had two Aden cannon fitted, as the lower pair of cannon troughs were plated over

Reference: ' A Short Illustrated History of the Royal Aerospace Establishment Bedford' by Arthur J Pearcy, Airlife

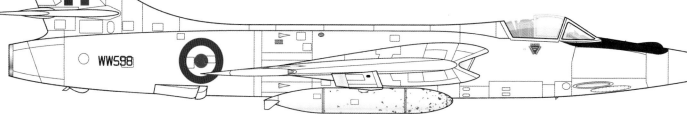

Gloster 'Gyron Junior' Javelin FAW.1, XA552, De Havilland Engine Company, summer 1961
XA552 was converted by Napier & Son to test the low speed handling qualities of the de Havilland Gyron Junior turbojet engine for eventual use in the Bristol 188 high-speed research aircraft programme. (see p39). It should be noted however that the engines used on the Bristol 188 were of considerably higher power. Finished in an overall gloss Royal Blue scheme with gold/orange lettering on the nose, and national markings thinly outlined in white, the serial number was applied to fin in white. From the photographic references used, it was impossible to discern with any real accuracy what the lettering was under the 'De Havilland Gyron Junior' script, so it has merely been represented by a dotted rectangle pending further information being available. In March 1963, XA552 was delivered to Rolls Royce at Filton where it undertook engine tests until May of the same year. However, after a mere eleven flying hours the engines were removed and used as spares for the Bristol 188 programme. With the exceptions of the engines and the colour scheme, the other most noticeable change from a standard Javelin FAW.1 was the truncated rear fuselage jet pipe area.

References: Warpaint 17 'Gloster Javelin' by Tony Butler AMRAeS, Warpaint Books Ltd;
'Postwar Military Aircraft 1: Gloster Javelin' by Maurice Allward, Ian Allan

Gloster Javelin FAW.2, XA778, A&AEE Boscombe Down, September 1967
XA778 was delivered to Boscombe Down in March 1961, and was flown against other aircraft to measure and calibrate airspeed. Finished in overall Day-Glo Orange, with a black anti-glare panel and canopy framing, the fuselage serials were white with those under the wings in black. The underwing flaps were painted in black and yellow target tug-style bands whereas the underfuselage tanks were finished in Golden Yellow on the port side and Light Aircraft Grey on the starboard. Note that the Day-Glo finish has started to fade, especially around the rear fuselage taking on a yellowish hue. By the time of its withdrawal in March 1969, XA778 was starting to look very worn, and was replaced by Javelin FAW.9, XH897.

Reference: 'Testing Colours - British Test, Trials and Research Aircraft of A&AEE, RAE & ETPS since 1960' by Adrian M Balch

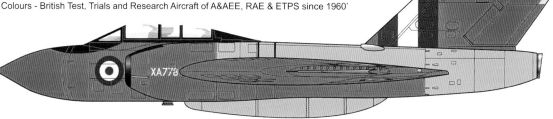

Left: Of striking appearance, Gloster Javelin, XA778, was photographed in September 1967 while still in use with the A&AEE, although by this time its Dayglo surfaces were looking rather tired. Delivered to Boscombe Down in March 1961, FAW.2, XA778, was a hybrid machine that had previously been modified to act as the prototype Javelin FAW.7 and, later, received FAW.8 flying controls. Withdrawn in March 1969, XA778 was replaced by FAW.9, XH897. (See profile above)

BAC TSR.2, XR219, flown by Roland 'Bee' Beamont, A&AEE Boscombe Down, 27 September 1964

There can be fewer aircraft in British aviation history as iconic, or as controversial, as the TSR.2. Conceived as a low-level, high-speed, strike aircraft, had it entered service, the TSR.2 would possibly have been the most advanced aircraft of its kind anywhere in the world. Powered by two Bristol Siddeley Olympus 22R reheat turbojets, each developing up to 30,600lb of thrust, the aircraft employed systems and avionics far in advance of technology in use anywhere else around the globe at the time. However, this was a governing factor leading to the TSR.2's eventual downfall and cancellation.

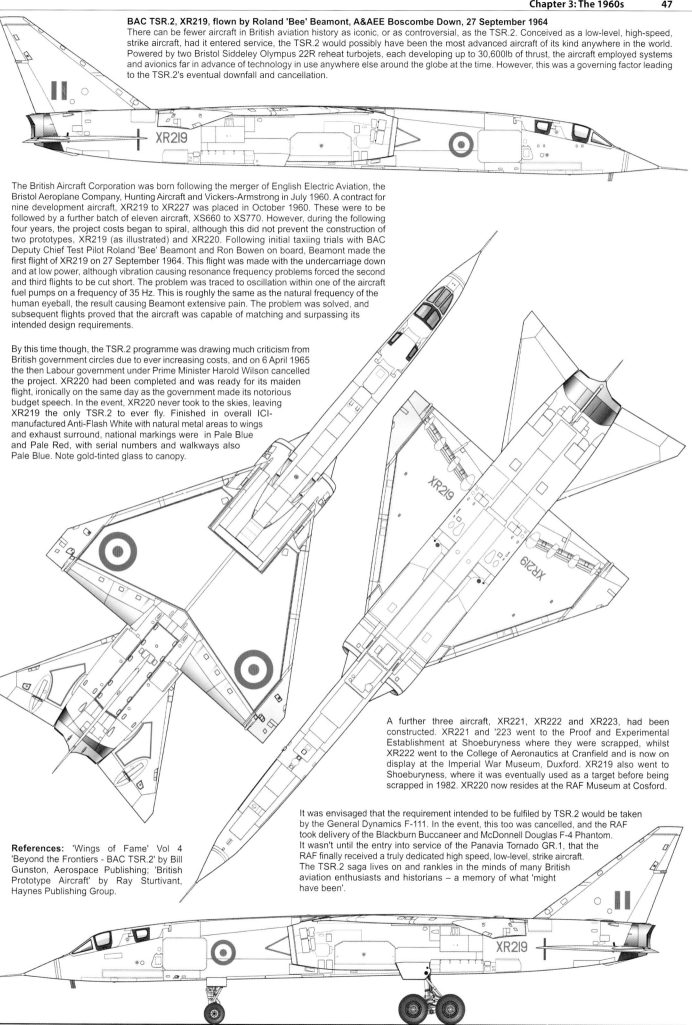

The British Aircraft Corporation was born following the merger of English Electric Aviation, the Bristol Aeroplane Company, Hunting Aircraft and Vickers-Armstrong in July 1960. A contract for nine development aircraft, XR219 to XR227 was placed in October 1960. These were to be followed by a further batch of eleven aircraft, XS660 to XS770. However, during the following four years, the project costs began to spiral, although this did not prevent the construction of two prototypes, XR219 (as illustrated) and XR220. Following initial taxiing trials with BAC Deputy Chief Test Pilot Roland 'Bee' Beamont and Ron Bowen on board, Beamont made the first flight of XR219 on 27 September 1964. This flight was made with the undercarriage down and at low power, although vibration causing resonance frequency problems forced the second and third flights to be cut short. The problem was traced to oscillation within one of the aircraft fuel pumps on a frequency of 35 Hz. This is roughly the same as the natural frequency of the human eyeball, the result causing Beamont extensive pain. The problem was solved, and subsequent flights proved that the aircraft was capable of matching and surpassing its intended design requirements.

By this time though, the TSR.2 programme was drawing much criticism from British government circles due to ever increasing costs, and on 6 April 1965 the then Labour government under Prime Minister Harold Wilson cancelled the project. XR220 had been completed and was ready for its maiden flight, ironically on the same day as the government made its notorious budget speech. In the event, XR220 never took to the skies, leaving XR219 the only TSR.2 to ever fly. Finished in overall ICI-manufactured Anti-Flash White with natural metal areas to wings and exhaust surround, national markings were in Pale Blue and Pale Red, with serial numbers and walkways also Pale Blue. Note gold-tinted glass to canopy.

A further three aircraft, XR221, XR222 and XR223, had been constructed. XR221 and '223 went to the Proof and Experimental Establishment at Shoeburyness where they were scrapped, whilst XR222 went to the College of Aeronautics at Cranfield and is now on display at the Imperial War Museum, Duxford. XR219 also went to Shoeburyness, where it was eventually used as a target before being scrapped in 1982. XR220 now resides at the RAF Museum at Cosford.

It was envisaged that the requirement intended to be fulfiled by TSR.2 would be taken by the General Dynamics F-111. In the event, this too was cancelled, and the RAF took delivery of the Blackburn Buccaneer and McDonnell Douglas F-4 Phantom. It wasn't until the entry into service of the Panavia Tornado GR.1, that the RAF finally received a truly dedicated high speed, low-level, strike aircraft. The TSR.2 saga lives on and rankles in the minds of many British aviation enthusiasts and historians – a memory of what 'might have been'.

References: 'Wings of Fame' Vol 4 'Beyond the Frontiers - BAC TSR.2' by Bill Gunston, Aerospace Publishing; 'British Prototype Aircraft' by Ray Sturtivant, Haynes Publishing Group.

Continued from page 44

Indeed, in a further reflection of the close ties between the wider industry and the test establishments, a number of aircraft types actually made their maiden flights from Boscombe Down rather than at the manufacturers' own airfields. These famously included the TSR.2, which first flew from Boscombe Down in September 1964, (interestingly, the second prototype TSR.2 was damaged while being transported by road to the Wiltshire airfield to make its first flight). In a wider context, an 'Approved Firm' scheme had been instituted during the 1950s between the industry and the A&AEE for data sharing and verification, particularly over performance testing by the aircraft companies of their products.

The Concorde programme was not the only important collaborative venture of the 1960s that illustrated the growing significance of international co-operation between allied countries into the creation of new designs. The increasing cost and complexity of new aircraft programmes, or the upgrading of existing types – and the increasingly long lead-time in creating new projects – was, even at that time, resulting in the growing necessity for more than one country to bear by means of a collaborative arrangement the substantial costs for R&D, promotion, prototype construction, test flying, and eventually the costs of production, for new aircraft ventures.

Further projects of the 1960s, such as the Anglo-French SEPECAT Jaguar programme that commenced in 1966 and led to the successful service introduction of the Jaguar twin-engined strike and training aircraft during the 1970s, were illustrative of this growing trend. Indeed, during the 1950s following the formation of NATO, (which actually took place in the late 1940s), a number of foreign aircraft types had been briefly evaluated by Boscombe Down test pilots in an effort to assess their wider suitability for their possible common adoption by a number of NATO air forces. Such exotic types as the Breguet Taon light strike fighter proposal from France had briefly taken the attention of the A&AEE test pilots, although in the event the concept that led to these trials of NATO standardisation on a single type was not carried through to a conclusion as originally intended.

Nevertheless, an excellent example of British ingenuity started to come to fruition during the 1960s, and in so doing demonstrated the necessary processes needed to successfully bring a concept into reality, to begin with through the initial research and development phases, to prototype building and flight testing, in order to evaluate the concept being developed, and thence to pre-production development and eventually production status. This project was the Hawker Siddeley Harrier V/STOL programme, which eventually saw the successful service introduction of the world's first vertical take-off front-line combat aircraft.

The road to the successful realisation of this project was a long one, and involved considerable work by the aircraft industry and both the RAE and the A&AEE, with extensive co-operation being achieved. It included a large amount of proving that

started, as far as flight testing was concerned, with the Rolls-Royce Thrust Measuring Rig, (the famous 'Flying Bedstead' of the 1950s), and thence to the Short SC.1 before the P.1127, Kestrel development aircraft and finally the Harrier production aircraft were successfully flown. The Harrier, which entered RAF service from 1969 onwards, and later the navalised Sea Harrier, was one of the finest examples of the endeavours to create the very best and most advanced front-line military aircraft by the post-war British aircraft industry.

Although the work of the RAE and the A&AEE was usually hidden from public view, it was thanks to the Harrier that the A&AEE became much more highly publicised during 1969. In that year a transatlantic air race was sponsored by the 'Daily Mail' newspaper. Amongst the contestants was a two-aircraft Harrier entry, comprising two of the very early Harrier GR.1 aircraft. Although technically RAF-operated Harriers, they were flown by two A Squadron pilots from Boscombe Down, and in the westbound race from the Post Office Tower in London to the Empire State Building in New York the Harrier entry was the winner. Considerable popular interest was generated in the event, and the two Harrier pilots, Squadron Leaders T Lecky-Thompson and Graham Williams, became genuine personalities.

On a more mundane but equally significant level, the A&AEE's work with the Harrier was a long and fruitful period in which much development work was accomplished from the late 1960s onwards, including considerable weapons clearance work and proving. Although the Harrier was a unique aircraft type because of its V/STOL capabilities, the variety of long-running development and clearance-for-service work that was performed by the A&AEE on the Harrier mirrored that performed on many other aircraft types for British military service. It must also be remembered that not all of this work was carried out in Britain. The Harrier, for example, underwent cold weather testing in Canada in 1969/1970, and hot weather trials in the Arizona desert in the United States, as a part of the testing for its acceptance for front-line service.

An important organisation returned to Boscombe Down in the 1960s in the form of the ETPS. Having spent two decades at Farnborough, the school returned to Boscombe Down in 1968, where it has remained ever since. During its time at Farnborough it had taken on, during 1963, a rotary wing course for prospective test pilots of helicopter designs. This reflected the, by then, great importance of the helicopter in many air forces and naval air arms. Indeed, the helicopter was no stranger to the test establishments at Farnborough and Boscombe Down. From the earliest days of military helicopter flying in the 1940s, helicopters had been tested for their service suitability at Boscombe Down and much R&D work had been undertaken at Farnborough. The ETPS itself had taken on charge a number of helicopter types during the later 1950s, and helicopter testing was to become as important as that carried out on fixed-wing aircraft in the decades that followed right up to the present day.

Below: De Havilland Devon C.2, VP975, belonging to RAE Farnborough's Air Transport Flight circa September 1964. (See profile opposite)

De Havilland DH 104 Devon C.1, VP959, RAE Farnborough Air Transport Flight, June 1962
The de Havilland Devon, essentially a military variant of the de Havilland DH 104 Dove civilian short-haul airliner, were mainly used for ferrying and transporting VIPs, such as VP959 of the RAE Air Transport Flight, although some were also used for test work as well. VP959 was finished in an overall silver scheme with white upper fuselage decking and rudder, with post-war national markings and black serials. Day-Glo areas were applied on the nose, rear fuselage, fin and dorsal strake. The flash above the cabin windows was black with a white panel in which the RAE title was in black.

Reference: 'Farnborough - 100 Years of British Aviation' by Peter J Cooper, Midland Publishing

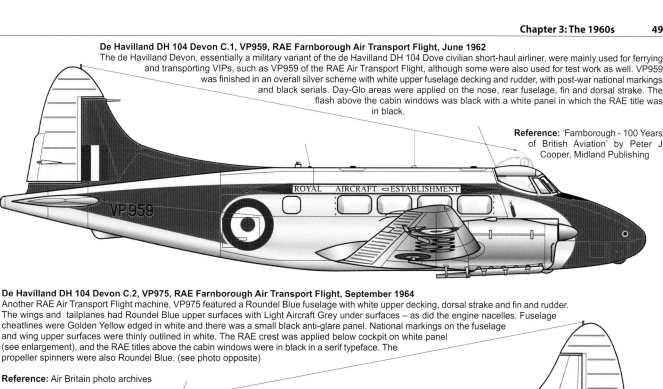

De Havilland DH 104 Devon C.2, VP975, RAE Farnborough Air Transport Flight, September 1964
Another RAE Air Transport Flight machine, VP975 featured a Roundel Blue fuselage with white upper decking, dorsal strake and fin and rudder. The wings and tailplanes had Roundel Blue upper surfaces with Light Aircraft Grey under surfaces – as did the engine nacelles. Fuselage cheatlines were Golden Yellow edged in white and there was a small black anti-glare panel. National markings on the fuselage and wing upper surfaces were thinly outlined in white. The RAE crest was applied below cockpit on white panel (see enlargement), and the RAE titles above the cabin windows were in black in a serif typeface. The propeller spinners were also Roundel Blue. (see photo opposite)

Reference: Air Britain photo archives

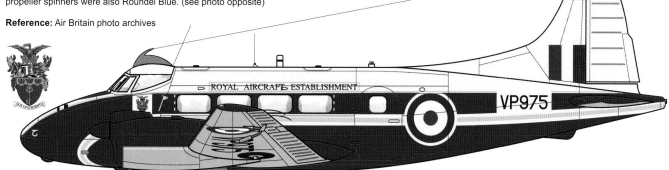

De Havilland DH 104 Devon C.1, VP980, Empire Test Pilots School, RAE Boscombe Down, September 1964
The ETPS operated VP980 in the ferrying and transport role in the early 1960s. Finished in an overall silver scheme with white upper fuselage decking, fin and rudder, with Roundel Blue cheatline above cabin windows, it carried ETPS titles on nose in black, the de Havilland logo on fin and had a black anti-glare panel. The wings, nacelles and tailplanes appear to be in natural metal finish. Post-war national markings were carried in all positions and the serials were black. Nose tip, probe and spinners were painted in Day-Glo orange. VP980, was also used by the Telecommunications Research Establishment (Royal Radar Establishment) at RAE Bedford, in the mid-1960s.

Empire Test Pilots School

Reference:
Air Britain photo archives

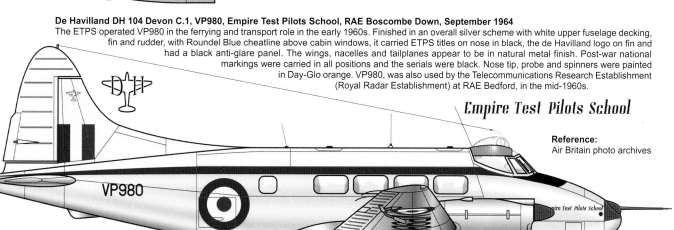

De Havilland DH 104 Devon C.2, WB530, RAE Bedford, April 1968
The Devon C.2 was a re-engined transport and communications version of the C.1, of which some forty or so were originally produced for the RAF. WB530 was serving with the RAE Air Transport Flight by the late 1960s and was finished in a Light Aircraft Grey fuselage with white upper decking, with silver wings, engine nacelles, with what appears to be areas left in primer (probably Zinc Chromate as illustrated), and tailplanes. The trim around the fuselage windows and on the nose was Roundel Blue with the anti-glare panel in a darker blue. The rear fuselage, fin and nose were covered in 'FabGlo' panels with the base Light Aircraft Grey exposed. The rudder was white and the spinners and serials were black. Note the small yellow diagonal flash above the fuselage cabin window. The nosewheel doors (shown inset) were finished in Day-Glo with Light Aircraft Grey hinges.

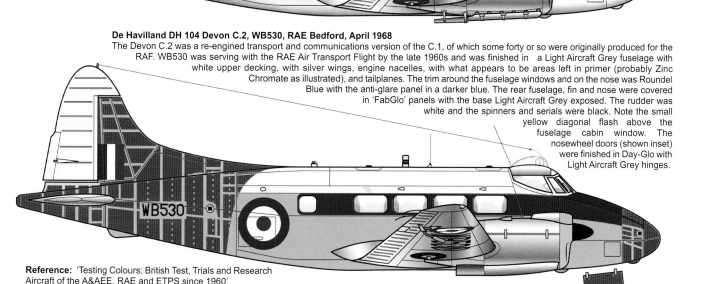

Reference: 'Testing Colours: British Test, Trials and Research Aircraft of the A&AEE, RAE and ETPS since 1960'

Above: Avro Lincoln B.2, RF533, seen at the Stansted Fire School on 29 October 1962 following its career with the Ministry of Supply who had undertaken numerous and varied research tasks using this airframe since 1948. RF533 later succumbed to fire.

Avro Lincoln B.2, RF533, Stansted Fire School, June 1961
RF533 is shown here as it appeared shortly after arriving at the Stansted Fire School, having reached the end of its useful life, and looking decidedly the worse for wear. Originally finished in the standard post-war Bomber Scheme of Medium Sea Grey upper surfaces with Anti-Searchlight Glossy Black side and under surfaces to pattern No 2, with red fuselage serials and white underwing serials, the Day-Glo nose cone, front and rear fuselage sections, fins and wing tips.sections, had faded to an orange-yellow hue. RF533 was destroyed by fire shortly afterwards.

Reference: 'Farnborough - 100 Years of British Aviation' by Peter J Cooper, Midland Publishing Ltd

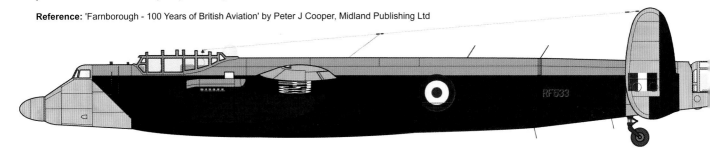

Avro Anson T.21, VS562, Aeroplane & Armament Experimental Establishment, Boscombe Down, 1962
VS562 was the prototype T.21 aircraft and was operated at a number of test and experimental establishments during its working life. When it was serving with the A&AEE at Boscombe Down in 1962 it carried an overall painted aluminium finish, with white fuselage upper decking. Day-Glo/'FabGlo' areas were applied to the nose and fin/rear fuselage. The cheatline is Day-Glo with Roundel Blue edging. Note the yellow prototype 'P' marking retained on the fuselage sides. Serials, spinners and anti-glare panel were all in black.

Reference: Warpaint No 53 'Avro Anson Mks 1-22' by Alan W Hall, Warpaint Books Ltd

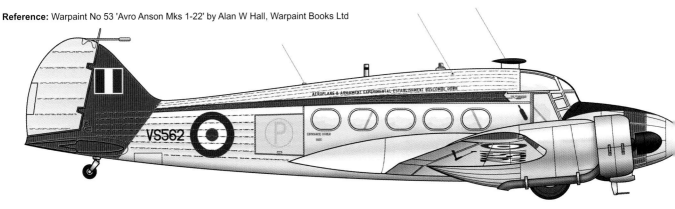

Below: Avro Anson T.21, VS562, as used by the A&AEE circa 1962. VS562 was the prototype T.21 Anson and was operated by several experimental establishments during its working life. Delivered in 1948, VS562's military flying career lasted until 9 April 1965 when it became maintenance airframe 8012M and still existed at Llanbedr as late as 1980.

Handley Page Hastings C.1A, TG618, Meteorological Research Flight, RAE Farnborough, August 1963
TG618 was one of a batch of 100 Hastings C.1s built by Handley Page at Radlett and delivered to the RAF between November 1947 and February 1950, some of which were converted to Met 1 and T.5 configuration. Finished in the standard overall aluminium/natural metal finish with white fuselage upper surfaces divided by a Roundel Blue cheatline, black serials and anti-glare panel, TG618's nacelles, cowlings, wings, tailplanes and radar pod were painted in aluminium – the radar pod having a black tip. There were Day-Glo sections on the fin, wing and tailplane tips, and the spinners were painted in Day-Glo too. The RAE crest was carried below and slightly to rear of cockpit (see inset), and the Meteorological Research Flight titling was applied in black above the fuselage cabin windows. TG618 was Struck Off Charge at the end of June 1968.

Reference: 'Testing Colours - British Test, Trials and Research Aircraft of A&AEE, RAE & ETPS since 1960' by Adrian M Balch, Airlife

Vickers Varsity T.1, WF417, Blind Landing Experimental Unit (BLEU), RAE Bedford, mid-1965
One of sixty Varsity T.1s delivered between September 1951 and September 1952, WF417 served with the A&AEE before being transferred to the BLEU at the end of November 1954, with which unit it was still serving in mid-1965. Painted aluminium overall with white upper fuselage, fin and rudder, the fuselage cheatline was in in Roundel Blue edged in Post Office Red with the B.L.E.U. initials in black, and the 'Blind Landing Experimental Unit' titles in white on the cheatline. Serials and anti-glare panel were black with the fin/rudder tip in Post Office Red.

Reference: Air Britain photo archives; photograph supplied by James Lawrence

Bristol 170 Freighter Mk.31C, XJ470 (c/n 13217), A&AEE Boscombe Down, July 1967
XJ470 was a specific one-off build for the Ministry of Supply, and was delivered to the A&AEE at Boscombe Down in March 1955 for heavy equipment transport duties, and as such was probably the only Bristol Freighter to carry RAF national markings. Finished in an overall painted aluminium scheme with white fuselage upper surfaces divided by a Day-Glo cheatline with blue trim, the engine nacelles and cowlings are believed to have been Light Aircraft Grey (as illustrated), although the cowlings were 'silver' at one stage (see photograph).

Reference: 'Testing Colours - British Test, Trials and Research Aircraft of A&AEE, RAE & ETPS since 1960' by Adrian M Balch, Airlife

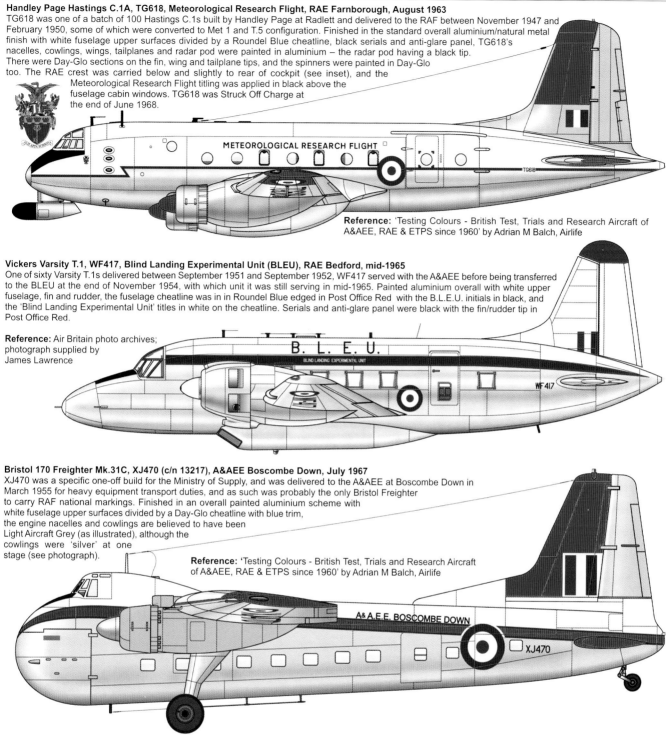

Below: Seen circa 1966/67, Bristol Freighter XJ470 was used by the A&AEE to transport equipment around Europe as required. Delivered in early 1955, XJ470 spent all its life with the A&AEE until retired in July 1968 – it was broken up the following year.

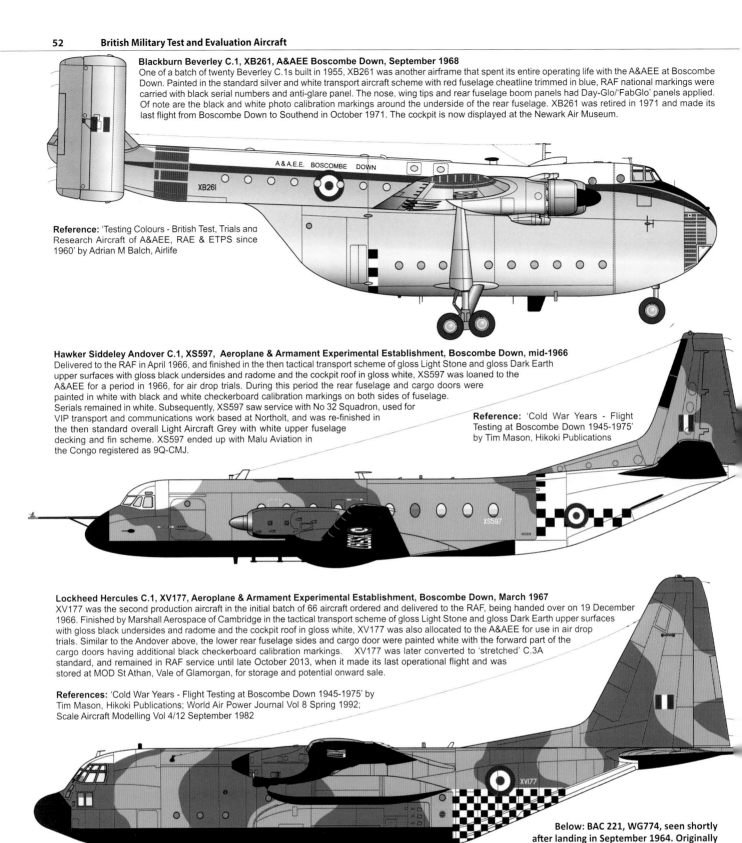

Blackburn Beverley C.1, XB261, A&AEE Boscombe Down, September 1968

One of a batch of twenty Beverley C.1s built in 1955, XB261 was another airframe that spent its entire operating life with the A&AEE at Boscombe Down. Painted in the standard silver and white transport aircraft scheme with red fuselage cheatline trimmed in blue, RAF national markings were carried with black serial numbers and anti-glare panel. The nose, wing tips and rear fuselage boom panels had Day-Glo/'FabGlo' panels applied. Of note are the black and white photo calibration markings around the underside of the rear fuselage. XB261 was retired in 1971 and made its last flight from Boscombe Down to Southend in October 1971. The cockpit is now displayed at the Newark Air Museum.

Reference: 'Testing Colours - British Test, Trials and Research Aircraft of A&AEE, RAE & ETPS since 1960' by Adrian M Balch, Airlife

Hawker Siddeley Andover C.1, XS597, Aeroplane & Armament Experimental Establishment, Boscombe Down, mid-1966

Delivered to the RAF in April 1966, and finished in the then tactical transport scheme of gloss Light Stone and gloss Dark Earth upper surfaces with gloss black undersides and radome and the cockpit roof in gloss white, XS597 was loaned to the A&AEE for a period in 1966, for air drop trials. During this period the rear fuselage and cargo doors were painted in white with black and white checkerboard calibration markings on both sides of fuselage. Serials remained in white. Subsequently, XS597 saw service with No 32 Squadron, used for VIP transport and communications work based at Northolt, and was re-finished in the then standard overall Light Aircraft Grey with white upper fuselage decking and fin scheme. XS597 ended up with Malu Aviation in the Congo registered as 9Q-CMJ.

Reference: 'Cold War Years - Flight Testing at Boscombe Down 1945-1975' by Tim Mason, Hikoki Publications

Lockheed Hercules C.1, XV177, Aeroplane & Armament Experimental Establishment, Boscombe Down, March 1967

XV177 was the second production aircraft in the initial batch of 66 aircraft ordered and delivered to the RAF, being handed over on 19 December 1966. Finished by Marshall Aerospace of Cambridge in the tactical transport scheme of gloss Light Stone and gloss Dark Earth upper surfaces with gloss black undersides and radome and the cockpit roof in gloss white, XV177 was also allocated to the A&AEE for use in air drop trials. Similar to the Andover above, the lower rear fuselage sides and cargo door were painted white with the forward part of the cargo doors having additional black checkerboard calibration markings. XV177 was later converted to 'stretched' C.3A standard, and remained in RAF service until late October 2013, when it made its last operational flight and was stored at MOD St Athan, Vale of Glamorgan, for storage and potential onward sale.

References: 'Cold War Years - Flight Testing at Boscombe Down 1945-1975' by Tim Mason, Hikoki Publications; World Air Power Journal Vol 8 Spring 1992; Scale Aircraft Modelling Vol 4/12 September 1982

Below: BAC 221, WG774, seen shortly after landing in September 1964. Originally built as a Fairey Delta FD.2, WG774 was reconstructed in 1960 to the form seen here. (See 4-view opposite)

BAC 221, WG774, SBAC show at Farnborough, 1966
Fairey's FD.2 WG774 (see also p31), was heavily modified by BAC (who by then owned Fairey) to test the new 'ogive' wing planform type envisaged to be used on the new BAC/Aerospatiale Concorde supersonic airliner, and re-named BAC 221. The resultant aircraft was only marginally recognisable from the previous design, exhibiting a considerably longer fuselage, and of course, the new wing, although it retained the 'droop snoot' of the FD.2. On initial roll-out, WG774 was completely unpainted and unmarked, but soon acquired an interim paint scheme of a mid-blue fuselage and fin with just the wings remaining in their original natural metal finish, albeit with red flashes on the chines, to give a more definite photographic shape against the sky.

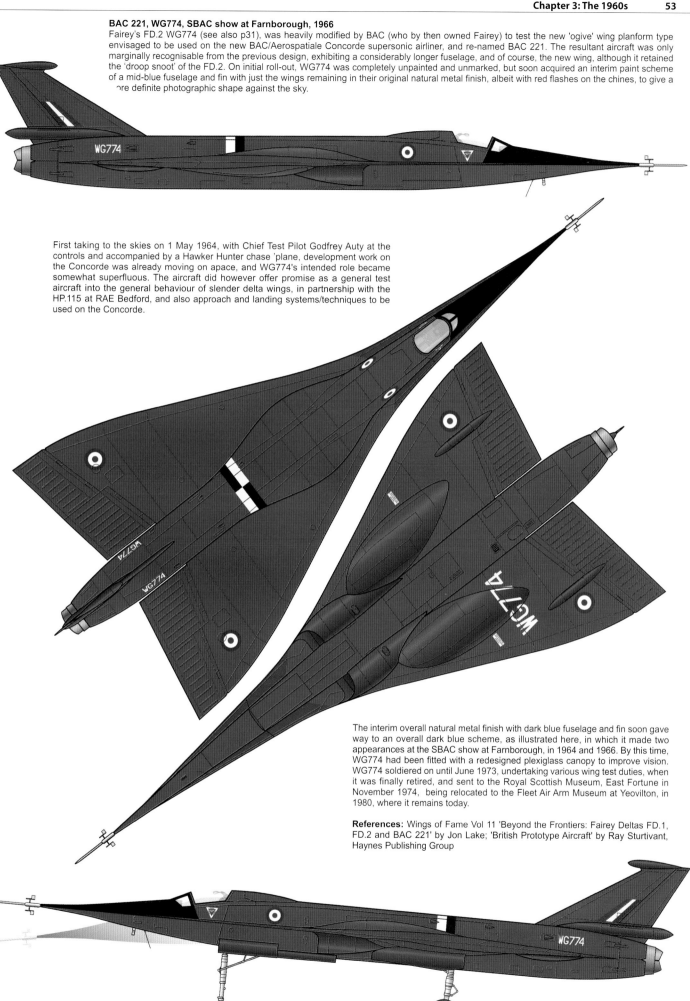

First taking to the skies on 1 May 1964, with Chief Test Pilot Godfrey Auty at the controls and accompanied by a Hawker Hunter chase 'plane, development work on the Concorde was already moving on apace, and WG774's intended role became somewhat superfluous. The aircraft did however offer promise as a general test aircraft into the general behaviour of slender delta wings, in partnership with the HP.115 at RAE Bedford, and also approach and landing systems/techniques to be used on the Concorde.

The interim overall natural metal finish with dark blue fuselage and fin soon gave way to an overall dark blue scheme, as illustrated here, in which it made two appearances at the SBAC show at Farnborough, in 1964 and 1966. By this time, WG774 had been fitted with a redesigned plexiglass canopy to improve vision. WG774 soldiered on until June 1973, undertaking various wing test duties, when it was finally retired, and sent to the Royal Scottish Museum, East Fortune in November 1974, being relocated to the Fleet Air Arm Museum at Yeovilton, in 1980, where it remains today.

References: Wings of Fame Vol 11 'Beyond the Frontiers: Fairey Deltas FD.1, FD.2 and BAC 221' by Jon Lake; 'British Prototype Aircraft' by Ray Sturtivant, Haynes Publishing Group

Above: First flown on 25 May 1957 and photographed at Wyton on 14 September 1963 is Westland Whirlwind HAS.7, XK907 '9', one of a batch intended for the RN but in this instance delivered instead to No.2 Rotary Wing, Empire Test Pilots School, Farnborough. At this time 'Empire Test Pilots School' was written in full across XK907's nose with the last two words visible in this image above the yellow and black probe.

Westland Whirlwind HAS.7, XK907/9, No 2 Rotary Wing, Empire Test Pilots School, RAE Farnborough, September 1963

Built and delivered to the Royal Navy's Fleet Air Arm in May 1957, XK907 had been transferred to the Empire Test Pilots School, No 2 Rotary Wing, at RAE Farnborough, by September 1963. Finished in overall Sky with Extra Dark Sea Grey upper surfaces, serials and the numeral '9' were in black. The 'Empire Test Pilots School' title was carried on the nose in red (see inset). The nose probe was yellow with black banding. XK907 was transferred to Boscombe Down on 6 March 1968, and then to Autair on 30 March 1971. By this time, the red 'Empire Test Pilots School' nose title had been removed and the ETPS crest on a white black-outlined rectangular background had been added, it is thought to both sides of the cabin. At the time of writing, the front cabin and engine section of XK907 were in open storage at the Midland Air Museum, Baginton, Coventry.

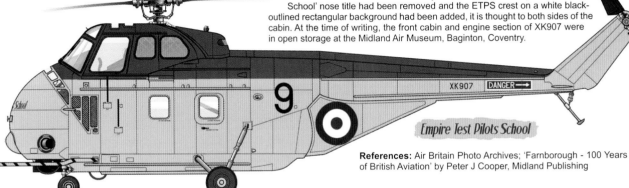

References: Air Britain Photo Archives; 'Farnborough - 100 Years of British Aviation' by Peter J Cooper, Midland Publishing

Westland Scout AH Mk 1, XP165/5, Rotary Wing Test Squadron, Empire Test Pilots School, RAE Farnborough, September 1966

XP165 was the first Scout AH.1 to be built and served with Fairey, Westlands and Blackburn before it went to Farnborough on 21 April 1964. Finished in overall Sky with Light Grey (BS381C: 631) upper surfaces, the serials and numeral '5' were in white, with the 'ETPS' title in red on the boom sides and the ETPS crest on a red outlined white rectangle on the engine bay sides. XP165 went to Boscombe Down on 24 January 1968 when the ETPS relocated there. It was withdrawn from service in June 1971 and is now an exhibit at the Helicopter Museum, Weston-Super-Mare.

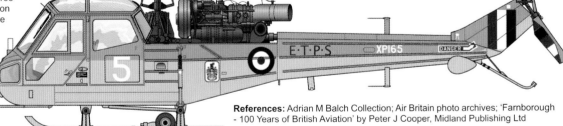

References: Adrian M Balch Collection; Air Britain photo archives; 'Farnborough - 100 Years of British Aviation' by Peter J Cooper, Midland Publishing Ltd

Westland Whirlwind HAR.5, XJ445, Instrument and Electrical Engineering (IEE) Flight, Royal Aircraft Establishment Farnborough, 1968

XJ445 was delivered from Westland's on 17 June 1958. Initially used in the development of all-weather instrumentation, automatic approach equipment, displays technology, it was finished in a unique scheme thought to have been overall Deep Cream (BS381C: 353) and Post Office Red (BS381C: 538) with post-war national markings on the boom fillet and black serials, and became the longest serving Whirlwind at Farnborough. XJ445 was passed to the Chemical Defence Establishment at Proton Down, Wiltshire for contamination/de-contamination tests in November 1971, and was known as 'The Red and Yellow Whirlwind' due to its scheme.

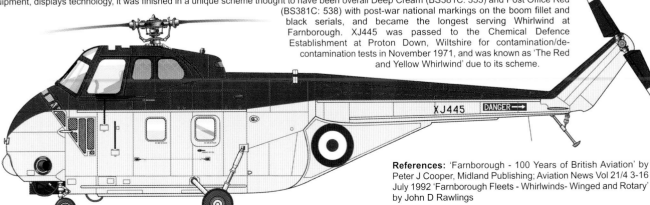

References: 'Farnborough - 100 Years of British Aviation' by Peter J Cooper, Midland Publishing; Aviation News Vol 21/4 3-16 July 1992 'Farnborough Fleets - Whirlwinds- Winged and Rotary' by John D Rawlings

Fairey FD.2, WG777, RAE. Farnborough, May 1966
WG777 was the sister aircraft to WG774 (see p31) and made its maiden flight on 15 February 1956. Initially, finished in overall natural metal, polished to a mirror-like sheen, both FD.2s appeared at the SBAC show at Farnborough in September 1956, WG774 piloted by Peter Twiss, and WG777 by Gordon Slade.

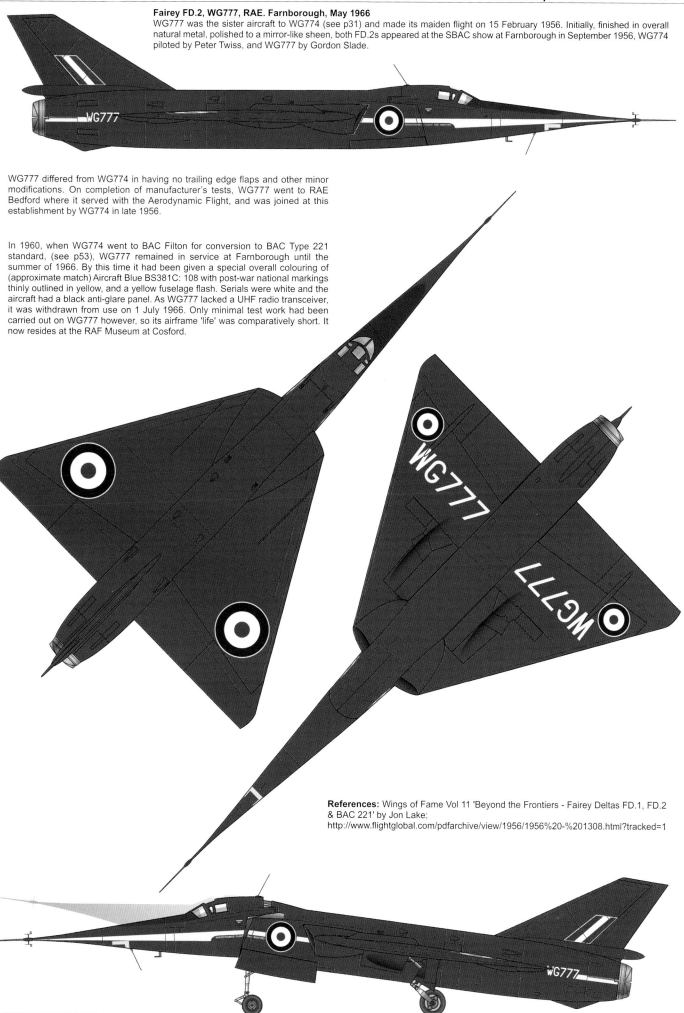

WG777 differed from WG774 in having no trailing edge flaps and other minor modifications. On completion of manufacturer's tests, WG777 went to RAE Bedford where it served with the Aerodynamic Flight, and was joined at this establishment by WG774 in late 1956.

In 1960, when WG774 went to BAC Filton for conversion to BAC Type 221 standard, (see p53), WG777 remained in service at Farnborough until the summer of 1966. By this time it had been given a special overall colouring of (approximate match) Aircraft Blue BS381C: 108 with post-war national markings thinly outlined in yellow, and a yellow fuselage flash. Serials were white and the aircraft had a black anti-glare panel. As WG777 lacked a UHF radio transceiver, it was withdrawn from use on 1 July 1966. Only minimal test work had been carried out on WG777 however, so its airframe 'life' was comparatively short. It now resides at the RAF Museum at Cosford.

References: Wings of Fame Vol 11 'Beyond the Frontiers - Fairey Deltas FD.1, FD.2 & BAC 221' by Jon Lake;
http://www.flightglobal.com/pdfarchive/view/1956/1956%20-%201308.html?tracked=1

Chapter 4: The 1970s

The onset of the 1970s continued very much the trend of the later 1960s, with reduced aircraft fleets at both Farnborough and Boscombe Down compared to the 1950s, and more problems for some of Britain's aircraft companies. The very high-profile financial difficulties that the famous engine company Rolls-Royce found itself in was one of a number of problems that plagued the wider aircraft industry during the decade, as comparatively reduced defence spending and the requirement for fewer front-line aircraft types continued to have a detrimental effect on the military infrastructure as well. Fortunately Rolls-Royce was saved, and continues to exist as one of the world's premier engine designers and manufacturers.

However, defence cuts instituted by the Labour Government of the mid-1970s, which were not reversed by the incoming Conservative administration at the end of the decade, which led to the abandonment of a conventional aircraft carrier-based Fleet Air Arm. During 1977 much of what was left of Britain's aircraft manufacturers was nationalised under the umbrella of a new entity named British Aerospace. This left only a small number of independent British companies, such as Westland Helicopters at Yeovil in Somerset. Westlands fortunately continued to be success story, and had become involved in useful foreign collaboration with France during the 1960s that

led to such projects as the Puma and Lynx helicopters – each of which has proven to be highly successful in military service.

Another significant collaborative programme, that is still with us today, gained momentum during the early 1970s – the MRCA or Multi-Role Combat Aircraft project, which eventually came to fruition as the Tornado. An international grouping named Panavia was formed in 1969 to oversee and create the multi-national programme, which included participation from Italy and West Germany as well as Britain. A very considerable amount of flight testing of the Tornado took place in all of the Panavia member countries, reflecting the fact that there were different versions of the type for strike and fighter roles, and each country was interested in a slightly different standard with various avionics installations, weapons capabilities and many other detail changes. The Tornado proved to be a highly successful combat aircraft, and is still undertaking front-line combat missions at the time of writing.

In the early part of the 1970s, the Ministry of Defence (MoD) in the form that is familiar to us today was first created. This had a considerable bearing on military aircraft procurement for the British armed forces, and therefore also for official flight testing
Continued on page 59

Above and Left: Gloster Javelin FAW.9, XH897, A&AEE Boscombe Down, seen in August 1968 at RAF Coltishall just weeks after receiving this outstanding colour scheme for its duties as a chase aircraft and for photographic calibration work. Whilst Javelin XA778's days were by now numbered, XH897 would continue to fly for almost seven more years – the last of the breed to do so.
Fred Martin Collection

(See 4-view opposite)

Gloster Javelin FAW.9, XH897, 'A' Flight, Aircraft & Armament Experimental Establishment (A&AEE) Boscombe Down, August 1970
This aircraft is probably the best known of all the test Javelins and was originally built as an FAW.7. It saw service with the RAF and was, throughout that time, on the strengths of Nos 5, 25 and 33 Squadrons, before being passed over to the A&AEE during the 1960s. XH897 served as a chase aircraft and also on photographic calibration work, hence the striking BS381C: 538 Post Office Red and white scheme. A black anti-glare panel was applied, and the fronts of engine intakes and the serials were also in black. 'A Flight FIGHTER TEST SQUADRON' markings were carried on the nose is in red on white section (see inset). Also note the red 'seadog' 'zap' on the outer faces of both engine intakes (see inset). XH897 was instrumental in the development of the Short SC.9, Panavia Tornado and Concorde SST programmes. XH897 was retired from service on 24 January 1975, when it made its last flight to Duxford – where it remains to this day as an exhibit.

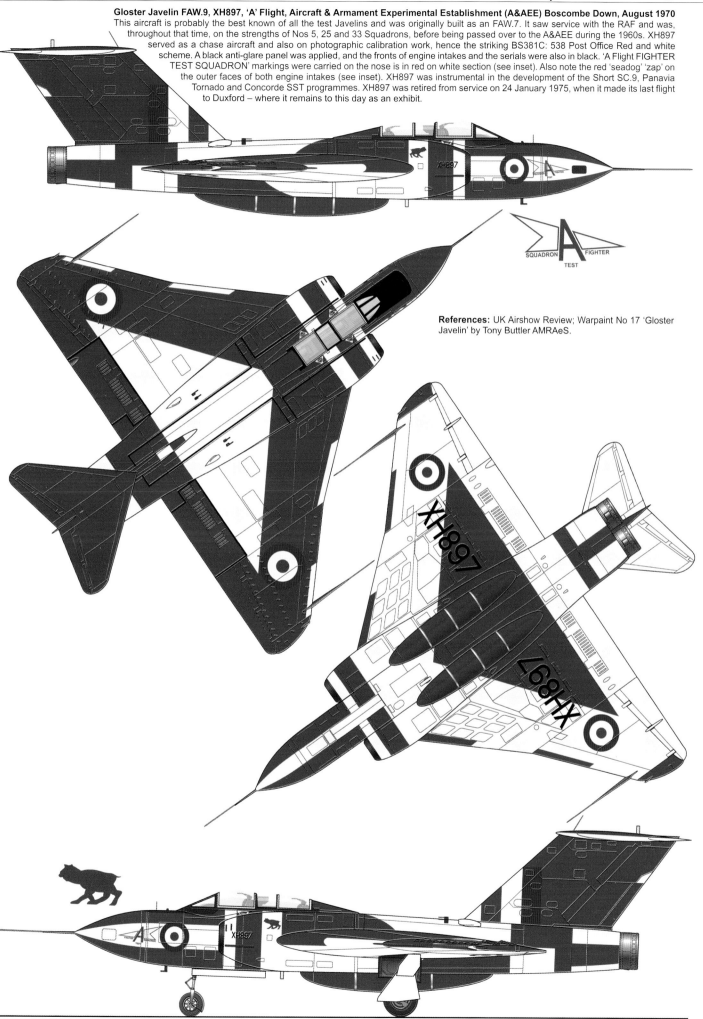

References: UK Airshow Review; Warpaint No 17 'Gloster Javelin' by Tony Buttler AMRAeS.

Hawker Hunter F.6 (P.1109B), WW598, Royal Aircraft Establishment Llandbedr, early 1970s
WW598 again, (see pp35 and 46), this time finished in an overall white scheme with Roundel Blue spine, fin, fuselage flash and tank upper surfaces. It also appears that the anti-glare panel was the same dark blue shade. Serials and 'Royal Aircraft Establishment' titles were in black. Note the red Welsh Dragon motif on the nose (inset). The nose bulge housed a camera. At this time WW598 was used as a chase aircraft for Llanbedr-based target drones, but went back to Hawker Siddeley Aviation in May 1974 and was converted to FGA.70A standard and passed on to the Lebanese Air Force,

Reference: 'Hawker Hunter 1951-2007 in UK and Foreign Service' by David J Griffin

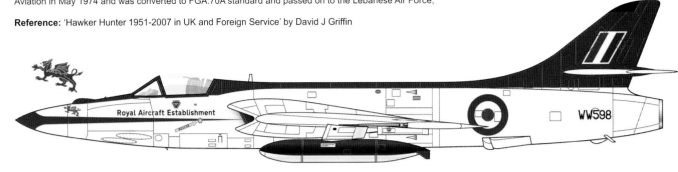

Hawker Hunter T.12, XE531, Instrument & Electrical Engineering (I&EE) Department, Royal Aircraft Establishment, Farnborough, July 1971
XE531 was built as a single-seat F.6 (with an Avon 203) but converted to FGA.9 spec (and re-fitted with Avon 207), before finally being converted to twin-seat T.12 standard. Finished in a striking overall gloss Ident Green, a special one-off colour which does not appear to have a BS381 code assigned to it, with gloss white spine, fin and rudder, nose fuselage flash and wing tanks/pylons, the serials were white and the anti-glare panel and tip of nose were black. The wing tank flashes were also Ident Green. An RAE crest and title (in white) were carried on the nose (see inset). XE531 later tested fly-by-wire systems from 1973, retaining the same scheme and was fitted with a Specto Avionics head-up display.

Reference: 'Testing Colours - British Test, Trials and Research Aircraft of A&AEE, RAE & ETPS since 1960' by Adrian M Balch, Airlife

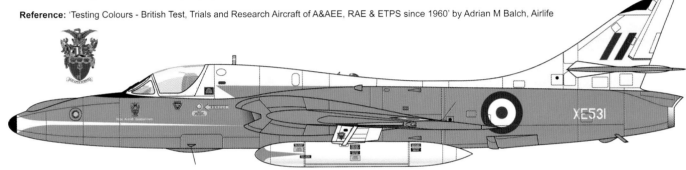

Hawker Hunter T.7, WV383, Flight Systems Department (FSD) RAE Farnborough, August 1974
WV383 was originally built as an F.4, before conversion to T.7 standard in 1956, and served with Nos 4, 20, 28 and 79 Squadrons before being passed to RAE Farnborough in 1971. Finished in an overall Light Aircraft Grey scheme with Roundel Blue fin/rudder, wing tips, nose flash and drop tank bands, the serials, nose tip and anti-glare panel were all in black. An RAE crest on white rectangular background was applied to the rear of the cockpit (see inset), and the RAE titling was in black. After its service at Farnborough, WV383 went to Cranfield, subsequently being used in the testing of night vision, FLIR (Forward Looking Infra-Red) and on-board camera systems. It was later repainted in the 'Raspberry Ripple' scheme and named 'HECATE - Lady of the Night' and last flew with QinetiQ in 1998. It is now an exhibit at the Farnborough Air Sciences Trust (FAST) Museum.

Reference: 'Forever Farnborough - Flying The Limits 1904-1996' by Peter J Cooper, Hikoki Publications

Hawker Hunter T.7A, XL616, Empire Test Pilots School, Aircraft & Armament Experimental Establishment (A&AEE) Boscombe Down, mid-1970s
XL616 was delivered to the ETPS in 1966 as one of three twin-seater Hunters, (the others being XL611 a T.7A and XL612 a T.7), to replace the Meteors then in use. Finished in overall Light Aircraft Grey with Post Office Red fuselage spine, fin and rudder, cheatline down the length of the fuselage, wing tips and drop tanks, the serials and anti-glare panel were in black. An ETPS crest on a Light Aircraft Grey rectangular background was originally carried behind cockpit, but appears to have been painted over when the red cheatline was added. XL616 was transferred to the Tactical Weapons Unit/45 Squadron in May 1976, and then passed onto 2 TWU at Lossiemouth before being retired in 1991.

References: 'Testing Colours - British Test, Trials and Research Aircraft of A&AEE, RAE & ETPS since 1960' by Adrian M Balch, Airlife;
'The Cold War Years - Flight Testing at Boscombe Down 1945-1975'

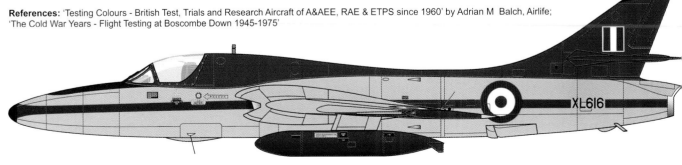

Continued from page 56

as well. The original Ministry of Defence had been created by Act of Parliament in 1946, with the new ministry being headed by a Minister of Defence. In the following few years the Ministry gradually took over more and more control over military-related matters from existing ministries and from the departments of the three services (Navy, Army and Air Force, which were absorbed in 1964). Finally, the defence functions of the Ministry of Aviation Supply as it was then known were taken over by the MoD in 1971, creating the entity that in roughly the same form has continued to exist in to the new century. By that step the MoD thus took on the responsibility for supplying military aircraft and guided weapons for the British armed forces.

In previous times much of this responsibility had rested with the Air Ministry of the 1930s, but was transferred early in World War Two to the Ministry of Aircraft Production (and from 1946 the Ministry of Supply). This procurement responsibility passed to the Ministry of Aviation in 1959, to the Ministry of Technology in 1967, and thence to the Ministry of Aviation Supply in 1970 before the whole process was absorbed into the MoD itself in 1971.

Within the MoD, a Procurement Executive was created in August 1971 to procure aircraft for the armed services, and thence by implication for official testing as well. Since that time, many of the aircraft involved in official test flying tended to be referred to (perhaps rather too loosely in specific cases) as MoD(PE) aircraft, as they were not assigned as front-line combat aircraft or in normal day-to-day operations with any of the services while involved in their test flying activities, but they nonetheless normally remained as military aircraft. (In 1999, the Procurement Executive became an Executive Agency within the MoD).

Continued on page 68

Blackburn Buccaneer S.1, XN923, Royal Aircraft Establishment Farnborough, 1970
XN923 was the second production Buccaneer S.1 and initially served at RAF West Freugh, Wigtownshire, an armaments training school five miles south east of Stranraer, Scotland, now known as MoD West Freugh and operated by QinetiQ, on behalf of the Ministry of Defence. Following this, it went to No 700Z Flight based at RAF Lossiemouth, Scotland before being returned to the RAE, serving at Brough, and then Farnborough where it stayed until retired in 1973. Finished in an overall white scheme, with Roundel Blue areas to the nose, wing tips and fin which were covered with 'FabGlo' strips and overpainted in Day-Glo to enhance visibility, an RAE crest was carried on the fin on a white rectangular background (see inset). Serials were in black.

References: 'Wings of Fame - Vol 14: 'Blackburn Buccaneer' by Denis J Calvert; 'Testing Colours - British Test, Trials and Research Aircraft of A&AEE, RAE & ETPS since 1960' by Adrian M Balch, Airlife

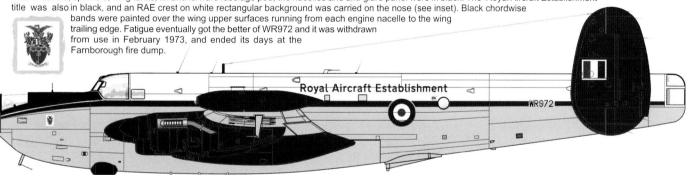

Avro Shackleton MR.3, WR972, Structures and Mechanical Engineering Flight, RAE Farnborough, June 1971
WR972 was used by Avro at Woodford for a variety of test work including airborne lifeboat trials, before going onto the A&AEE at Boscombe Down in late December 1956. It was then passed onto RAE Farnborough in April 1961 where it was used for parachute drag tests and general towing work. It was also used over the Larkhill ranges on Salisbury Plain, on a series of bomblet deployment runs. Finished in an overall Light Aircraft Grey scheme with white fuselage top decking and Roundel Blue cheatline, spinners, wing tanks, fin and forward fuselage pod, the nacelles and anti-glare panel were in black. The 'Royal Aircraft Establishment' title was also in black, and an RAE crest on white rectangular background was carried on the nose (see inset). Black chordwise bands were painted over the wing upper surfaces running from each engine nacelle to the wing trailing edge. Fatigue eventually got the better of WR972 and it was withdrawn from use in February 1973, and ended its days at the Farnborough fire dump.

References: 'Testing Colours - British Test, Trials and Research Aircraft of A & AEE, RAE & ETPS since 1960' by Adrian M Balch; 'Farnborough - 100 Years of British Aviation' by Peter J Cooper, Midland Publishing; 'Shackleton - Guardian of the Sea Lanes' by Richard A Franks, Dalrymple & Verdun; Scale Aircraft Modelling Vol 12/9 June 1990 - Aircraft in Detail- Avro Shackleton by Alan W Hall; http://avroshackleton.com/marktree.html

Below: In March or April 1968, Avro Shackleton MR.3, WR972, was repainted to a style which complied with the RAE's standard colour scheme as witnessed by this September 1968 image taken at Coltishall. WR972 was SOC at Farnborough in early 1973 and used for fire practice. [Fred Martin Collection]

English Electric Canberra B.2/8 (hybrid), WJ643, Royal Aircraft Establishment, Farnborough, February 1972
WJ643 arrived at Farnborough on Christmas Eve 1969 after previously being operated from RAF West Freugh, in Wigtownshire, Scotland by the RAE and Ferranti Ltd, in various trials including the development of a laser rangefinder for the Harrier and Jaguar, and nav-attack and aiming systems development. Finished in Dark Sea Grey and Dark Green upper surfaces with gloss black under surfaces, 'FabGlo' panels were applied to the nose and wing tips. The fuselage and underwing serials were white. (see also p72)

Reference: 'Forever Farnborough - Flying the Limits 1904-1996' by Peter J Cooper, Hikoki Publications

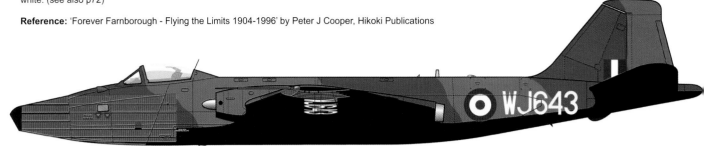

English Electric Canberra B.2, WH876, B Flight, A&AEE Bomber & Maritime Flight Test Squadron, Aeroplane & Armament Experimental Establishment, Boscombe Down, August 1972
After its regular RAF service, WH876 was converted to U.14 drone standard in 1961 by Short Brothers, Belfast. It was passed onto No 728B NAS at Hal Far, Malta, where it was used as a pilotless aircraft engaged in missile development work. By December 1961, it had returned to the UK, to Pershore in Worcestershire for storage, and was re-converted back to B.2 standard in 1963, when it was passed on to the A&AEE early in 1964. During the early 1970s, WH876 acquired an in-flight refuelling probe, although this was never set up to operate, Finished in an overall white scheme with light blue trim and blue-grey rudder and elevator, the fuselage serials were also in light blue, with those under the wings presumed to be in black. The serial number was repeated on wing tanks in white. The wing, fin and tailplane leading edges were in Day-Glo, with an A&AEE crest on light blue background on fuselage and an A&AEE badge on both sides of the fin (see inset). National insignia appears to be in the 'bright' shades of blue and red. WH876 went on to become an ejection seat test aircraft before being passed on to Martin Baker Aircraft Ltd at Chalgrove, Oxfordshire, and used as a parachute trials aircraft, before being broken up for scrap at Boscombe Down in 1990.

Reference: Air Britain photo archives

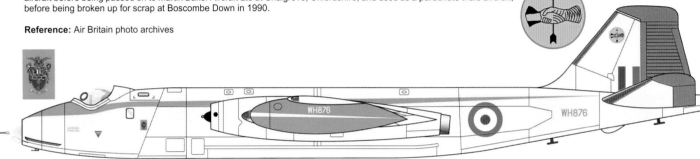

English Electric Canberra PR.7, WH774, Royal Radar Establishment, Pershore, Worcestershire, September 1972
WH774 became operational with the Royal Radar Establishment (RRE) in August 1955 and was heavily involved in radar development and research trials. A number of different systems were fitted, and the aircraft displays a characteristic radar fairing on top of the fuselage and specially modified wing tanks to house further equipment. Finished in overall High Speed Silver, with black serials and Day-Glo trim, an RRE badge was carried on both sides of the fin (see inset). The serial number was repeated on the nosewheel doors. WH774 was later painted in the 'Raspberry Ripple' scheme.

References: Airliners.net; 'Testing Colours - British Test, Trials and Research Aircraft of A&AEE, RAE & ETPS since 1960' by Adrian M Balch, Airlife

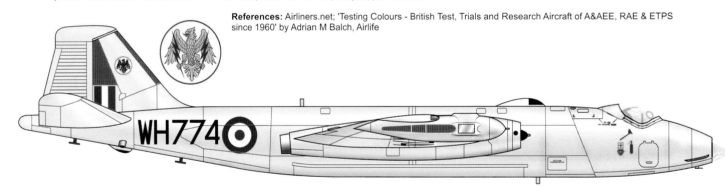

English Electric Canberra PR.3, WE173, Meteorological Research Flight, Farnborough, September 1972
WE173 was originally painted in overall High Speed Silver and delivered to the Meteorological Research Flight (MRF) in 1965. It was repainted in overall Light Aircraft Grey with white fuselage top decking divided by a Signal Red cheatline in 1972 and used in high-altitude stratospheric research work. The serial number and anti-glare panel remained in black. The 'Barber's pole' nose probe was finished in red and white rings and a Meteorological Research Flight badge was carried on both sides of the fin with the RAE crest on the forward fuselage (see insets). WE173 was retired from service on 31 March 1981 and ended up on RAF Coltishall's fire dump.

Reference: 'Testing Colours - British Test, Trials and Research Aircraft of A&AEE, RAE & ETPS since 1960' by Adrian M Balch, Airlife

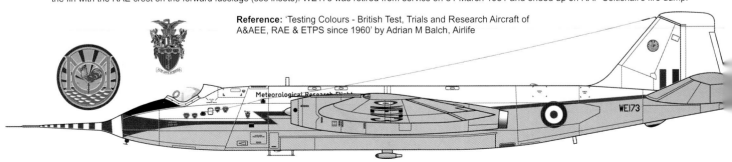

English Electric Canberra B.2, WJ638, Aeroplane & Armament Experimental Establishment (A&AEE) Boscombe Down, June 1970
WJ638 was originally modified from a B.2 to U.10 drone configuration and undertook various test work, then, in March 1964, it was delivered to Boscombe Down, where it was reconfigured back to B.2 standard to be used as an ejection seat trials aircraft. The navigator's compartment was altered to accommodate two ejection seats mounted side by side, with cameras on the wings to record the test firings. Finished in an overall white scheme with 'FabGlo' trim on the nose, forward fuselage, wing tips, rear fuselage and fin, the serials were in black. An A&AEE badge was applied to both sides of the fin (see inset). The extreme rear section of fuselage and the rudder trim tab were painted in light blue-grey. Miniature ejection seat test firing symbols were applied to the nose. WJ638 was mainly operated over the Larkhill Ranges in Wiltshire and ended its days at Predannack as a fire rescue hulk.

Reference: 'Testing Colours - British Test, Trials and Research Aircraft of A&AEE, RAE & ETPS since 1960' by Adrian M Balch, Airlife

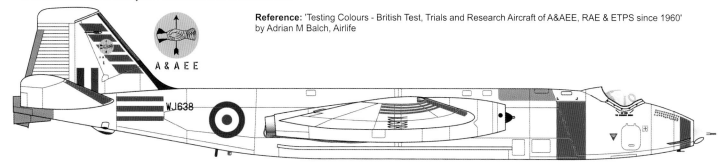

English Electric Canberra B.2/8 (hybrid), WJ643, Royal Aircraft Establishment, Farnborough, January 1975
WJ643 was used (at this time) on electro-optical sensor trials, but had originally been used by Ferranti in the late 1950s as a 'target aircraft' in conjunction with Airpass radar-equipped Dakota TS423 (see p28).
Finished in overall Light Aircraft Grey with white fuselage top decking and tops to the engine nacelles, it had Roundel Blue cheatlines on fuselage and engine nacelles, with Roundel Blue wing tips, fin and rudder. Serials, anti-glare panel and radome were all in black..

Reference: 'Testing Colours - British Test, Trials and Research Aircraft of A&AEE, RAE & ETPS since 1960' by Adrian M Balch, Airlife

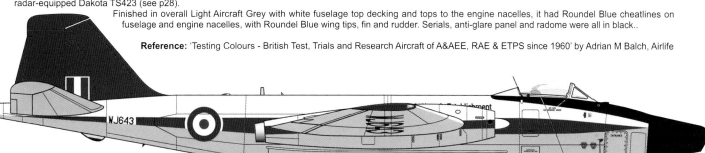

Handley Page Hastings C.1A, TG500, Aeroplane & Armament Experimental Establishment (A&AEE) Boscombe Down, March 1971
One of the three Hastings operated by the A&AEE during the 1960s and early 1970s (the other two being TG503 and WD496 – see below), TG500 was from the initial batch, and made its first flight in May 1947. It stayed with Handley Page for general test work before being passed on to Boscombe Down in 1949, where it undertook general transport work around the globe on behalf of the A&AEE. Finished in Light Aircraft Grey overall with white upper fuselage decking and rudder, the fin was Post Office Red, as was the fuselage cheatline which was edged in Roundel Blue. Engine cowlings were natural metal, with spinners, anti-glare panel, nose radome and 'A&AEE BOSCOMBE DOWN' titling all in black. TG500 was scrapped at Bicester in 1972.

Reference: 'Testing Colours - British Test, Trials and Research Aircraft of A&AEE, RAE & ETPS since 1960' by Adrian M Balch, Airlife

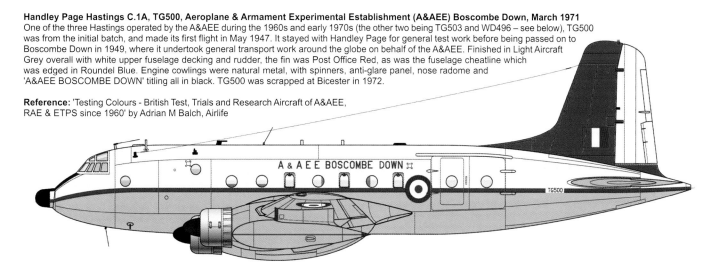

Handley Page Hastings C.2, WD496, Aeroplane & Armament Experimental Establishment (A&AEE) Boscombe Down, June 1972
WD496 was one of three Hastings, (see TG500 above), operated in the 1960s and early 1970s by the A&AEE at Boscombe Down, and was fitted with a nose-mounted air data probe for general test measuring work. Finished in Light Aircraft Grey overall with white upper fuselage decking and rudder, the fin, wing tips and cheatline were Post Office Red, the cheatline edged in Roundel Blue. Serial numbers, spinners and anti-glare panel were in black with the 'A&AEE BOSCOMBE DOWN' title is in Roundel Blue. The nose probe was also in Post Office Red. By the early 1970s, WD496 was starting to look the worse for wear and was finally scrapped in 1973.

Reference: 'Testing Colours - British Test, Trials and Research Aircraft of A&AEE, RAE & ETPS since 1960' by Adrian M Balch, Airlife

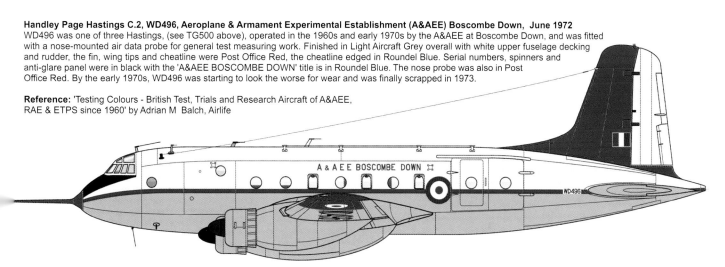

Vickers V.475D Viscount, XR802, Empire Test Pilots School, Aeroplane & Armament Experimental Establishment (A&AEE) Boscombe Down, July 1970
Originally, XR802 operated on the civilian circuit in the United States with Capital Airlines, then Northeast Airlines, before being resold to Vickers-Armstrong as G-ARUU. It was then sold on to the Ministry of Aviation and in turn passed over to Farnborough for general test and training work. It was then allocated to Boscombe Down in 1968, Finished in overall aluminium, including the wings, nacelles and tailplanes, with white upper fuselage decking, fin and rudder, it featured a Roundel Blue trim around the cabin windows and a black mid-fuselage cheatline edged in white. Serials were in black. The tip of the fin and wing tips were in Day-Glo. 'EMPIRE TEST PILOTS SCHOOL' title was in black and the ETPS crest on a white rectangle outlined in red, was carried on the nose (see inset). XR802 was eventually scrapped in 1972.

Reference: 'Testing Colours - British Test, Trials and Research Aircraft of A&AEE, RAE & ETPS since 1960' by Adrian M Balch, Airlife

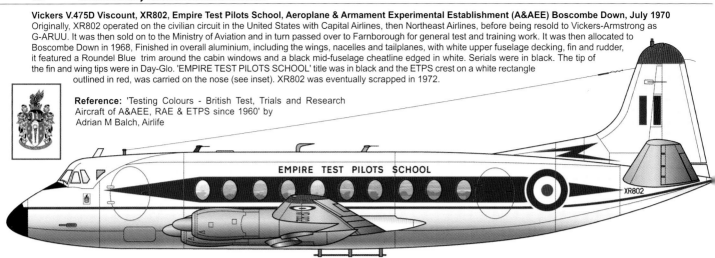

Armstrong Whitworth Meteor NF.11 Hybrid, WD790, Radar Research Establishment, Pershore, Worcestershire, September 1971
WD790 was the 39th production NF.11 and was designated (albeit off the record) as a Meteor NF.111/2 when it was modified upto NF.12 standard. Initially serving with the Telecommunications Research Establishment (TRE) in 1952 it then went to the Ferranti Flying Unit in 1958, where it was heavily involved in trials in the development of the radar system for TSR.2 and the AI Mk 23 system used on the Lightning. WD790 was also used in development work on Red Brick and Indigo Corkscrew radar systems for Bloodhound and Thunderbird SAM systems. Finished in Dark Sea Grey and Dark Green upper surfaces with Light Aircraft Grey undersides, a new pointed nose cone was fitted which was white with a silver tip. Serials were in black. Underwing tanks and pylons are thought to have been in Medium Sea Grey (as illustrated). Engine intake rings were brown and the tip of the rear fuselage was Day-Glo. WD790 transferred from Pershore in 1977 to RAE Llanbedr, then went to Bedford and was repainted in the Raspberry Ripple scheme.

References: 'Testing Colours - British Test, Trials and Research Aircraft of A&AEE, RAE & ETPS since 1960' by Adrian M Balch, Airlife; 'Meteor - Gloster's First Jet Fighter' by Steven J Bond, Midland Counties Publications; Wings of Fame Vol 15: 'Variant Briefing - Gloster Meteor Part 2'

Left: Vickers Viscount XR801 (foreground) and XR802 photographed at Farnborough in September 1962 after having been purchased from civilian ownership and allocated to the ETPS earlier that year. They served with the ETPS and other agencies until taken out of service in 1972 and were scrapped at Coventry in 1974. (See profile at top of page)

Left: Armstrong Whitworth Meteor NF.11, WD790, belonging to the RRE is seen in flight at Finningley in September 1970. Built originally as an NF.11, a quick glance at the fin shows it to have the later 'scalloped' fin leading edge as used by both the NF.12 and later NF.14, a feature that sometimes led to WD790 being referred to, unofficially, as an NF.11½! Fred Martin vcollection (See profile above)

Scottish Aviation Twin Pioneer Srs 3, XT610/22, Empire Test Pilots School, A&AEE Boscombe Down, August 1972
In the summer of 1972 XT610 was finished in the overall painted aluminium scheme, including the wings, struts, tailplanes nacelles and cowlings, with white fuselage top decking and both faces of the fins and rudders and a Roundel Blue fuselage cheatline. Anti-glare panel was black and the wing tips were Day-Glo. The fuselage serial was in white on the blue cheatline with underwing serials and the numeral '22' in black. The ETPS crest on the outer face of the nacelles was on a white rectangular background (see inset). Later, the following summer, XT610 had been re-finished in Light Aircraft Grey overall including wings, struts, tailplanes, nacelles and cowlings, but retained a white fuselage top decking albeit with a Post Office Red cheatline. The fins and rudders were repainted in Day-Glo. and the fuselage serials in black.

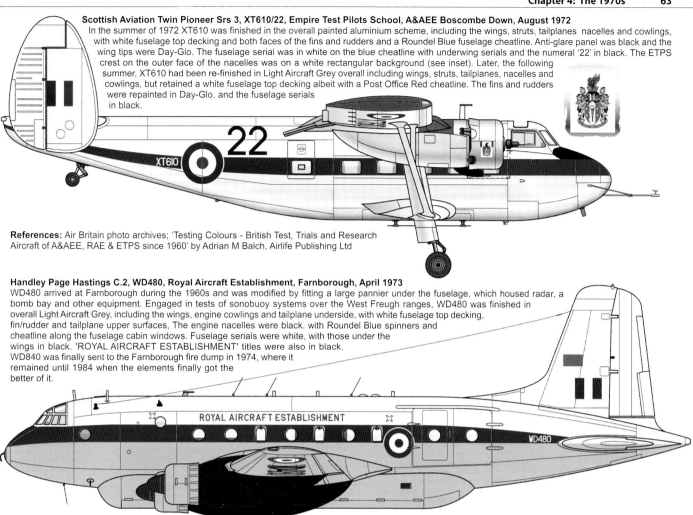

References: Air Britain photo archives; 'Testing Colours - British Test, Trials and Research Aircraft of A&AEE, RAE & ETPS since 1960' by Adrian M Balch, Airlife Publishing Ltd

Handley Page Hastings C.2, WD480, Royal Aircraft Establishment, Farnborough, April 1973
WD480 arrived at Farnborough during the 1960s and was modified by fitting a large pannier under the fuselage, which housed radar, a bomb bay and other equipment. Engaged in tests of sonobuoy systems over the West Freugh ranges, WD480 was finished in overall Light Aircraft Grey, including the wings, engine cowlings and tailplane underside, with white fuselage top decking, fin/rudder and tailplane upper surfaces, The engine nacelles were black. with Roundel Blue spinners and cheatline along the fuselage cabin windows. Fuselage serials were white, with those under the wings in black. 'ROYAL AIRCRAFT ESTABLISHMENT' titles were also in black.
WD840 was finally sent to the Farnborough fire dump in 1974, where it remained until 1984 when the elements finally got the better of it.

References: 'Testing Colours - British Test, Trials and Research Aircraft of A&AEE, RAE & ETPS since 1960' by Adrian M Balch, Airlife; Warpaint No 62 'Handley Page Hastings' by Alan W Hall, Warpaint Books Ltd

Right: Circa 1971 image of Scottish Aviation Twin Pioneer, XT610 '22', as used by the ETPS following delivery in 1965. Completely repainted in 1973, XT610 remained in service until withdrawn from use in February 1975.
(See profile at top of page)

Right: Handley Page Hastings C.2, WD480, belonging to the Royal Aircraft Establishment as seen in March 1969.
(See profile above)

Blackburn Beverley C.1, XB259, Royal Aircraft Establishment, Farnborough, October 1971

XB259 was the first production Beverley and was a lifelong resident at Farnborough, arriving on 16 September 1959. Initially, the aircraft was in the standard overall painted silver finish, with the black and yellow 'target-towing' stripes added to the under surfaces a little later. During 1966, it was repainted in overall gloss white, with the fin outer sides, wing-tips and nose painted Day-Glo and black engine nacelles, spinners, main fuselage underside and anti-glare panel. Engine cowlings and undercarriage-to-fuselage struts were in silver. Serials and 'ROYAL AIRCRAFT ESTABLISHMENT' titles were black. In mid-1971, the Day-Glo areas had faded almost to a yellow, so were overpainted in orange. XB259 served at Farnborough until late 1972, when it was retired and sold to Court Line, although it was never delivered as the airline ceased trading. At the time of writing, XB259 is on display at Fort Paull, a preserved coast artillery fort near Hull.

Reference: 'Testing Colours- British Test, Trials and Research Aircraft of A&AEE, RAE & ETPS since 1960' by Adrian M Balch, Airlife Publishing Ltd

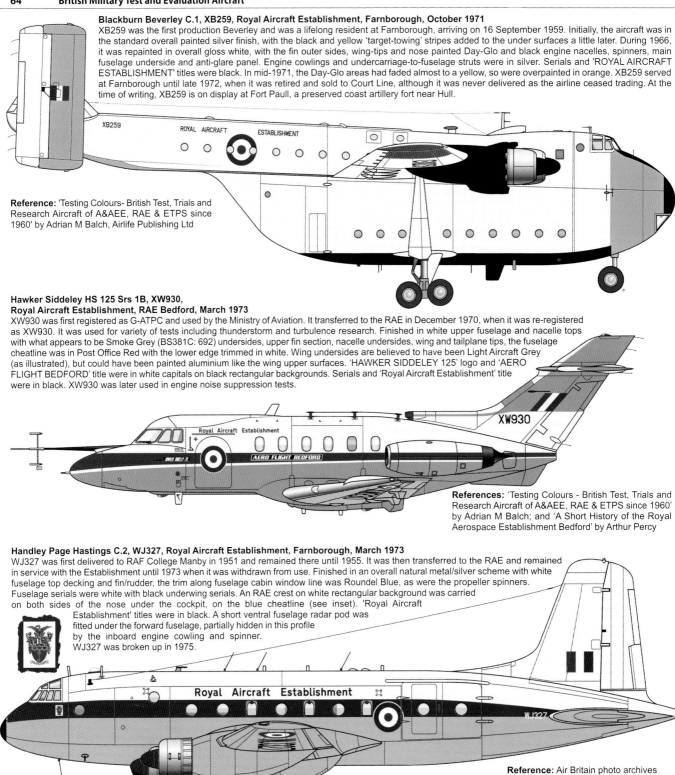

Hawker Siddeley HS 125 Srs 1B, XW930,
Royal Aircraft Establishment, RAE Bedford, March 1973

XW930 was first registered as G-ATPC and used by the Ministry of Aviation. It transferred to the RAE in December 1970, when it was re-registered as XW930. It was used for variety of tests including thunderstorm and turbulence research. Finished in white upper fuselage and nacelle tops with what appears to be Smoke Grey (BS381C: 692) undersides, upper fin section, nacelle undersides, wing and tailplane tips, the fuselage cheatline was in Post Office Red with the lower edge trimmed in white. Wing undersides are believed to have been Light Aircraft Grey (as illustrated), but could have been painted aluminium like the wing upper surfaces. 'HAWKER SIDDELEY 125' logo and 'AERO FLIGHT BEDFORD' title were in white capitals on black rectangular backgrounds. Serials and 'Royal Aircraft Establishment' title were in black. XW930 was later used in engine noise suppression tests.

References: 'Testing Colours - British Test, Trials and Research Aircraft of A&AEE, RAE & ETPS since 1960' by Adrian M Balch; and 'A Short History of the Royal Aerospace Establishment Bedford' by Arthur Percy

Handley Page Hastings C.2, WJ327, Royal Aircraft Establishment, Farnborough, March 1973

WJ327 was first delivered to RAF College Manby in 1951 and remained there until 1955. It was then transferred to the RAE and remained in service with the Establishment until 1973 when it was withdrawn from use. Finished in an overall natural metal/silver scheme with white fuselage top decking and fin/rudder, the trim along fuselage cabin window line was Roundel Blue, as were the propeller spinners. Fuselage serials were white with black underwing serials. An RAE crest on white rectangular background was carried on both sides of the nose under the cockpit, on the blue cheatline (see inset). 'Royal Aircraft Establishment' titles were in black. A short ventral fuselage radar pod was fitted under the forward fuselage, partially hidden in this profile by the inboard engine cowling and spinner. WJ327 was broken up in 1975.

Reference: Air Britain photo archives

Gloster Meteor T.7, XF274, Royal Aircraft Establishment, Farnborough, June 1973

XF274 was the last Meteor T.7 to enter trials service. It originally served with the A&AEE, coded '5', before serving at Farnborough. Finished in overall Light Aircraft Grey with white upper fuselage decking and topsides to the engine nacelles, with blue cheatlines, fin bullet fairing and trim, the wing leading edges and wing tips were also white. Fuselage and underwing serials were black and the RAE crest was carried on both sides of the fin (see inset). XF274 was written off in an accident on 14 February 1975, when the aircraft was attempting an asymmetric approach. The aircraft rolled towards the dead engine, and spun in to the ground tragically killing both crew.

Reference: 'Meteor - Gloster's First Jet Fighter' by Steven J Bond, Midland Counties Publications

De Havilland Comet 2E, XV144/144, Blind Landing Experimental Unit, Royal Aircraft Establishment Bedford, June 1970
This aircraft originally served with BOAC (British Overseas Airways Corporation) as G-AMXK in the late 1950s but was sold to the Ministry of Supply in October 1960. Put in to storage, it was then sent to RAE Bedford in the mid-1960s, serving with the Establishment until May 1971, when it was passed onto RAE Farnborough. Finished in overall high speed silver with white upper fuselage decking and fin and a dark blue trim around cabin windows with black pinstripes, the serials, codes and 'BLIND LANDING EXPERIMENTAL UNIT' titles were in black. Note the small Union Flag on nose. Sadly, XV144's fate, like many other such aircraft of the period, was to be sent to be scrapped, in 1974.

Reference: 'Testing Colours - British Test, Trials and Research Aircraft of A&AEE, RAE & ETPS since 1960' by Adrian M Balch, Airlife

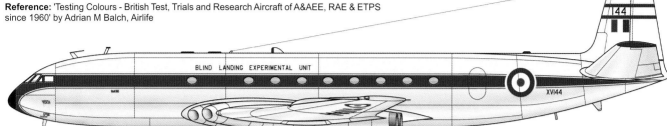

De Havilland Comet 2E, XN453/453, Royal Aircraft Establishment Farnborough, April 1972
XN453 was previously registered as G-AMXD, (one of two Comet 2 airliners fitted with Avon 504s in the inner nacelles and Avon 524s in the outer ones, and was used by BOAC for proving flights during 1957-1958 – see also profile above), but it was passed over to the RAE at Farnborough in 1959 for use as a radio and navigation aid test aircraft. Finished in overall Light Aircraft Grey with white upper fuselage decking, fin and rudder, it also had Roundel Blue trim along the fuselage cabin windows and blue bars across the fin and rudder. The fuselage serials were white, while those under the wings were black, as were the 'last three' on the fin and the 'Royal Aircraft Establishment' title on the fuselage. Note the small ventral fairing with portholes under the forward fuselage. XN453 was scrapped at Farnborough in 1991.

Reference: 'Testing Colours - British Test, Trials and Research Aircraft of A&AEE, RAE & ETPS since 1960' by Adrian M Balch, Airlife

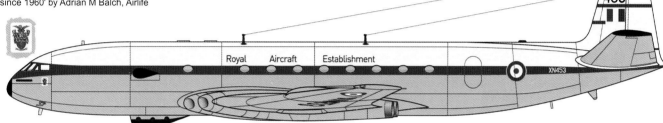

De Havilland Comet 3B, XP915/915, Royal Aircraft Establishment Farnborough, April 1972
Looking distinctly narwhal-like, with its long nose probe, XP915 was originally registered as G-ANLO, the Comet 3 prototype (and the only Comet 3 to fly). A larger and much improved aircraft over the Comet 2, with more advanced Rolls-Royce Avon engines, a 15ft longer fuselage with room for more passengers, and ability to carry 20% more fuel, XP915 served with the Blind Landing Experimental Unit at RAE Bedford from June 1961. Finished in overall high speed silver with white upper fuselage decking, fin and rudder, the cheatline trim was Roundel Blue with the fuselage and underwing serials in black. The 'last three' on the fin and 'Royal Aircraft Establishment' titles on the fuselage sides were in black. A black photo-calibration 'cross' was carried on the upper decking and the black and white photo-calibration discs applied to the front and rear of the fuselage. XP915/G-ANLO had the distinction of not only being the only Comet 3 to fly, but the first airliner to circumnavigate the globe. In January 1971, whilst at Bedford, it was severely damaged when it overshot the runway. After repair, it was passed onto the RAE, its eventual fate being as a test rig for the then new HS Nimrod.

Reference: 'Testing Colours- British Test, Trials and Research Aircraft of A&AEE, RAE & ETPS since 1960' by Adrian M Balch, Airlife

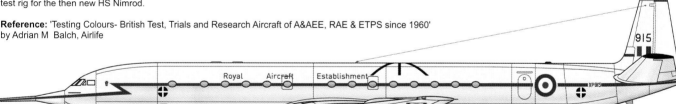

De Havilland Comet 4, XV814/814, Royal Aircraft Establishment Farnborough, April 1972
Another ex-BOAC Comet, XV814 was delivered to Farnborough in the late 1960s/early 1970s, (the actual date is unconfirmed), and served on a number of test programmes. Finished in overall Light Aircraft Grey with white upper fuselage decking, fin and rudder, the trim along the fuselage cabin windows and the two bars across the fin and rudder were Roundel Blue. The fuselage serials were white (on the blue trim), while those under the wings were black. The 'last three' on the fin, 'Royal Aircraft Establishment' titles on the fuselage and 'AVIONICS DEPT' on wing pod were black. A large underfuselage fairing was fitted to allow carriage of various equipment. Repainted in the 'Raspberry Ripple' scheme in March 1977, XV814 was decommissioned and used as a spares aircraft for Comet 4C, XS235 'Canopus', which, although no longer airworthy, at the time of writing still conducts taxi-runs at Bruntingthorpe, Leicestershire.

Reference: 'Testing Colours - British Test, Trials and Research Aircraft of A&AEE, RAE & ETPS since 1960' by Adrian M Balch, Airlife

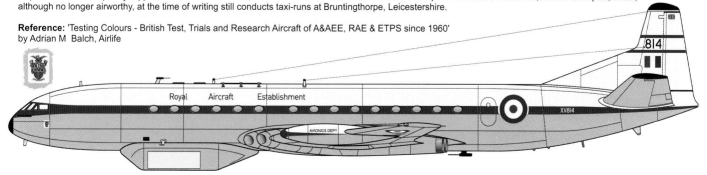

McDonnell Phantom FG.1, XT597, Aircraft & Armament Experimental Establishment (A&AEE), Boscombe Down, March 1975
XT597 was first delivered in 1968 and this illustration shows the aircraft in its initial guise when serving with the Royal Navy Test Squadron in the overall Extra Dark Sea Grey upper surfaces with white undersides scheme. The fin and the outer wing section upper surfaces were in Post Office Red – although they should have been Signal Red, but were painted Post Office Red in error. 'A&AEE' titles and serials were in white as was the nose probe, with red banding, that starts horizontally at the nose cone before running vertically around the rest of the probe.

Reference: 'Cold War Years - Flight Testing at Boscombe Down 1945-1975' by Tim Mason, Hikoki Publications

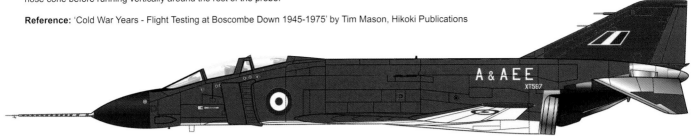

Hawker Siddeley Andover C.1, XS646, Royal Aircraft Establishment Farnborough, April 1975
This aircraft previously served with the RAF in the Middle East, before being passed over to the RAE at Farnborough in January 1973 for use on general systems trials, tests and evaluation. Finished in the overall Light Aircraft Grey with white upper fuselage decking and fin scheme, the rudder was in Post Office Red, with a Roundel Blue cheatline along the line of the fuselage cabin windows. The 'Royal Aircraft Establishment' title, serial number (note its non-standard, mid-fuselage, position), and 'last three' on fin, were all in black. Propeller spinners were Post Office Red. At the time of writing, XS646 was still flying, with the Defence Evaluation and Research Agency (DERA)/QinetiQ, (the British multinational defence technology company headquartered in Farnborough), finished in a variation of the 'Raspberry Ripple' scheme, engaged on radar trials fitted with a Blue Vixen-esque nose radome, although it is unconfirmed exactly what system was being tested.

Reference: 'Forever Farnborough - Flying The Limits 1904- 1996' by Peter J Cooper AMRAeS, Hikoki Publications Ltd

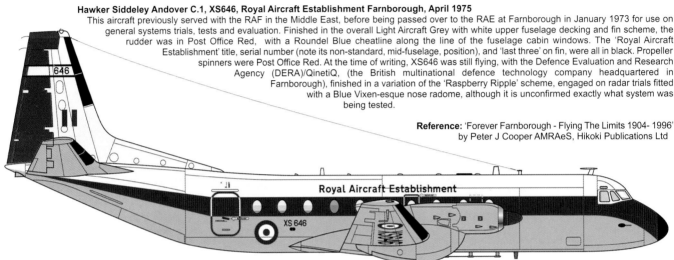

Vickers VC 10-1103, XX914/914, Aero Flight Systems, Royal Aircraft Establishment, Bedford, July 1974
This aircraft was originally registered as 9G-ABQ for Ghana Airways, but delivery was cancelled and instead the aircraft went to British United Airways, (before being merged into British Caledonian), as G-ATDJ. It then went to the RAE at Bedford in March 1973 and was used as a flying laboratory and general test aircraft. Finished in overall Light Aircraft Grey with white fuselage top decking, engine pods and tailplanes, the fin and rudder were Post Office Red, with Post Office Red, white and Golden Yellow fuselage cheatlines. The 'Royal Aircraft Establishment' title was in black and the 'Aero Flight BEDFORD' title just to the rear of the cockpit windows, was in white. XX914 was withdrawn from service in July 1983 and broken up, the remnants being sent to the RAF Defence Movements School at Brize Norton where they still were as late as 2006.

References: 'Testing Colours - British Test, Trials and Research Aircraft of A&AEE, RAE & ETPS since 1960' by Adrian M Balch, Airlife; 'A Short Illustrated History of the Royal Aerospace Establishment Bedford' by Arthur Pearcy, Airlife

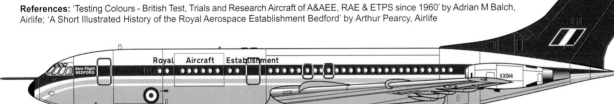

Westland Scout AH.1, XP165, Empire Test Pilots School, Aircraft & Armament Experimental Establishment, Boscombe Down, March 1971
XP165 was actually the first Scout AH.1 to be built, and first flew on 29 August 1960. It initially served on test work with Fairey, Blackburn, Westland and the RAE before going to the A&AAE. Finished in overall Post Office Red with a white flash down the side, the serials were in black. The ETPS crest was on a silver background on fuselage sides. (see inset)

Reference: 'Testing Colours - British Test, Trials and Research Aircraft of A&AEE, RAE & ETPS since 1960' by Adrian M Balch

Westland Wessex Mk 5 (Hybrid), XL728, Radio & Navigation Flight, RAE Farnborough, September 1972
XL728 originally started life as an HAS.1 but was upgraded to Mk 5 standard becoming known as a Mk 5 (Hybrid). It was the second pre-production Wessex and spent all of its life at Farnborough. Finished in Light Aircraft Grey with white fuselage top decking, it had a Roundel Blue fuselage cheatline/flash and black serials and 'Royal Aircraft Establishment' titles. Note the modified weapons platform above mainwheel, used to mount a variety of external radio and aerial equipment. XL728 was later repainted in the 'Raspberry Ripple' scheme, but was struck off charge in 1985 and ended its days on the Pendine Ranges, in Carmarthenshire on the southwest coast of Wales, where it was eventually destroyed.

References: 'Testing Colours - British Test, Trials and Research Aircraft of A&AEE, RAE & ETPS since 1960' by Adrian M Balch, Airlife Publishing Ltd; 'Farnborough - 100 Years of British Aviation' by Peter J Cooper, Midland Publishing; 'Forever Farnborough - Flying the Limits 1904-1996' by Peter J Cooper

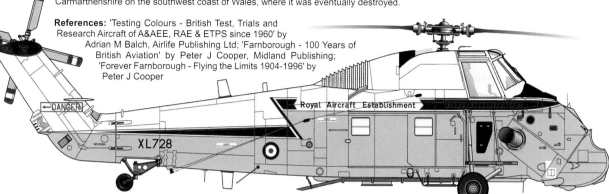

Westland Wessex HAS.1, XM330, Weapons Flight, Royal Aircraft Establishment Farnborough, March, 1973
A number of Wessex were stationed at Farnborough from the 1970s onwards, supplanting or replacing the Whirlwinds then in use. XM330 was one of them and was finished in overall RAF Blue Grey with a white fuselage 'flash' and was used by the Weapons Unit in the development of helicopter offensive and defensive systems. The 'Royal Aircraft Establishment' title was applied on the 'flash' in black, and the serials were white. The RAE crest was carried on a white background on the nose. During the following years, this scheme gave way to the more standardised 'Raspberry Ripple' version.

Reference: 'Testing Colours - British Test, Trials and Research Aircraft of A&AEE, RAE & ETPS since 1960' by Adrian M Balch, Airlife Publishing Ltd

Westland Wessex HU.5, XS241, Avionics and Instrument & Electrical Engineering (AIEE) Flights, RAE Farnborough, July 1975
Another of the many Wessex that were stationed at Farnborough from the 1970s onwards, XS421 carried out a variety of roles, mainly associated with avionics and sensor systems. Finished in the Dark Green and Light Stone upper surfaces with Light Stone undersides scheme, it also featured a white fuselage 'flash' with 'Royal Aircraft Establishment' title in black, and the RAE crest on the nose is superimposed on a white rectangular background. This aircraft went on to be painted in the 'Raspberry Ripple' scheme.

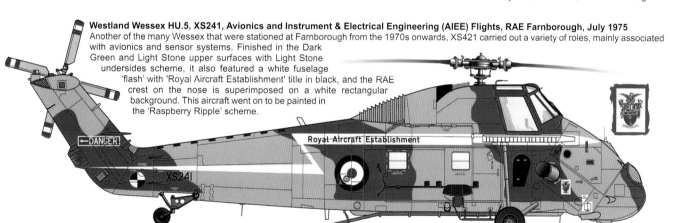

Reference: 'Forever Farnborough - Flying the Limits 1904-1996' by Peter J. Cooper AMRAeS, Hikoki Publications

Westland Sea King HAS.1, XV651/064, Royal Signals and Radar Establishment Pershore, Worcestershire, 1975
Built as HAS.1 and fist flown on 17 October 1969, XV651 was delivered to the RAE at Boscombe Down on 7 November 1969. It was later fitted with a Ferranti Sea Spray radar system, in a Lynx nose cone, as part of the Westland Lynx helicopter trials at the Royal Signals and Radar Establishment (RSRE), Pershore in Worcestershire. Finished in overall RAF Blue Grey with serials, codes and 'ROYAL NAVY' title in white, the anti-glare panel was in black. The code number '64' was carried on the fuselage sides and upper nose and repeated on the forward fuselage below cockpit window on port side only. The Lynx radome was in light tan. XV651 was converted to HAS.5 standard in 1986 and served with 826 NAS, then was with DERA at Fleetlands by 2003, and later still served with 771 NAS at St Mawgan from March 2005.

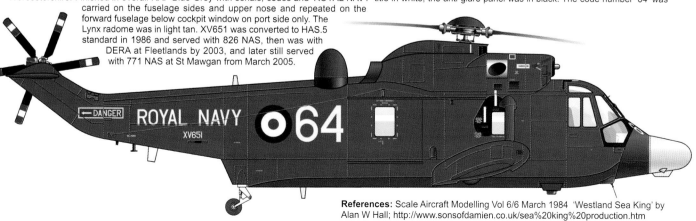

References: Scale Aircraft Modelling Vol 6/6 March 1984 'Westland Sea King' by Alan W Hall; http://www.sonsofdamien.co.uk/sea%20king%20production.htm

Continued from page 59
By the middle years of the 1970s, the number of aircraft at both Farnborough and Boscombe Down was somewhat less than in the heyday of the late World War Two and early post-war periods. At Boscombe Down, just short of fifty aircraft were assigned in 1975, while at Farnborough some forty were on strength (there had been approximately eighty at Farnborough in the early 1950s, before the new RAE at Bedford took on some of Farnborough's flight test duties). However, these totals varied from time to time depending on the trials being undertaken and on other factors such as overseas deployments for cold weather testing or many other factors. The number of service personnel at Boscombe Down had noticeably fallen over the years, as more tasks were civilianised and the number of aircraft that were assigned had decreased.

Indeed, a number of changes had taken place during the previous years to the aircraft-operating units within the A&AEE structure. The original four squadrons of the post-war years were added to in 1960 by a Support Squadron to assist in foreign trials and a variety of other duties, but in 1964 a fifth 'lettered' squadron, 'E' Squadron, had been created specifically to cover transport aircraft trials. The naval aircraft 'C' Squadron was eventually disbanded in 1971, and in 1974 this fate awaited 'E' Squadron. Increasingly, aircraft flying was concentrated into just three squadrons, 'A', 'B' and 'D' Squadrons, which was theoretically a more efficient organisation but in practice reflected the smaller number of new types that were being brought forward for service evaluation and release.

Nevertheless, the amount and variety of work continued throughout the 1970s to be considerably varied, while advances were made with telemetry for recording test results, and increasing miniaturisation took place. A considerable amount of development work was undertaken towards the capability to fly in adverse weather particularly at low level, and in the accurate aiming of weapons. This was partly through American experience in the Vietnam War during the 1960s, where early guided weapons such as the Martin 'Bullpup' air-to-surface missile had proved to be less than successful on many occasions.

Equipment to improve precision targeting capability or to allow safe flight in adverse weather or at night, such as Forward Looking Infra Red (FLIR) devices, underwent considerable testing and development work at the RAE during this period. Just to prove that much of the behind-the-scenes development effort that took place often did not need to be flown in the latest high-performance types, some of the RAE's FLIR research was performed with flight testing carried out in a converted Vickers Varsity twin-engined transport. Weapons development work, including the then relatively new concept of laser-guided munitions, was performed at the RAE site at West Freugh in Scotland and at a variety of weapons ranges.

Left and below: Two images of the Handley Page HP.115, XP841, as used by Aero Flight, RAE Bedford. Both photos were taken at Farnborough in September 1964, and both have the titles 'Aero Flight' & 'R.A.E. Bedford' on the nose, but in the non-flying image sunlight, reflecting on the highly-polished natural metal nose cone, serves to obliterate any wording. (See 4-view opposite)

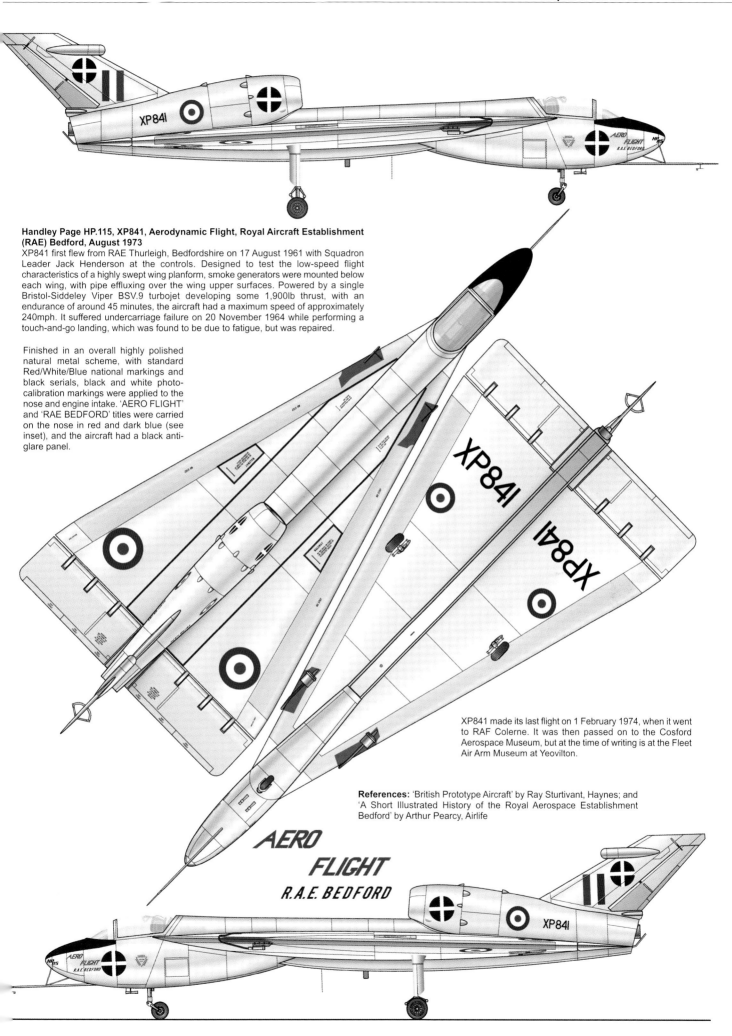

Handley Page HP.115, XP841, Aerodynamic Flight, Royal Aircraft Establishment (RAE) Bedford, August 1973

XP841 first flew from RAE Thurleigh, Bedfordshire on 17 August 1961 with Squadron Leader Jack Henderson at the controls. Designed to test the low-speed flight characteristics of a highly swept wing planform, smoke generators were mounted below each wing, with pipe effluxing over the wing upper surfaces. Powered by a single Bristol-Siddeley Viper BSV.9 turbojet developing some 1,900lb thrust, with an endurance of around 45 minutes, the aircraft had a maximum speed of approximately 240mph. It suffered undercarriage failure on 20 November 1964 while performing a touch-and-go landing, which was found to be due to fatigue, but was repaired.

Finished in an overall highly polished natural metal scheme, with standard Red/White/Blue national markings and black serials, black and white photo-calibration markings were applied to the nose and engine intake. 'AERO FLIGHT' and 'RAE BEDFORD' titles were carried on the nose in red and dark blue (see inset), and the aircraft had a black anti-glare panel.

XP841 made its last flight on 1 February 1974, when it went to RAF Colerne. It was then passed on to the Cosford Aerospace Museum, but at the time of writing is at the Fleet Air Arm Museum at Yeovilton.

References: 'British Prototype Aircraft' by Ray Sturtivant, Haynes; and 'A Short Illustrated History of the Royal Aerospace Establishment Bedford' by Arthur Pearcy, Airlife

Above: The longest-lived Shackleton MR.1/T.4, VP293, first flew in July 1951. Converted to a T.4 from August 1956, it was later stored until selected for use by the RAE in January 1964 for trials work – for which it received a most distinctive colour scheme. The latter was retained, with variations, until VP293 was retired on 23 May 1975 and later sold to the Strathallen Aircraft Collection where it arrived on 3 May 1976, when this image was taken. Fred Martin collection

Avro Shackleton T.4, VP293, 'Zebedee' of the Weapons Flight, RAE Farnborough, 1973
VP293 was originally an MR.1 and first flew on 18 July 1951. After serving with several Coastal Command squadrons throughout the mid-1950s, it was converted to T.4 standard at Avro Langer between August 1956 and March 1958, following which it was sent to the A&AEE, Boscombe Down for official clearance of mods before being transferred to the Maritime Operational Training Unit (MOTU) at RAF Kinloss on 1st March 1960. Following further modifications at Avro Langar and Avro Bracebridge Heath between April 1962 and February 1963, it was taken on the strength of the RAE Farnborough for trials work in January 1964. Finished in the standard RAF Coastal Command scheme of Dark Sea Grey overall with white fuselage top decking, the nose, fins, extreme rear fuselage and wing leading edges and tips were painted in Day-Glo. Forward sections of the engine nacelles were in black. The propeller spinners were painted in differing combinations of black and white, white and Day-Glo or black, white and Day-Glo and the propeller blades were painted in combinations of black and white stripes or black with red and white tips – see separate variations. The serials were in red, with those under the wings outlined in white. Upper wing roundels had white outlines and the anti-glare panel was black. The aircraft was nicknamed 'Zebedee' after the 1960s/1970s 'Magic Roundabout' children's TV programme character because of the internal equipment having to be mounted on springs to dampen vibration due to the Shackleton's 'choppy' flight characteristics, and the fact that the type suffered from landing 'bounce'. A cartoon of the 'Zebedee' character was applied on tip of tail and reportedly on fuselage sides. VP293 was retired from use in 1975, and was eventually sold to the Strathallan Collection in 1976. After more than a decade on outside display, the aircraft was broken up in 1988 due to corrosion. At the time of writing, the nose section of VP293 survives, looked after by the Shackleton Preservation Trust on behalf of it's owner Norman Thelwell. The nose section is trailer mounted and used by the Trust at various events around the country to promote the work being carried out at Coventry on another Shackleton, WR963.

References: 'Testing Colours - British Test, Trials and Research Aircraft of A&AEE, RAE & ETPS since 1960' by Adrian M Balch; Air Britain photo archives

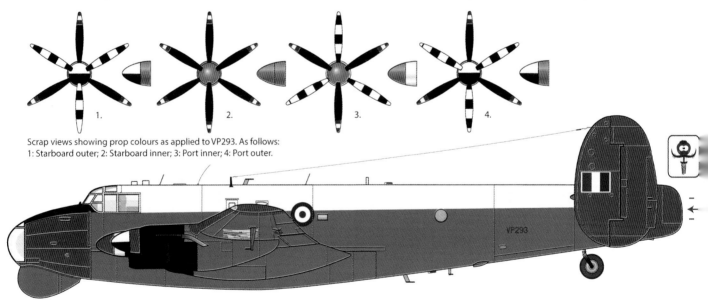

Scrap views showing prop colours as applied to VP293. As follows:
1: Starboard outer; 2: Starboard inner; 3: Port inner; 4: Port outer.

Armstrong Whitworth Argosy C.1, XN817/817, Aeroplane & Armament Experimental Establishment (A&AEE) Boscombe Down, April 1974
XN817 was delivered to the A&AEE Boscombe Down on 24 July 1961 and remained there until 1984 when it was retired. The aircraft was mainly used for parachute extraction tests as evidenced by the black and white photo-calibration squares on the rear fuselage. Finished in the overall Light Aircraft Grey with white fuselage and tail boom upper surfaces scheme, it had Roundel Blue cheatline with Post Office Red fins, wing tips and spinners. The anti-glare panel, serials and radome were in black. Following the tragic crash of the ETPS Argosy XR105 on 27 April 1976, XN817 became the last Argosy in service. On 1 October 1984, XN817's nosewheel leg collapsed at RAE West Freugh, Wigtownshire, Scotland; an incident that resulted in its forced retirement.

Reference: 'Testing Colours- British Test, Trials and Research Aircraft of A&AEE, RAE & ETPS since 1960' by Adrian M Balch

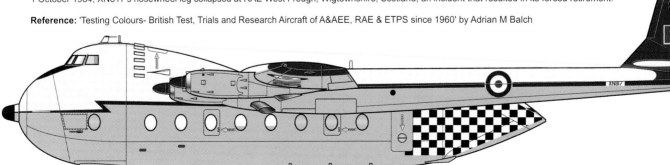

Vickers Varsity T.1, WF425, Meteorological Research Flight, RAE Farnborough, June 1974
For many years the UK's national meteorological service maintained the Meteorological Research Flight (MRF) based at the RAE at Farnborough using a number of aircraft, which performed a wide variety of measurements, including this Varsity T.1. Built in 1952, WF425 was finished in a Light Aircraft Grey overall scheme including the fuselage, fin, rudder, wings, tailplanes, engine nacelles and cowlings, with just the upper fuselage decking in white. 'Fabglo' strips were applied on the fin, rear fuselage, tailplanes and wings. The serials, 'Meteorological Research Flight' title and anti-glare panel were all in black as were the propeller spinners. The fuselage nose tip was painted aluminium. The RAE crest was applied on a white panel below cockpit and the Meteorological Research Flight badge was positioned behind the cockpit glazing (see insets). WF425 was scrapped in 1993

Reference: 'Testing Colours - British Test, Trials and Research Aircraft of A&AEE, RAE & ETPS since 1960' by Adrian M Balch, Airlife Publishing Ltd

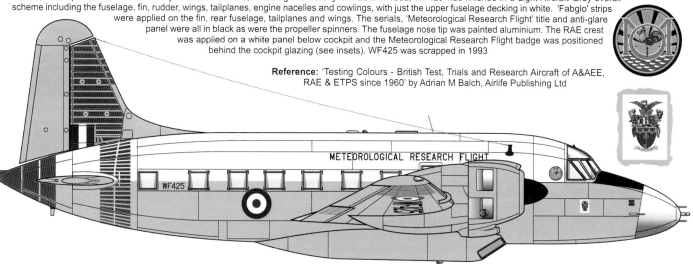

De Havilland Sea Vixen FAW.1, XJ476, Aircraft & Armament Experimental Establishment (A&AEE) Boscombe Down, June 1974
XJ476 was one of the first batch of pre-production Sea Vixens and spent part of its life at the Woomera ranges in Australia, before returning to Boscombe Down to be used as a test aircraft on the Red Top missile programme. Probably originally delivered in its original Royal Navy Extra Dark Sea Grey and white scheme, at some stage prior to arriving at Boscombe Down, (maybe in Australia) it had been repainted overall white, with just the national markings and black serials and anti-glare panel. The radome was dark grey.

Reference: Scale Aircraft Modelling Vol 14/1, October 1991, Aircraft in Detail 'De Havilland Sea Vixen' by Alan W Hall

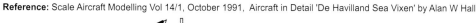
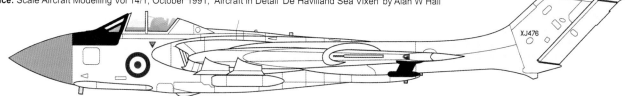

Vickers V.837 Viscount, XT575, Royal Radar Establishment, Pershore, Worcestershire, July 1974
First flown in February 1960, XT575 was originally operated by Austrian Airlines as OE-LAG 'Franz Schubert', and served as a civil airliner with this airline and TABSO (Bulgarian Civil Air Transport) until it was sold to the Ministry of Aviation and then onto the RAE in the 1960s, where it was modified for radar development trials and fitted with a large ventral fuselage radome forward of the wing for Nimrod ASW electronic trials. Finished in overall aluminium, including the wings, nacelles and tailplanes, with white upper fuselage decking, fin and rudder, it had Roundel Blue trim around the cabin windows. Serials were white on the blue rear fuselage trim and black under the wings. the anti-glare panel was black and there was a Day-Glo strip on fin. A Royal Radar Establishment badge was on a white disc was carried on both sides of the nose under the cockpit glazing. (see inset). XT575 was withdrawn from RAE service in February 1991 and stored at Thurleigh Airfield, Bedfordshire, until July 1993 when it was sold to International Turbine Service Inc, Texas, USA, primarily for the Rolls-Royce Dart engines (four installed and two spares), after which the airframe was broken up and the forward fuselage section donated for preservation to the Brooklands Museum, Weybridge, Surrey, where, at the time of writing public access is available to the interior.
Reference: Airliners.net

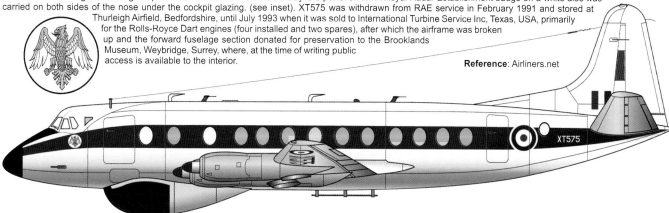

Folland Gnat T.1, XP505, Aero Flight Systems, RAE Bedford, July 1974
XP505 first flew on 21st September 1962 and began its career with the manufacturers, on loan from the Ministry of Aviation (MoA), entering RAF service with the CFS in February 1966 but went back to MoA charge in April and returned to Hawker-Siddeley at Dunsfold. In January 1969 HS sold XP505 to the Ministry of Technology and was sent to the A&AEE at Boscombe Down for a few weeks 'before being overhauled at Bitteswell and allocation to RAE Bedford's 'Aero Flight' where it served on gust and turbulence research. During the mid-1970s, XP505 was finished in Light Aircraft Grey overall with white spine, fin/rudder and Roundel Blue rear fuselage trim and tailplane fillets. It had a black anti-glare panel, and wing and tailplane leading edges. Serials were white on the blue fuselage trim and black underwing, with the fuselage roundels thinly outlined in white. 'Aero Flight BEDFORD' titles on intake were red. XP505 was later being repainted in the 'Raspberry Ripple' scheme, and was not retired until the 1980s, thus becoming the last flying Gnat in UK service. Sold to the Science Museum, XP505 was on display at the Museum's central London site until 1992 when it was moved into obscurity at their out-station at Wroughton, where at the time of writing, it remains to this day.

References: 'A Short Illustrated History of the Royal Aerospace Establishment Bedford' by Arthur Pearcy; Scale Aircraft Modelling Vol 8/2 November 1985

Above: Hunter F.6, XE601, (upgraded to FGA.9 although never officially redesignated as such), spent most of its service life operated jointly by the ETPS and A&AEE in several trials, including simulated biological warfare for which two special spray tanks were carried on the inner pylons, although the underwing tanks in this photo are thought to be smoke generators. This photo was probably taken in the early 1990s, although still in the Light Aircraft Grey and red scheme. At a later stage of its life, XE601 was repainted in the 'Raspberry Ripple' colour scheme. XE601was finally retired at Boscombe Down in July 1999.

Hawker Hunter F.6 (modified to FGA.9 standard), XE601, Empire Test Pilots School, A&AEE Boscombe Down, October 1974
Built in 1956, XE601 never entered RAF service but was retained by the Hawker Aircraft Company as a certification and trials aircraft. Subsequently converted to FGA.9 standard (via F.6A spec), it first flew as an FGA.9 in April 1965, although it was never officially classified as an FGA.9 and was always referred to by its original F.6 designation. Finished in overall Light Aircraft Grey with Post Office Red fuselage dorsal spine, fin/rudder, wing tips and cheatline down the full length of the fuselage, the serials, nose tip and (initially) fin tip were black. XE601 was purchased by the Canadian Northern Lights Group, with a view to relocating the aircraft to Canada, but before this happened, it was bought by Andy Foan of Skyblue Aviation (now Skyblue Aero Services), and is now flown by Andy Foan with the Hunter Flying Club as G-ETPS.

Reference: Airliners.net

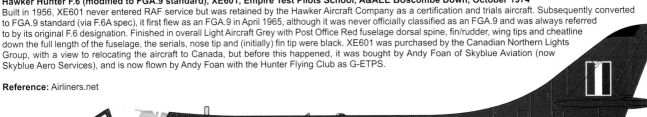

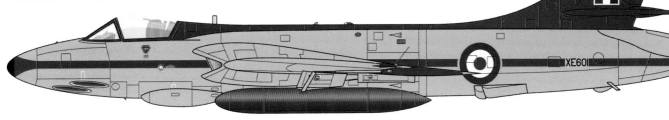

Hawker Hunter T.7, XL563, Institute of Aviation Medicine (IAM), RAE Farnborough, April 1975
Built at Kingston, Surrey, XL563 was the first production T.7 and first flew on 11 October 1957. The earlier part of its service was as a trials aircraft both at Boscombe Down with the A&AEE, and with the manufacturer's, Hawkers, as a support aircraft for the P.1127 VTOL/STOL project during September 1960. Allotted to the Bristol Aircraft Company in January 1961 for use as a chase aircraft in support of the Bristol 188 project to monitor the over water supersonic flight trials, XL563 remained at Filton until January 1963, when it was transferred to Farnborough and taken on charge by the RAF Institute of Aviation Medicine (IAM) in May 1963, under whose name it operated for over 30 years until its retirement in July 1993, having accrued a total of 2,979.40 flying hours. During these years this Hunter performed many varied but essential tasks in undertaking valuable aeromedical flight research on behalf of the IAM. Contrary to popular belief, this aircraft was not on the strength of the Royal Aircraft Establishment (later Defence Research Agency DERA) as it remained with IAM, although it was occasionally used by, and flown by, RAE pilots for trials or continuation training work. Finished in overall white with Post Office Red fin/rudder, nose flash and wing tips, the anti-glare panel, canopy framing, nose tip and serials were black. 'RAF Institute of Aviation Medicine' title was also in black (see inset). Drop tank pylons were in Light Aircraft Grey. Two years later in 1977, XL563 was repainted in the 'Raspberry Ripple' scheme. From August 1993 XL563 was used for valuable engineering training work prior to it being stripped of internal equipment ready for its new role as a ground display aircraft on the lawns outside the Officers Mess at the eastern end of Farnborough airfield. On display for some years, in late March 1999, XL563 was dismantled and moved to Kempston near Bedford, to be returned to flying condition, but this fell through, and the aircraft was moved to premises in Southmoor, near Oxford, where it remained in outside storage in a dismantled condition until it was transported to the Farnborough Air Sciences Trust (FAST) Museum premises in December 2014, where, at the time of writing, it awaits re-assembly and refurbishment by a team of dedicated volunteers

References: 'Farnborough - 100 Years of British Aviation' by Peter J Cooper, Midland Publishing Ltd;
'Forever Farnborough - Flying the Limits 1904-1996' by Peter J Cooper, Hikoki Publications; Airliners.net photo

THE WOODFIRE WAY

NINJA Electric BBQ Grill & Smoker UK

ONE TWO COMBO

The Woodfire Way - For Beginners
The Woodfire Way 2 NEXT LEVEL Combined

FULL-COLOUR

S.J. Peel

HOME CHEF BOOKS

Introduction

Introducing "The Woodfire Way One Two Combo", an eco-friendly and dynamic guide to mastering the art of outdoor barbecuing with the Woodfire grill, the perfect alternative to traditional charcoal and gas methods. This comprehensive book is designed for those new to Woodfire cooking, featuring an overview of the grill's components, usage instructions, maintenance tips, and much more.

Explore dozens of full-page recipes with vibrant, full-colour images, easily adaptable for different meats, fish, and vegetables, with only minor adjustments and a dash of creativity. With diverse recipes for various cuts of meat, vegetables, and mouth-watering seasonings, rubs, and sauces, you'll be well on your way to becoming a Woodfire pro.

This user-friendly guide includes UK metric measurements, effortless cooking charts, Woodfire maintenance and usage guidance, and lined pages for jotting down your culinary creations. Delight in flavourful seasonings, rubs, sauces, and marinades, and prepare scrumptious outdoor BBQ dishes using ingredients readily available in the UK.

With a focus on popular meat cuts, this book encourages you to experiment and hone your skills. Discover jerky preparation guides, tantalising marinades, and a glossy cover for effortless cleaning, making "The Woodfire Way" your essential companion for eco-friendly and versatile outdoor cooking.

Remember that these full-page recipes are designed for mixing and matching with other meats, fish or vegetables not included in these recipes, so feel free to experiment with various sauces or seasonings.

Regarding salt, we prefer sea salt, and regarding oil, we prefer olive oil, but you are free to choose your desired salt and oil. We have also included metric and imperial measures in the recipes for those using either, as we are aware that many in the UK still use a mix of both measurements, including spoons and cups.

For more air fryer dishes compatible with the Woodfire, see our **"Air Fryer UK Recipes - Ultimate UK Cookbook".**

Visit: homechefbooks.com
or facebook.com/groups/woodfire

Contents

Contents

Let's Break It Down

Nonstick Grill Grate: Suitable for all cooking functions. Place foil trays or other oven-proof dishes on top when necessary.

Removable Smoke Box: Ensure it is in place before adding pellets.

Digital Controls

Grease Tray Underneath: Ensure it is in place before cooking.

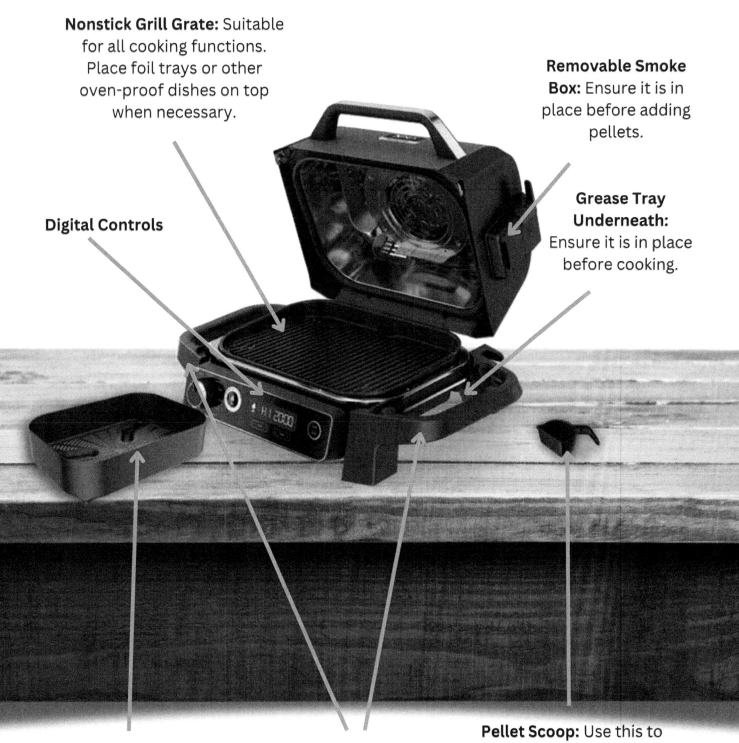

Air Fryer Basket: Fits up to 1.36 kg. For Air Frying, Roasting, Dehydrating and more.

Carry Handles: Only to be carried when switched off and cold.

Pellet Scoop: Use this to pour pellets into the smoke box, no more than twice per cook. Always close the smoke box lid after filling.

To fit the grill grate, position it flat atop the heating element and gently press down until it slots into place.

Functions

OFF: Ensure the dial is in the OFF position when the unit is not in use. Turn the dial clockwise to select a cooking function. Note that the unit is switched on when the display is lit.

Cooking Functions: SMOKER, Grill, AIR FRY, ROAST, BAKE, DEHYDRATE, and REHEAT.

START/STOP: Press to initiate or halt the current cooking function, or press and hold for 4 seconds to bypass preheating.

TEMP: Adjust the temperature using the (- TEMP +) button.

TIME: Modify the timer with the (- TIME +) button.

WOODFIRE FLAVOUR TECHNOLOGY: Press the button to infuse smoky flavour after selecting a cooking function. This feature is compatible with GRILL, AIR FRY, BAKE, ROAST, and DEHYDRATE functions. When activated, a flame icon will illuminate the display screen.

Wood Pellets

Ninja recommends using only their brand of products. However, some individuals use similarly sized pellets designed for the purpose but at a significantly lower cost, such as Traeger pellets. Use 1 scoop of pellets for each session and no more than 2 per cook.

Ninja has collaborated with Bear Mountain BBQ to develop their wood pellet blends. The All-Purpose blend combines cherry, maple, and oak, resulting in a smoother, sweeter flavour. The Robust blend incorporates the same woods as the All-Purpose blend, adding hickory for a smokier and richer taste.

To use, fill the pellet scoop, lift the Woodfire smoke box, and pour in the pellets. The pellets used in the Woodfire system are solely for adding flavour and do not contribute to cooking or seasoning your food in any other way. Expect one scoop to last about 45 minutes.

We are not affiliated to Ninja or Bear Mountain BBQ.

Preheating

Preheating and Tips: Once you have selected the function, time, and temperature, pressing START will cause the unit to begin preheating automatically (unless you use the SMOKER or DEHYDRATE functions without WOODFIRE FLAVOUR TECHNOLOGY).

- Preheat times by temperature: HI 10-12 mins, MED 8-10 mins, LO 7-9 mins.
- Ignition times for smoking will take an additional 5-7 minutes.
- Ensure ingredients are cool, but not ice-cold, before placing them on the grill.
- To achieve the best smoke flavour, minimise the time the lid is open when adding or turning food.
- For consecutive smoking sessions, refill the smoke box when half the pellets have burned.
- DO NOT reignite pellets, and DO NOT refill more than two times.

Cleaning

The grill grate and air fryer basket can be removed. Once the grill has cooled down, clean the grate from the rest of the Woodfire. The grate is not dishwasher safe, so use soap, water, and a cloth or non-abrasive pad. Disposable baking tins can be used at times.

To clean the Woodfire's exterior, thoroughly wipe it down with a damp cloth. If you have used the WOODFIRE FLAVOUR or SMOKER functions, empty the pellet smoke box. Next, remove the drip pan, dispose of its contents, and wash it with warm soapy water.

One - The Set Up

Position the Woodfire on a flat, level surface. Open the lid and install the grill grate by laying it flat over the heating element so that it sits securely in place. Fit the grease tray, preferably lined with tin foil, and slide it into position beneath the grill.

Two - Programing and Preheating

Switch the unit on by rotating the dial clockwise from the OFF position to select GRILL. Use the buttons on either side of TEMP to adjust the temperature and the buttons on either side of TIME to set the cooking duration.

Press START to initiate preheating. Allow the Woodfire to preheat fully before adding food, as not doing may result in overcooking and an extended preheating time. While preheating is strongly advised, you can bypass it by pressing the START/STOP button for 4 seconds.

Four - Cook

Once the Woodfire has been preheated, "ADD FOOD" will appear on the screen. Open the lid to place ingredients on the grill, then close the lid. The Woodfire will start cooking, and the timer will commence counting down. When complete, the Woodfire will beep and "END" will appear on the screen. Remove from the Woodfire and serve.

One - The Set Up

Position the Woodfire on a flat, level surface. Open the lid and install the grill grate by laying it flat over the heating element so that it sits securely in place. Fit the grease tray, preferably lined with tin foil, and slide it into position beneath the grill.

Two - Add Food

Add food and close the lid.

Three - Add Pellets

Open a bag of Woodfire pellets, and using the supplied pellet scoop, reach into the bag, fill the scoop to the top, and level it off. The scoop is designed to measure the pellets required for a single smoking session. With the smoke box lid held open, pour the pellets into the smoke box until it is full. Then, close the smoke box lid.

Four - Program and Cook

Switch the grill on by turning the dial clockwise from the OFF position to select the SMOKER function. Use the buttons on either side of TEMP to adjust the temperature and the buttons on either side of TIME to set the cooking duration. Press the button to the right of the display labelled START/STOP to commence cooking. Close the lid, and the Woodfire will start cooking as the timer counts down. No preheat is needed for SMOKER.

Four - Remove and Serve

When complete, the grill will beep, and an END message will appear on the screen. Remove from the Woodfire and serve.

Tips

- To achieve a smokier outcome, use cooler ingredients but avoid using ice-cold food.
- For the best smoke flavour, minimise the time the lid is open when turning food.
- If you want to add one more scoop of pellets and you have let the others finish burning, pour another full scoop. Press and hold the WOODFIRE FLAVOUR button for 3 seconds to ignite the newly filled box of pellets.
- Avoid adding oil to the meat when smoking, or use only a tiny amount if necessary.

Functions Explained

SMOKER

The integrated smoke box burns natural wood pellets to create authentic BBQ flavours. A convection fan evenly circulates heat and smoke around food, ensuring rich, fully developed woodfire flavours.

GRILL

Grilling serves as the principal function of the Woodfire, commonly used for general barbecuing and imparting smoky flavours. The smoking feature can be employed with other settings, and it is worth noting that, unlike traditional smoking methods, the Woodfire's SMOKER function adds smoky nuances without cooking the food. Electricity cooks the food. Therefore, the grilling function is predominantly utilised when barbecuing items such as steaks, peppers, chops, sausages, etc.

AIR FRY

Air frying replicates the deep-frying process by employing hot air circulation and minimal oil. It functions by circulating hot air at high speed around the food, yielding a crispy exterior and a cooked interior akin to traditional fried dishes. However, air fryers are favoured for their capacity to produce healthier alternatives to conventionally fried meals, utilising considerably less oil and decreasing overall fat content.

ROAST

This function allows you to cook food with a roasting technique similar to an oven. Using this mode, hot air is circulated the food, evenly cooking it and producing a tender interior with a nicely browned exterior. The ROAST method is beneficial for cooking various meat joints, whole chicken, and root vegetables.

BAKE

The BAKE function allows you to cook various dishes using a baking technique similar to a conventional oven. You can even add a smoky flavour while baking.

DEHYDRATE

This function removes moisture from foods by circulating low-temperature, dry air around them. This process preserves the food and concentrates flavours while maintaining its nutritional content. Dehydration is commonly used for snacks such as fruit and vegetable crisps and dried herbs. It offers a convenient and efficient alternative to traditional food dehydrators or sun-drying methods.

REHEATING

The REHEAT function carefully reheats food to help retain flavours and texture.

Recipes & Cooking Times

The Woodfire is undoubtedly a versatile cooking appliance. Its confined space, under-grill grate, and overhead element significantly reduce cooking times, especially for popular items like steaks, chops, and fish. With these features, a dish that might take 15 minutes on a regular barbecue could be ready on the Woodfire in 10 or 12 minutes. Adapting to this increased speed may take a little getting used to.

Our recipes provide time frames for you to adapt to your preference, but remember, perfect cooking relies on more than just time and temperature. Factors such as food quality, size, quantity, preheating, external temperature, and food's initial temperature all come into play. Seasonings and rubs also matter. For instance, excess salt can dry out the food, so we suggest that when you add extra seasoning when more is required for your taste, you do so without extra salt.

Grill grate cooking with the hood open is akin to conventional barbecuing: the food cooks on one side before being flipped. To do this, close the hood, set the dial to GRILL and the temperature to HI or a temperature you would usually barbecue certain foods. Next, select the timer for the duration you plan to barbecue and press START/STOP to begin preheating. Preheating helps eliminate potential germs and prepare the grill grate for the food. Once you see the ADD FOOD message, lift the hood, which turns off the overhead element but leaves the under-grill grate element on. You may find this method slower than using the flames of a conventional open barbecue, so you can adjust the cooking times as needed.

Mastering the Woodfire involves a learning curve; our guides are designed to assist with that. We're confident you'll create delicious dishes on the Woodfire in no time.

Heating Elements Utilisation

GRILL

In GRILL mode, the under-plate heating element becomes active when the hood is open, warming the grill rack and rising heat, similar to a traditional BBQ. This specific heating element is not utilised in any other cooking mode. With the hood closed during GRILL mode, the overhead heating element comes into play. If the hood is lifted while cooking, the overhead element will temporarily switch off until the hood is shut again. Nevertheless, the under-plate element continues to function consistently.

For instance, and this is purely down to personal preference, GRILL mode with the hood open is often used for items that you may want to flip continually on a BBQ, such as burgers, seafood, thin steaks, sliced or chopped fruits and vegetables, or for toasting one side of a bun or bread roll. On the other hand, foods like pizza, which benefit from simultaneous top and bottom cooking, are suited to GRILL mode with the hood closed.

AIR FRY and ROAST

The ROAST and AIR FRY modes utilise the overhead element and high fan speeds to circulate the hot air around the food from the top and sides (ROAST) all sides (AIR FRY). Other than temperature presets and ranges, they operate fundamentally similarly, allowing diverse applications.

DEHYDRATE, BAKE, REHEAT, AND SMOKER

These modes engage the overhead heating element and lower fan speeds, circulating heated air around the food from all directions, akin to cooking in a traditional oven. Both temperature settings and cooking times are crucial factors in these modes. If you prefer to have all sides of your food cooked simultaneously, using either the air fryer basket or an ovenproof rack might be beneficial, or you could employ firm, sliced vegetables, like carrots, to elevate the food off the grill grate or rack.

Woodfire Recipes

Though the Woodfire excels at creating mouth-watering air-fried and baked dishes, its true allure lies in its smoking, dehydrating, and outdoor electric barbecuing capabilities. It's these exceptional features that have taken centre stage in our exploration. You should have little trouble working with other meats in many of these recipes.

In the upcoming sections, we shall embark on a thrilling culinary journey, unveiling an assortment of delectable Woodfire recipes guaranteed to tantalise your taste buds. Be prepared to discover the magic of smoky flavours, the irresistible charm of outdoor barbecuing, and the satisfying simplicity of perfectly dehydrated treats.

The convection fan within the Woodfire helps retain moisture. However, a little spray of water or apple cider vinegar every hour or two can work wonders for meets that need a long time to cook.

Wrapping food in foil or butcher's paper is unnecessary when smoking on the Woodfire.

Slice the meat against the grain. The grain refers to the direction of the fibres.

The flavourful outer crust on meat that looks blackened is called the bark.

When smoking, always use pellets of your choice.

Sides, Snacks & Meat-Free Dishes

The role of side dishes can be overlooked in BBQ, where the spotlight often shines on perfectly smoked brisket or chargrilled chicken. However, these accompaniments are far more than mere afterthoughts; they are pivotal in creating a balanced and satisfying culinary experience.

Side dishes offer a counterpoint to the main event, providing complementary flavours and textures that can enhance and elevate the enjoyment of the grilled meat or fish. For example, the creaminess of macaroni and cheese can beautifully offset the smokiness of BBQ ribs. At the same time, the crunch and tang of coleslaw can provide a refreshing contrast to a rich, pulled pork sandwich.

Moreover, BBQ side dishes create opportunities to cater to diverse palates and dietary needs. For example, vegetarian and vegan guests can enjoy sides like grilled vegetables or a hearty potato salad. Those with a spice preference might enjoy collard greens slow-cooked with garlic and chilli, while others may prefer the sweet comfort of BBQ beans.

Additionally, side dishes often carry cultural and regional significance. A serving of collard greens can evoke the culinary traditions of the American South, while potato salad, although initially a European dish, might pay homage to Midwestern heritage. These sides offer a sense of place and history, grounding the BBQ experience in time-honoured traditions and creating a deeper connection with our food.

Visually, side dishes add vibrancy and colour to the BBQ spread, making the meal more appealing. The bright yellows and reds of grilled corn and bell peppers, the deep green of collard greens, or the creamy hues of coleslaw and potato salad create an inviting mosaic that stimulates the appetite.

Brussels Sprouts & Chestnuts

4 bacon rashers, chopped but not too small that they may fall through the air fryer basket holes

Chestnuts, tinned and drained or from vacuum packs				225 g	1/2 lb
Balsamic vinegar	30 ml	2 tbsp	Brussels sprouts	900 g	2 lb
Sea salt		1/2 tsp	Olive oil	30 ml	2 tbsp
Ground black pepper		1/2 tsp			

Place the air fryer basket on the grill grate in the Woodfire and turn the dial to AIR FRY. Set the temperature to 200C and the timer for 20 minutes. Press START/STOP to preheat. Halve the raw Brussels sprouts, combine them in a large bowl with the other ingredients, and toss to coat evenly.

When the ADD FOOD message appears, open the lid, transfer the sprouts mixture to the air fryer basket, and close the lid to cook. Toss the sprouts every 5 minutes. Once they are lightly browned, fork-tender and the bacon is cooked, remove the basket and transfer the sprouts to a serving bowl. Season with additional salt and pepper to taste.

Serves 4 to 6, Preparation time approx 20 mins, Cooking time approx 20 minutes

Bacon-Wrapped Brussels Sprouts

Brussels Sprouts	900 g	2 lb	Sea salt		1 tsp
Olive oil	30 ml	2 tbsp	Ground black pepper		1 tsp
Balsamic vinegar	30 ml	2 tbsp	6 to 8 fatty bacon rashers		

Toothpicks or longer skewers if you wish to thread several sprouts on one stick. (Soak the toothpicks, cocktail sticks or skewers in water for 20 minutes prior to use)

Position the air fryer basket on the grill grate, turn the Woofire dial to AIR FRY, and set the temperature to HI and the timer for 20 minutes. Press START/STOP to start preheating.

In the meantime, discard any old or loose leaves from the Brussels sprouts. Place the sprouts in a large bowl with the other ingredients, excluding the bacon, tossing until evenly coated. Cut the bacon into strips, ensuring they are long enough to wrap around each sprout once but not so wide as to hide the sprout. Secure each bacon-wrapped sprout with a toothpick or thread them onto long skewers. Continue with the rest.

Once the ADD FOOD message appears, lift the lid and arrange the bacon-wrapped sprouts in the air fryer basket, ideally in a single layer, to ensure optimal airflow. Close the lid to start cooking. Stir the sprouts approximately every 5 minutes to ensure even cooking. Remove the basket from the grill once the sprouts become lightly browned, are easily pierced with a fork, and the bacon is fully cooked. Transfer the sprouts to a serving dish and season with additional salt and pepper to taste.

Serves 4 to 6, Preparation time approx 10 minutes, Cooking time approx 20 minutes

BBQ Beans

1 tin kidney beans, rinsed and drained			1 tin baked beans, rinsed and drained		
1 tin white beans, rinsed and drained			Dijon mustard	30 ml	2 tbsp
Brown sugar	10 g	1 tbsp			
barbecue sauce of choice (or use the recipe below)					

BBQ Sauce

Tomato ketchup	45 ml	3 tbsp	Clear honey	45 ml	3 tbsp
Worcestershire sauce	30 ml	2 tbsp			

Combine the ingredients in a baking dish or tin, cover them with aluminium foil, and close the lid. Turn the Woodfire dial to BAKE, set the temperature to MED, and set the timer for 30 minutes. Press START/STOP to start preheating.

Once the ADD FOOD message appears, open the lid, carefully place the covered dish onto the grill grate, and close the lid to begin cooking. Monitor the beans after the first 20 minutes, stir them, and check and stir every few minutes afterwards. The dish is ready when the beans are thoroughly cooked and the mixture is smooth. Remove the dish from the Woodfire, and serve.

Serves 6 to 8, Preparation time approx 10 minutes, Cooking time approx 30 minutes

Beer Cheese Sauce

Unsalted butter		2 tbsp	Garlic powder		1 tsp
Plain flour		2 tbsp	Dried parsley		1/2 tsp
Ground black pepper		1/2 tsp	Beer (preferably lager)	250 ml	1 cup
Cheddar cheese, freshly grated, not from a packet of grated cheese, as freshly grated melts easier				225 g	8 oz

This tangy, tasty, all-around cheese sauce is excellent for burgers, steaks, and dips. If you don't fancy the beer, replace it with a clear vegetable stock.

Turn the Woodfire dial to GRILL, set the temperature to MED, and the timer for 20 minutes. Press START/STOP to preheat. While preheating, mix everything except the beer and cheese. While mixing, add a little beer at a time until you have a lump-free batter and you have used up the all of the beer. Gently stir in the cheese and place all ingredients in a baking tray or tin.

When the ADD FOOD message appears, open the lid, place the tray on the grill grate, and close the lid to start cooking. Check the sauce and stir after 10 minutes, and check and stir every few minutes until the ingredients have melded to your liking. If the sauce might need more time, leave the tray in the Woodfire while it absorbs the residual heat. For the last few minutes of the cook, adding bread rolls or pretzels to the grill will warm them up nicely. Sprinkle on some freshly grated cheese to garnish.

Serves 2 to 4, Preparation time approx 10 minutes, Cooking time approx 20 minutes

Cajun Corn on the Cob

Unsalted butter, room temperature	60 g	2 oz	1/4 tsp ground black pepper		1/4 tsp
4 to 6 corn cobs			2 tsp Cajun seasoning		2 tsp
Olive oil	30 ml	2 tbsp	Juice of 1/2 lime		
Sea salt		1/4 tsp	Fresh coriander, chopped		1 tbsp

Combine the butter, Cajun seasoning, lime juice, and coriander in a small bowl and evenly coat each cob with oil, salt, and pepper.

Turn the dial to GRILL, set the temperature to HI, and set the timer for 15 minutes. Press START/STOP to begin the preheating process.

When the ADD FOOD shows, open the lid and place the cobs on the grill grate. Close the lid to start cooking. Check and turn the cobs halfway through. Once complete, remove the cobs and serve hot with the Butter.

Serves 4 to 6, Preparation time approx 15 mins, Cooking time approx 15 minutes

Crispy Collard Greens or Kale

450 g/1 lb collard greens or 200 g/5 oz kale				
Coarse sea salt		1 tsp	Coconut oil	15 ml	1 tbsp

Position the air fryer basket onto the grill grate, close the lid, and turn the Woodfire dial to AIR FRY. Adjust the temperature to 150C and set the timer for 10 minutes. Press the START/STOP button to start preheating. In a large bowl, prepare the greens, ensuring that the stems are removed. Drizzle the greens with coconut oil.

Once the ADD FOOD notification appears, open the lid and carefully transfer the greens to the air fryer basket or a rack, spreading them out in a single layer. Close the lid to commence cooking. Check on the greens periodically, tossing them in the basket for even cooking. Remove the greens from the basket once the edges have attained a light brown colour and the greens are crispy. Transfer the greens to a salad bowl, sprinkle with salt, and serve immediately to enjoy their fresh, crispy texture.

Serves 1 to 2, Preparation time approx 10 minutes, Cooking time approx 10 minutes

Crispy Topping Onions

4 large onions, peeled and thinly sliced and separated, not diced (onions of choice)

Spray oil

Set the Woodfire dial to AIR FRY, adjust the temperature to 130C, and timer to 25 minutes. Do not place the air fryer basket inside during preheating. Close the lid and press START/STOP to start preheating.

Lightly mist the air fryer basket with oil, add the thinly sliced onions, and give them a gentle spray before tossing. When the ADD FOOD message appears, set the basket on the grill grate and shut the lid to start cooking.

Toss the onions every 5 minutes until they're cooked to your liking. Once done, immediately serve them on burgers, salads, and main dishes, or let them cool before storing them in an airtight container for up to a month.

Preparation time approx 15 minutes, Cooking time approx 25 minutes

Grilled Butternut Squash

1 butternut squash, skin on, sliced in half lengthways, seeds removed, and scored as in the photograph					
Seasoning of choice (or refer to our seasoning recipes)					1 tbsp
Olive oil	30 ml	2 tbsp			

Mix the seasoning and olive oil, then arrange the sliced squash on a large tray and gently rub the mixture into them. Set the Woodfire dial to GRILL, the temperature to HI, and the timer for 30 minutes, then press START/STOP to start preheating. When you see the ADD FOOD message, place the squash skin-side down on the grill grate – no need to flip them in this recipe.

Once they're fork-tender and have slightly dark, crispy edges on the outer skin, remove the squash. Add a pinch of salt and pepper, and serve with fried onions or your favourite topping.

Serves 2, Preparation time approx 20 mins, Cooking time approx 30 minutes

Grilled Peach Salad

10 to 16 bite-sized mozzarella balls (Bocconcini)			A large bowl of rocket or salad greens of choice		
6 to 10 slices of smoked ham, chicken, turkey, serrano, or meat substitute					
4 large peaches, soft but not overripe, cut in halves and de-stoned					
Olive oil for brushing the peach halves	30 ml	2 tbsp			
Dressing					
Olive oil	45 ml	3 tbsp	White balsamic vinegar	30 ml	2 tbsp
Clear honey	15 ml	1 tbsp	1 red chilli, finely chopped		
1 garlic clove, finely grated					

Turn the Woodfire dial to GRILL, set the temperature to HI, and the timer for 15 minutes. Close the lid and press START/STOP to start preheating.

Dressing: Combine the olive oil, vinegar, and honey, then stir in the chilli and garlic.

Once the ADD FOOD message appears, open the lid, place the peach halves, cut side down onto the grill grate. Leave the lid open while you cook on the hot grate until the undersides look grilled and have started to caramelise. This process will likely take less time than 15 minutes.

While the peaches are grilling, prepare the salad and cold meats as you wish. Once the peaches are done, place them into the salad and drizzle on the dressing. Serve with crusty fresh bread.

Serves 2, Preparation time approx 10 minutes, Cooking time approx 15 minutes

Halloumi Wraps

Block of halloumi, cut to 8 slices	225 g	1/2 lb	Salad items of choice		
4 large tortillas					

First, assemble your chosen ingredients in a large bowl for the salad, cover it with cling film, and refrigerate until needed.

Select GRILL, set the temperature to HI and the timer to 8 minutes. Press START/STOP. When preheating is complete, and the ADD FOOD message appears, place halloumi slices on the grill grate and close the lid. Add some slices of onion, peppers or mushroom to the grill alongside the halloumi if you like.

After up to 4 minutes, flip the halloumi. Once cooked, remove it from the Woodfire. Place tortillas on the grill, using the residual heat to warm them. When warmed, remove the tortillas, add salad and halloumi, fold, and serve.

Serves 2 to 4, Preparation time approx 20 mins, Cooking time approx 8 minutes

Honey Corn Cobs

3 to 4 whole sweetcorn cobs, husks removed			1 jalapeno, deseeded and finely chopped		
Unsalted butter, softened	90 g	3 oz	1 garlic clove, finely grated		
Fresh coriander, finely chopped		2 tbsp	Clear honey	30 ml	2 tbsp
Fresh oregano, chopped		1 tbsp	Lime zest, finely grated		1 tsp
Fresh lime juice	30 ml	2 tbsp	Sea salt		1/2 tsp
Ground black pepper		1/4 tsp			

Turn the Woodfire dial to GRILL, set the temperature to HI, and the timer for 20 minutes. Press START/STOP to start preheating. While the grill is preheating, combine all ingredients, excluding the sweetcorn cobs.

Once the ADD FOOD message appears, lift the lid and position the sweetcorn cobs on the grill grate, generously brushing them with the prepared mixture. Close the lid to commence cooking.

Halfway through, check the sweetcorn to prevent it from burning, turning each cob and applying more of the mixture. Once cooked, remove the grilled sweetcorn and serve, offering additional butter or a sprinkle of grated cheese.

Serves 3 to 4, Preparation time approx 10 minutes, Cooking time approx 20 minutes

Meat-Free Skinless Sausages

1 tin cooked chickpeas			Nutritional yeast	30 g	1 oz
Vital wheat gluten	60 g	2 oz	Soy sauce	30 ml	2 tbsp
Tomato ketchup	125 ml	1/2 cup	Dijon mustard	30 ml	2 tbsp
Dried oregano		1 tsp	Paprika		1 tsp
Ground coriander		1 tsp	Sea salt		1/2 tsp
Ground black pepper		1/2 tsp	Spray oil		

Blend all ingredients, excluding the vital wheat gluten, in a food processor until well combined. Alternatively, mash and mix manually, then transfer to a bowl. Incorporate the wheat gluten and mix well. Hand-knead the mixture into dough, ensuring an even distribution of ingredients. Aim for a firm yet elastic consistency, being cautious not to over-knead into stiffness or looseness. It might take some practice, but the outcome is worth it for these tasty vegan sausages.

Partition the dough into eight equal sections and gently mould each into a sausage-like form. Situate each sausage on a small square of cling film, roll slightly more, and twist the cling film at both ends to secure and encapsulate them. Next, wrap each cling film-wrapped sausage in a foil square, rolling tightly and twisting the foil ends. Chill all the wrapped sausages in the fridge for at least 30 minutes.

Set the Woodfire dial to GRILL, the temperature to MED, and set the timer for 20 minutes. Press START/STOP to begin preheating. When the ADD FOOD message appears, remove the sausages from their wrappings, carefully position them on the grill grate, lightly oil them, and close the lid to cook. After approximately 8 minutes, open the lid and delicately flip the sausages. Keep an eye on them, flipping occasionally until they are cooked to your liking.

Serves 2 to 4, Preparation time approx 30 minutes, Cooking time approx 20 minutes

1 tin of pinto or kidney beans			Tomato ketchup	45 ml	3 tbsp
Sea salt		1/2 tsp	Garlic granules		1/2 tsp
Onion granules		1/4 tsp	Plain flour		2 tbsp
1 medium onion, diced			1/2 green bell pepper or 1 jalapeno, finely chopped		

After draining and rinsing the beans, puree them using a blender or manually. Combine with the rest of the ingredients and shape into 4 to 6 burgers. If the texture is too loose, add more flour until you reach the desired consistency. Chill the burgers in the fridge while the Woodfire preheats.

Load your preferred pellets into the smoke box, turn the dial to BAKE and press the WOODFIRE FLAVOUR button. Adjust the temperature to MED, set the timer for 20 minutes, and press START/STOP to start preheating. When the ADD FOOD message appears, position the burgers on the grill grate. Add a thin layer of oil to the burgers for a crisper finish. Close the lid to continue cooking.

After cooking for 8 minutes, open the lid and flip the burgers, then close the lid and continue cooking until they are to your liking by checking on them every few minutes. Once done, remove them from the Woodfire and use them as desired, such as on a flavourful burger with a generous serving of salad and sauce.

Serves 2 to 4, Preparation time approx 30 minutes, Cooking time approx 20 minutes

Mexican Mac & Cheese

Enough cooked macaroni to 3/4 fill a 23 x 33 cm baking dish (or a dish size close to it and any shape as long as it fits easily in the Woodfire)

6 rashers of thin raw bacon, diced			Cheddar cheese, grated	350 g	12 oz
Parmesan cheese, grated	60 g	2 oz	Panko or coarse breadcrumbs	70 g	3/4 cup
Milk	160 ml	2/3 cup	Cooked kidney bean	100 g	3 oz
1 red or orange bell pepper, chopped			Fresh coriander, chopped		1 tbsp
4 jalapenos, deseeded and chopped			Ground black pepper		1 tsp
3 garlic cloves, finely chopped			1 onion, finely chopped		

Combine pasta, bacon, cheddar, milk, peppers, jalapenos, kidney beans, black pepper, garlic, and onion in a baking dish. Place it on the Woodfire grill grate. Add pellets of choice to the smoke box, set the Woodfire dial to BAKE, the temperature to 150C, the timer for 40 minutes, and press the WOODFIRE FLAVOUR button. Press START/STOP to start cooking. If preheating activates, hold the START/STOP button down for 4 seconds to stop the preheating process.

Cook until the cheese has melted, then mix well. Cover with breadcrumbs and top with Parmesan cheese. Close the lid and continue cooking until done to your liking, ensuring the Parmesan doesn't burn. Allow it to rest for a few minutes before serving with a sprinkling of fresh coriander.

Serves 4 to 6, Preparation time approx 20 minutes, Cooking time approx 40 minutes

Mushroom Skewers

Balsamic vinegar	30 ml	1/2 cup	Low-sodium soy sauce	30 ml	2 tbsp
2 garlic cloves, finely grated			Ground black pepper		1/2 tsp
Medium to small mushrooms or choice, sliced or halved to 1 to 2 cm thick				450 g	1 lb
Fresh parsley, for garnish, chopped	1 tbsp				
4 or more long wooden skewers, soaked in water for 20 minutes before use					

Combine all the ingredients, excluding the parsley, in a large bowl. Ensure the mushrooms are thoroughly coated, then allow the mixture to rest for 20 minutes. Once you're ready to cook, turn the Woodfire dial to GRILL, set the temperature to HI, and the timer for 12 minutes. Press START/STOP to begin preheating.

During preheating, thread the sliced mushrooms onto the skewers. Once the ADD FOOD message appears, lift the lid, position the skewers on the grill grate, and close the lid to commence cooking. Halfway through, check and flip the mushrooms, brushing on more marinade. Once cooked to your liking, remove the skewers from the Woodfire and serve, garnishing with a sprinkle of parsley and/or toppings such as toasted sesame seeds for added flavour.

Serves 2 to 4, Preparation time approx 20 minutes, Cooking time approx 12 minutes

Paprika Chips

4 Russet or King Edwards potatoes, peeled and patted dry (or potatoes of choice)				
Sea salt	1/2 tsp	Olive oil	30 ml	2 tbsp
smoked paprika (or to your taste)	2 tbsp			

Slice the potatoes, combine them with the other ingredients, and toss until the chips are thoroughly coated. Position the air fryer basket on the grill grate and close the lid. Turn the dial to AIR FRY, set the temperature to HI, and the timer for 20 minutes. Press START/STOP to start preheating.

Once the ADD FOOD message appears, open the lid and transfer the chips into the air fryer basket, then close the lid to start cooking. Be aware that cooking might require less than 20 minutes, so checking on the chips periodically is advisable. Cook until the chips are golden brown, shaking the basket occasionally to ensure even cooking.

Serves 2 to 4, Preparation time approx 20 minutes, Cooking time approx 20 minutes

Smoked Garlic Bread & Cheese

1 loaf of bread, round, and enough for 4 people					
Cheese of choice (ideally a mix of cheddar and mozzarella), grated					
Salted butter, room temperature	120 g	4 oz	Fresh parsley, finely chopped		1 tbsp
10 garlic cloves, peeled and finely grated					

In a small bowl, combine butter, garlic, and parsley, mixing well. Using a bread knife, slice the bread into 6 segments, like pizza slices, cutting halfway through or slightly deeper, ensuring the loaf remains intact. Add pellets of choice to the smoke box and turn the dial to BAKE. Press WOODFIRE FLAVOUR, set the temperature to 180C, and the timer for 10 minutes. Press START/STOP to begin preheating.

While the Woodfire preheats, prepare the bread. Place it on a double-layer of tin foil and gently pull the cuts open by up to 1 cm, keeping the loaf together. Fill the cuts with the garlic butter and cheese mixture. When the ADD FOOD message appears, open the lid, place the loaf (and tin foil) on the grill grate, and close the lid to start cooking.

Check on the loaf occasionally, and once the cheese has melted and you're satisfied, remove the bread and allow it to cool for a few minutes before serving.

Serves 2 to 4, Preparation time approx 15 mins, Cooking time approx 10 minutes

Smoked Hasselback Potatoes

Olive oil	15 ml	1 tbsp	Ground black pepper		1/2 tsp
Sea salt		1/2 tsp	1 onion, sliced (thin enough to hold open the cuts)		
2 to 4 medium-sized floury potatoes (Maris Piper or King Edward will work well)					

Add your choice of pellets to the smoke box, turn the Woodfire dial to AIR FRY, and press WOODFIRE FLAVOUR. Set the temperature to 180C and the timer for 15 minutes. Press START/STOP to preheat. While preheating, slice the potatoes, being careful not to cut all the way through to maintain their structural integrity. Insert small onion slices between the potato cuts to pry them open slightly. Drizzle the potatoes with olive oil, then season with a light sprinkling of salt and pepper.

While preheating, slice the potatoes, being careful not to cut all the way through to maintain their structural integrity. Insert small onion slices between the potato cuts to pry them open slightly. Drizzle the potatoes with olive oil, then season with a light sprinkling of salt and pepper.

When the ADD FOOD message appears, lift the lid and position the potatoes on the grill grate. Close the lid to start cooking. Monitor the potatoes approximately every 5 minutes, cooking them until they are done to your liking.

Serves 2 to 4, Preparation time approx 20 minutes, Cooking time approx 15 minutes

2 heads of cauliflower		
Mustard maple sauce (or refer to our sauce recipes for mustard maple)	125 ml	1/2 cup

Position the cauliflower heads on the grill grate and close the lid. Add your chosen pellets to the smoke box. Set the dial to SMOKER, the temperature to 120C, and the timer for 2 hours. Press START/STOP to begin cooking.

Once cooking is complete, open the lid, remove the cauliflower heads, and slice them into cauliflower steaks. Sprinkle some seasoning over them and serve with a dipping sauce or dressing, such as ranch-style or blue cheese.

Place a small heatproof water dish in the Woodfire on the grill grate during cooking to ensure extra-moist cauliflower.

Serves 4 to 6, Preparation time 10 mins, Cooking time approx 2 hours

Smoked Sweet Potato Wedges

Seasoning of choice (or refer to our seasoning recipes)				1 tbsp
4 to 6 large sweet potatoes, cut into wedges		Smoked paprika		1/2 tsp
Olive oil	30 ml	2 tbsp		

First, place the basket inside the unit and add your preferred pellets to the smoke box. Select AIR FRY and press the WOODFIRE FLAVOUR button. Adjust the temperature to 200C and set the timer for 25 minutes. Press START/STOP to begin preheating.

In a large bowl, mix the ingredients thoroughly. When the ADD FOOD message appears, place the seasoned wedges into the air fryer basket in a single layer. Close the lid and press START/STOP to begin cooking.

After 10 minutes, flip the wedges over and continue to check on them every few minutes until they're cooked to your liking. Serve with your favourite dip.

Serves 4 to 6, Preparation time approx 15 mins, Cooking time approx 25 minutes

Smoky Grilled Queso

225 g/8 oz mild cheddar cheese, grated, or 225 g/ 8 oz processed cheese slices

Butter	60 g	2 oz	Spring onions, finely chopped	80 g	3 oz
2 garlic cloves, finely grated			2 tomatoes, average-sized, chopped		
Ground cumin		1/2 tsp	Onion powder		1/2 tsp
Cayenne pepper		1/2 tsp	Cornflour		1 tbsp
Evaporated milk	350 ml	1 1/3 cup	Fresh coriander, finely chopped		1 tbsp
Green chillies or jalapenos, finely chopped				90 g	3 oz

Add pellets of choice to the smoke box, turn the Woodfire dial to GRILL, and press the WOODFIRE FLAVOUR button. Set the temperature to medium and the timer for 30 minutes. Press START/STOP to preheat.

While preheating, mix onions, garlic, tomatoes, chillies or jalapenos in a baking tray or tin. When the ADD FOOD message appears, lift the lid, place the tray on the grill grate, and close the lid to start cooking so these ingredients can absorb a smoky flavour.

After 10 minutes, add the remaining ingredients to the tray and stir. Close the lid to continue cooking. Stir the ingredients every 5 minutes. Continue until the ingredients have melded to your preference. If the queso might need more time, leave the tray in the Woodfire while it absorbs the residual heat.

Serves 2 to 4, Preparation time approx 10 minutes, Cooking time approx 30 minutes

Smoky Potato Salad

Fresh dill, chopped		1 tbsp	Dijon mustard	15 ml	1 tbsp
Soured cream	125 ml	1/2 cup	Fresh parsley, chopped		1 tbsp
Sherry vinegar	15 ml	1 tbsp	1 red onion, peeled, diced		
Olive oil	15 ml	1 tbsp	Sea salt		1 tsp
New potatoes, halved or quartered (or baby potatoes)				900 g	2 lb

Place potato pieces in a large bowl, cover with water, and soak for 30 minutes to remove excess starch. Drain and rinse the potato pieces and dry them with a towel. Dry the bowl and combine pieces with the oil and the salt, tossing until evenly coated.

Add your choice of pellets to the smoke box and place the air fryer basket on the grill grate. Set the dial to AIR FRY and press the WOODFIRE FLAVOUR button. Set the temperature to 180C and the timer to 25 minutes, then press STOP/START for the preheating to begin.

When the ADD FOOD message displays, place the potato pieces into the preheated air fryer basket within the Woodfire. Close the lid to initiate the cooking process. Flip the potato pieces occasionally until they are cooked to your liking. Once done, remove them from the basket and allow them to cool to room temperature.

While the potatoes are cooling, combine the remaining ingredients in a separate bowl. Once the potato pieces have cooled, add them to this mixture and stir gently to ensure an even coating. Serve the dish immediately for the best flavour and texture.

Serves 2 to 4, Preparation time approx 15 minutes, Cooking time approx 25 minutes

Smoky Salsa

4 large tomatoes			Fresh coriander, chopped		1 tbsp
1/2 large red onion			Freshly squeezed lime juice	30 ml	2 tbsp
4 garlic cloves			Sea salt		1/2 tsp
2 jalapenos			Olive oil	30 ml	2 tbsp

Place all the vegetables in a large bowl or plastic bag and mix well with the olive oil or brush the vegetables with the oil instead.

Place the tomatoes, red onion, garlic cloves, and jalapenos on the grill grate and close the lid. Add your preferred pellets to the smoke box, set the dial to SMOKER, set the temperature to 120C and the timer for 2 hours, then press START/STOP to begin cooking.

Check the vegetables occasionally and remove them once they're done, ensuring they don't burn. Remove any stems and garlic skin. Blend all ingredients in a food processor to your desired consistency.

Serves 4 to 6, Preparation time 15 mins, Cooking time approx 2 hours

Smoky Wedges

Maris Piper or other floury potatoes, cut into wedges of no more than 2.5 cm / 1 inch thick				900 g	2 lb
Olive oil	30 ml	2 tbsp	2 cloves of garlic, peeled and crushed		
Fresh Rosemary, finely chopped		1 tbsp	Sea salt		1 tsp
Fresh thyme, finely chopped		1 tbsp	Soured cream	250 ml	1 cup

Place potato wedges in a large bowl, cover with water, and soak for 30 minutes to remove excess starch. Drain and rinse the potatoes, then dry them with a towel. In the dried bowl, combine wedges, oil, herbs, garlic, and salt, tossing until evenly coated. Add your chosen pellets to the smoke box.

Place the air fryer basket on the grill grate. Set the dial to AIR FRY and press the WOODFIRE FLAVOUR button. Set the temperature to 190C and the timer to 25 minutes, then press STOP/START for the preheating to begin.

When ADD FOOD appears, place the wedges in the preheated air fryer basket inside the Woodfire. Close the lid and cook, flipping the wedges occasionally. Once cooked, remove and serve with a soured cream dip, tomato sauce, or one of our sauce recipes.

Serves 2 to 4, Preparation time approx 40 mins, Cooking time approx 25 minutes

Southern-Style Coleslaw

Mayonnaise	250 ml	1 cup	Dijon mustard	30 ml	2 tbsp
Apple cider vinegar	30 ml	2 tbsp	Sugar	20 g	2 tbsp
Sea salt		1 tsp	Onion powder		1 tsp
Celery seeds		1 tsp	Loose coleslaw mix of choice	450 g	1 lb

Combine everything other than the coleslaw mix in a large bowl. Next, introduce the coleslaw mix, tossing gently until thoroughly coated with the dressing.

For optimal flavour infusion, refrigerate the coleslaw for at least an hour before serving. However, if needed, it can be stored in the refrigerator for up to two days, but it will release more liquid the longer it is stored. You may need to drain some excess liquid before tossing again and serving. Give the coleslaw a final toss before serving for the best presentation and taste.

Serves 2 to 4, Preparation time approx 15 minutes, Cooking time approx 0 minutes

Stuffed Portobello Mushrooms

4 to 6 medium-large portobello mushrooms			Ground black pepper		1/2 tsp
Cheese of choice, grated	150 g	5 oz	A little parsley or fresh herb of choice		
3 garlic cloves, grated					

Start by cleaning your mushrooms, removing the stems and gills and dicing the stems and gills. Next, mix the cheese, garlic, diced stems and gills, and herbs in a bowl. Finally, fill each mushroom cup with the mixture.

Turn the dial to GRILL, set the temperature to HI, and the timer for 10 minutes. Press START/STOP to begin preheating. Once the ADD FOOD message appears, place the mushrooms on the grill grate and close the lid to start cooking.

Once cooked, remove them from the Woodfire and garnish them with ground black pepper and fresh herbs. Serve with soured cream for dipping.

Serves 2 to 3, Preparation time approx 15 mins, Cooking time approx 10 minutes

Twice Baked Filled Jacket Potatoes

4 large baking potatoes, such as Maris Piper			Olive oil	15 ml	1 tbsp
Sea salt		1/2 tsp	Chives, finely chopped		1 tbsp
Filling					
6 rashers of streaky bacon			3 spring onions, finely chopped		
Unsalted butter	120 g	4 oz	Double cream	80 ml	1/3 cup
Cheddar cheese, grated	225 g	8 oz	Ground black pepper		1/4 tsp

Set the Woodfire dial to BAKE, adjust the temperature to HI, and set the timer for 2 hours. Close the lid and press START/STOP to preheat. While preheating, pierce the potatoes with a fork and rub them with olive oil and salt. When the ADD FOOD message appears, position potatoes and bacon on the grill grate. Close the lid to start cooking.

After roughly 20 minutes, flip the potatoes and remove the bacon, then close the lid to continue cooking. Monitor the potatoes until a knife easily pierces them. Once done, remove the potatoes but keep the Woodfire on, regardless of the remaining time, with the lid up. Cut the potatoes in half lengthwise, scoop out most of the insides, and place in a large bowl. And mash until smooth.

Gently melt the butter and cream on low heat in a saucepan, or place the butter and cream in an ovenproof dish, place it on the grill grate, close the lid for a few minutes, and then add it to the mashed potato bowl. Incorporate the remaining fillings, excluding bacon and using only half of the grated cheese, into the bowl with the potato and mix.

Fill the emptied potato skins with the potato mixture and top with the remainder of the grated cheese and the bacon (but only if the bacon needs further cooking). Reopen the lid, place the filled potato halves on the grill grate, and close the lid to resume cooking. Monitor until the topped cheese has thoroughly melted, and the potatoes are heated (about 20 minutes). Finish by garnishing the potato halves with bacon, chopped chives, and optional sour cream before serving.

Serves 4, Preparation time approx 15 minutes, Cooking time approx 2 hours

Toppings of choice (we're going with 60 g / 2 oz of pepperoni)					
Ready-made pizza sauce	125 ml	1/2 cup	Seasonings of choice		1/2 tsp
Mozzarella cheese, grated	6	2 oz			
Pizza Dough (or use ready-made pizza dough)					
Plain flour / all-purpose flour, plus extra for dusting				200 g	7 oz
Instant-dried yeast		2 tsp	Granulated sugar		1/2 tsp
Sea salt		1/2 tsp	Olive oil, plus extra to drizzle		1/2 tbsp
Granulated sugar		1/2 tsp	Cornmeal or polenta for rolling		1/2 tbsp
Water	125 ml	1/2 cup	Water	125 ml	1/2 cup

Pizza Dough:

If using ready-made dough, follow the rolling, adding the toppings and cooking part. Combine flour, yeast, salt, and sugar in a mixing bowl. Create a well in the centre, add oil, then about 100 ml water and mix by hand to form a dough. Place the dough on a floured surface and knead until smooth. Let it rest under the upturned bowl for 15 minutes. Roll out a dough ball on a lightly floured surface up to 20 cm wide by 30 cm long but no less than .5 cm thick in the middle. Or split the dough into 2 separate small pizzas. Using your fingertips, create a thicker crust around the edges. The centre should be about .5 cm thick, and the crust approximately 1 cm deep. Spread sauce over the dough, followed by mozzarella and your chosen toppings. Drizzle with a touch of olive oil and let the pizza rest on a sheet of baking paper while you begin heating the Woodfire.

Pizza:

Add your preferred pellets to the smoke box, choose GRILL, press WOODFIRE FLAVOUR, set the temperature to HI and the timer for 10 minutes and press START/STOP. Once the Woodfire has preheated, slide the pizza off the baking paper onto the grill grate. Close the lid to continue cooking. Check the pizza after 4 minutes and then every couple of minutes until it's done to your liking.

Serves 1 to 2, Preparation time 30 mins, Cooking time approx 10 minutes

Jerky: A Wholesome and Flavourful Snack

The Woodfire is perfect for creating delicious jerky. Originating from ancient food preservation techniques, jerky is a delectable snack created by dehydrating lean cuts of meat, often marinated in various spices, herbs and flavourings. This tasty and protein-rich snack offers a range of benefits, making it an excellent choice for those seeking a nutritious and convenient food option.

Historical Background

Preserving meat through dehydration dates back thousands of years and was adopted by numerous cultures globally. 'jerky' originates from the Quechua word 'ch'arki', meaning 'dried meat'. Spanish explorers who arrived in the Americas in the 16th century learned about this preserved meat from indigenous people, spreading jerky-making techniques across Europe.

Meat Selection and Preparation

Beef is the traditional choice for making jerky, but other meats like poultry, pork, game, and fish are also used. High-quality jerky requires lean cuts of meat, as excess fat can spoil during dehydration. The meat is sliced thinly, marinated, and dried at low temperatures to eliminate moisture, inhibit bacterial growth, and extend shelf life.

Nutritional Advantages

Jerky is an outstanding source of protein, vital for tissue maintenance, repair, and immune function. A 28-gram serving of beef jerky contains around 9 grams of protein, making it a satisfying and convenient protein-rich snack. Moreover, jerky is relatively low in calories and fat, especially when compared to other snacks like crisps or sweets.

Health Benefits

Jerky's low-carbohydrate content suits those following low-carb or ketogenic diets. Additionally, it contains essential nutrients like iron, zinc, and B vitamins, contributing to overall health and well-being. However, it is important to consider the high sodium content in some jerkies and choose brands with lower salt levels, particularly for those monitoring their sodium intake.

During dehydration, check the jerky hourly to ensure it is done to your liking.

Jerky: A Wholesome and Flavourful Snack

Incorporating a marinade in the jerky-making process is essential for achieving a tender and flavoursome snack. A well-prepared marinade not only infuses taste but also tenderises the meat. Here's a concise guide on effectively using jerky marinades, which are interchangeable with all meats and fish:

1. Select your meat: Opt for lean cuts like beef, pork, chicken, or game, and ensure you trim any visible fat which can spoil during dehydration.
2. Prepare the meat: Slice the meat into thin, even strips, roughly 3 to 6 millimetres thick. Cutting across the grain (aka: against the grain) yields more tender jerky.
3. Create the marinade: Combine liquid ingredients (e.g., soy sauce, Worcestershire sauce, or vinegar), spices, and herbs in a bowl. Add sugar or honey for sweetness. Consider a small amount of fruit juice (such as pineapple or papaya) containing natural enzymes to tenderise the meat further, or use the following recipes.
4. Marinate the meat: Place meat strips in a resealable plastic bag or non-reactive container and pour the marinade over them. Massage the bag or stir the contents to ensure an even coating.
5. Refrigerate: Seal the bag or cover the container, and refrigerate for at least 4 to 8 hours. Avoid marinating for more than 24 hours, which may result in excessively soft jerky.
6. Drain and dry: Remove the meat from the marinade, allowing excess liquid to drip off. Gently pat the meat dry with kitchen paper to eliminate surface moisture and expedite dehydration.
7. Dehydrate the meat: Arrange marinated meat strips on the Woodfire grill grate, air fryer basket or wire racks in the middle of the Woodfire. Ensure even spacing and no overlapping.   **Follow the information on Page 7.**
8. Cool and store: After dehydrating, allow the jerky to cool at room temperature before transferring it to an airtight container. Consume within 1-2 weeks if stored at room temperature, or extend its shelf life by refrigerating or freezing.

Beef Jerky

Ingredients:

- 200 g dark brown sugar
- 250 ml soy sauce
- 45 ml (3 tbsp) Worcestershire sauce
- 1 tbsp smoked paprika
- 1 tsp unseasoned meat tenderiser
- 1 tsp freshly ground black pepper
- 1 tsp chilli flakes
- 1 tsp onion powder
- 1/2 tsp garlic powder

Smoky Lamb

Ingredients:

- 1 tbsp onion salt
- 30 ml (2 tbsp) Liquid Smoke
- 30 ml (2 tbsp) soy sauce
- 30 ml (2 tbsp) Worcestershire sauce
- 1 tsp hickory seasoning
- 5 drops Tabasco sauce

Malaysian Pork

Ingredients:

- 30 ml (2 tbsp) soy sauce
- 30 ml (2 tbsp) Worcestershire sauce
- 1 tbsp brown sugar
- 1 tbsp chilli sauce
- 15 ml (2 tbsp) sesame oil
- 1 tsp garlic powder
- 1 tsp onion powder
- 1 tsp black pepper

Lemon Salmon

Ingredients:

- 15 ml (1 tbsp) soy sauce
- 15 ml (1 tbsp) lemon juice
- 1 tbsp brown sugar
- 1 tsp ground black pepper
- 15 ml (1 tbsp) Liquid Smoke
- 1/2 tsp garlic powder

Maple Syrup

Ingredients:

- 15 ml (1 tbsp) honey
- 30 ml (2 tbsp) pure maple syrup
- 2 tbsp sugar
- 15 ml (1 tbsp) Liquid Smoke
- 1 tsp sea salt
- 1 tsp ground black pepper
- 120 ml cold water

Sweet Coconut

Ingredients:

- 30 ml (2 tbsp) soy sauce
- 2 tbsp coconut sugar
- 15 ml (1 tbsp) Liquid Smoke
- 15 ml (1 tbsp) apple cider vinegar
- 1 tsp sea salt
- 1 tsp ground black pepper

Orange Game

Ingredients:

- 100 ml soy sauce
- 60 ml (4 tbsp) orange juice
- Zest of 1 orange
- 15 ml (1 tbsp) honey
- 3 cloves garlic, finely grated
- 1 onion, finely grated
- 1 jalapeno, finely grated
- 1 tbsp brown sugar
- 1 tbsp freshly ground black pepper
- 1 tbsp red pepper flakes
- 1 tbsp ground ginger
- 1 tsp onion powder
- 1 tsp cumin

Balsamic

Ingredients:

- 30 ml (2 tbsp) soy sauce
- 45 ml (3 tbsp) barrel-aged balsamic
- 15 ml (1 tbsp) Liquid Smoke
- 1 tsp sea salt
- 1 tsp ground black pepper
- 1 tsp garlic powder
- 1 tsp onion powder
- 1 tsp chilli flakes

Fish Wine

Ingredients:

- 120 ml red wine
- 45 ml (3 tbsp) fish sauce
- 1/2 tsp black pepper

Smoky Turkey

Ingredients:

- 30 ml (2 tbsp) soy sauce
- 30 ml (2 tbsp) Worcestershire sauce
- 1 tbsp brown sugar
- 1 tbsp garlic powder
- 1 tsp onion powder
- 15 ml (1 tbsp) Liquid Smoke

Kung Pao

Ingredients:

- 60 ml (4 tbsp) soy sauce
- 60 ml (4 tbsp) sweet sherry
- 5 dried red chillis, chopped
- 30 ml (2 tbsp) Szechuan peppercorns, crushed
- 1 tbsp garlic granules
- 1 tbsp ground ginger
- 1 1/2 tbsp sugar

Mexican Heat

Ingredients:

- 30 ml (2 tbsp) Worcestershire sauce
- 1 tsp garlic powder
- 2 tbsp brown sugar
- 1 tsp smoked paprika
- 2 tsp chilli flakes
- 3 jalapeno peppers, diced
- 30 ml (2 tbsp) red wine vinegar

Air-Fried Smoked Lobster

2 to 4 lobster tails (if using frozen tails, give them plenty of time to thaw in the refrigerator)					
Unsalted butter	60 g	2 oz	Ground black pepper to taste		
Lemon zest		1 tsp	2 to 4 lemon wedges		
1 garlic clove					

Butterfly the lobster tails by cutting lengthwise through the centres of the hard top shells and meat using kitchen shears. Ensure you don't cut through the bottoms of the shells. Gently spread the tail halves apart. Position the tails in the air fryer basket away from the Woodfire, with the lobster meat facing up.

In a small saucepan over medium heat, melt the butter. Add lemon zest and garlic, heating until the garlic is fragrant, approximately 30 seconds. Transfer 2 tbsp of the butter mixture to a small bowl and brush it onto the lobster tails. Dispose of any remaining brushed butter to avoid contamination from uncooked lobster. Season the lobster with salt and pepper.

Add pellets of choice to the smoke box, turn the Woodfire dial to AIR FRY, and press the WOODFIRE FLAVOUR button. Set the temperature to 190C and the timer for 10 minutes. Press START/STOP to preheat. Once preheating finishes, place the air fryer basket containing the lobster tails onto the grill grate and close the lid to begin cooking. Check the tails after 6 and 8 minutes to assess doneness. When satisfied, remove them from the Woodfire. Spoon the reserved butter over the lobster, and garnish with parsley, a little pepper, and lemon wedges.

Serves 2 to 4, Preparation time approx 15 mins, Cooking time approx 10 minutes

Breaded Prawns & Dip

Plain flour	60 g	1/2 cup	Garlic powder		1 tbsp
2 large eggs, beaten			Prawns, peeled, deveined	450 g	1 lb
Water, room temperature	30 ml	2 tbsp	Spray oil		
Breadcrumbs	100 g	1 cup	Smoked paprika		1/2 tsp
Ground cumin		1 tbsp			
Dipping sauce					
Freshly squeezed lime juice	30 ml	2 tbsp	Tomato ketchup	125 ml	1/2 cup
Sea salt		1/4 tsp	Fresh coriander, finely chopped		2 tbsp
Ground black pepper		1/4 tsp			

Prepare 3 bowls: one with flour, another with eggs and water, and the last with breadcrumbs, cumin, and garlic powder. Dip the prawns in the flour, the egg, and the breadcrumb mixture, shaking off excess breadcrumbs. Place the air fryer basket in the Woodfire. Set the dial to AIR FRY, temperature to 180C, and timer for 10 minutes. Press START/STOP to preheat.

While the Woodfire preheats, combine tomato ketchup, coriander, lime juice, and salt and pepper in a small bowl. When the ADD FOOD message appears, open the lid, place prawns in a single layer in the air fryer basket, and spray them with cooking oil. Close the lid to cook. After 5 minutes, open the lid, toss the prawns, and close the lid to continue cooking. Once golden brown, remove the prawns and serve with the dipping sauce.

Serves 2, Preparation time approx 15 mins, Cooking time approx 10 minutes

Garlic Prawns

Olive oil		30 ml	2 tbsp	Large raw prawns, peeled, deveined	450 g	1 lb
4 garlic cloves, grated				Freshly squeezed lemon juice	5 ml	1 tsp
Ground black pepper			1/4 tsp			

Combine the oil, garlic and pepper in a large bowl. Add the prawns and ensure they are evenly coated. Refrigerate the bowl of prawns for 1 hour to marinate them, then mix in the lemon juice before cooking.

Set the Woodfire to GRILL and the temp to HI, and set the timer for 10 minutes. Press START/STOP to begin. Place the prawns onto the grill when preheated completes and ADD FOOD is displayed. Close the lid again to start cooking.

Flip the prawns halfway through. Once the cooking is complete, serve the prawns with a sauce of choice for dipping and sprinkle with the chopped coriander.

Serves 2, Preparation time approx 15 mins, Cooking time approx 10 minutes

Grilled Oysters

20 fresh closed or pre-shucked oysters (if closed, shuck them when ready to grill and leave the meat attached to the shell to prevent it from falling out)					
Fresh parsley, chopped		2 tbsp	Unsalted butter, softened	90 g	3 oz
Parmesan cheese, grated	50 g	2 oz	2 garlic cloves, finely grated		
Mature cheddar cheese, grated	60 g	2 oz	Ground black pepper		1/2 tsp
Dried oregano		1/2 tsp			

Turn the Woodfire dial to GRILL, adjust the temperature to HI, set the timer for 10 minutes, and press START/STOP to start preheating. In a frying pan, gently melt the butter and stir in the garlic, pepper, and oregano. When the ADD FOOD message appears, lift the lid and place the oysters on the grill grate. Pour a little of the butter sauce onto each oyster. Close the lid to start cooking.

Combine the cheese and parsley in a bowl. After 3 minutes of cooking the oysters, lift the lid and sprinkle the cheese and parsley mixture onto each oyster. Close the lid and cook for another minute or until the cheese has melted. Remove the oysters and serve with crusty bread or your choice of sides.

Serves 2 to 4, Preparation time approx 10 minutes, Cooking time approx 10 minutes

Grilled Sardines

8 to 12 whole sardines, approximately 15 to 30 cm long, with the innards removed (although sardines typically do not require descaling due to their small scales, any large scales should be removed)				
Olive oil	30 ml	2 tbsp	Ground black pepper	1/4 tsp
3 garlic cloves, finely grated			Coarse sea salt for garnishing	1 tsp
Zest of 1/2 lime or lemon				

In a large dish or tray, combine the olive oil, garlic, zest, and black pepper, and mix well. Add the sardines to the mixture, ensuring they are coated. Cover the dish or tray with cling film and refrigerate for 1 hour.

When you're ready to cook, set the Woodfire dial to GRILL, adjust the temperature to HI, set the timer for 10 minutes, and press START/STOP to begin preheating. Once the ADD FOOD message appears, lift the lid and place each sardine across the grill grate. Close the lid to continue cooking. After 4 minutes, open the lid and gently roll the sardines over. Close the lid and continue cooking. Check on them periodically until they are cooked to your liking. Serve with a sprinkle of sea salt and your favourite sides.

Serves 2 to 4, Preparation time approx 1 hour, Cooking time approx 10 minutes

Grilled Seasoned Cod

Our "Best of British Fish" seasoning (refer to our seasonings or use a one of your choice)			2 tsp
2 to 4 cod fillets, skin on (or other white fish)	Olive oil	30 ml	2 tbsp

Coat all sides of the fish with olive oil and apply the seasoning evenly. Add your preferred pellets to the smoke box. Set the Woodfire to GRILL and press the WOODFIRE FLAVOUR button. Adjust the temperature to HI and the timer to 10 minutes, then press START/STOP to begin preheating.

When the ADD FOOD message displays, open the lid, place the fish on the grill grate skin side down and close the lid. Flip the fish halfway through cooking so the skin side is on the top. Sprinkle more seasoning on the skin and close the lid to continue cooking. When cooking is complete and to your liking, remove the fish and serve with whatever you feel will complement the fish.

Serves 2 to 4, Preparation time approx 15 mins, Cooking time approx 10 minutes

Marinated Smoke Grilled Octopus

1 whole octopus, approx weight	1.5 kg	3 lb 5 oz	Olive oil	125 ml	1/2 cup
2 bay leaves			White wine vinegar	125 ml	1/2 cup
1 onion, peeled, quartered			1 garlic clove, crushed		
1 carrot, chopped			Dried oregano		1 tbsp
1 stick celery, chopped			1/2 lemon		
Ground black peppercorns		1 tbsp	Coarse sea salt		1 tsp

Thoroughly rinse the octopus under cold running water. Remove the beak, ink sac, and eyes if not prepared. Place the octopus in a large pan with bay leaves, onion, carrot, celery, and peppercorns. Add enough cold water to cover the octopus. Cover the pan with a lid and bring it to a boil, then simmer on low heat for 1 hour with the lid on. After 1 hour, test one of the tentacles with a knife to ensure it goes through without much resistance. Remove from heat and allow the octopus to cool completely in the liquid.

After cooling, take out the octopus and slice it into pieces. Whisk together olive oil, salt, vinegar, garlic, and oregano in a large bowl. Add the octopus pieces and let them marinate in the refrigerator for 2 hours.

Add your preferred pellets to the smoke box when ready to grill. Set the Woodfire dial to GRILL, press the WOODFIRE FLAVOUR button, set the temperature to HI, the timer for 10 minutes, and press START/STOP to start preheating. Once the ADD FOOD message appears, lift the lid and place the octopus pieces on the grill grate, then close the lid to begin cooking. After 3 minutes, lift the lid to check on the octopus and flip the pieces over. Check every 2 minutes thereafter until the octopus is cooked to your liking. Remove from the grill and serve.

Serves 2 to 4, Preparation time approx 3 hours, Cooking time approx 10 minutes

Masala Fish

Pollock or cod fillets or another flaky fish, with one side having skin				450 g	1 lb
Sea salt		1 tsp	Chilli powder		1/2 tsp
Lemon juice	15 ml	1 tbsp	Coriander, finely chopped		1/2 tsp
1 garlic clove, finely grated			Amchoor (amchur) powder		1/2 tsp
Ground turmeric		1/2 tsp	Olive oil	15 ml	1 tbsp
Garam masala		1/2 tsp	Butter	30 g	1 oz

Season the fish with salt and refrigerate for 30 minutes to firm slightly. Combine all the other ingredients except the fish and butter in a separate bowl. Remove the fish from the fridge, rinse off the salt, and pat it dry with kitchen paper.

Turn the Woodfire dial to GRILL, set the temperature to HI, the timer for 10 minutes, and press START/STOP to start preheating. While preheating, score the fish's skin and brush the flesh with the mixture, avoiding the skin.

Once the ADD FOOD message appears, open the lid, place the fish on the grill grate with the skin side down, and close the lid to start cooking. After 3 minutes, open the lid and gently flip the fish. Add butter to each fillet, allowing it to melt into the scores as it cooks. Cook for a few more minutes or until cooked to your liking.

Serves 2, Preparation time approx 40 minutes, Cooking time approx 8 minutes

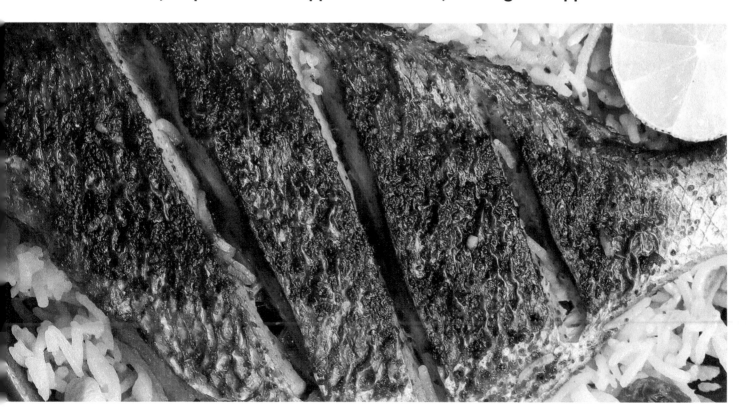

Scallops & Asparagus Spears

Fresh scallops, cleaned and prepared	450 g	1 lb	Sea salt		1/4 tsp
Olive oil	30 ml	2 tbsp	Ground black pepper		1/4 tsp
Asparagus spears (or broccoli stems)	450 g	1 lb	Fresh herbs of choice, chopped, to garnish		

Pat the scallops dry with a tea towel or kitchen roll and place them in a large bowl with the asparagus, olive oil, salt, and pepper. Gently massage the ingredients together to ensure an even coating. Turn the Woodfire dial to GRILL, set the temperature to HI, and set the timer for 15 minutes. Press START/STOP to start preheating.

When the ADD FOOD message appears, open the lid, place the asparagus on the grill in line with the grooves, and close the lid. Cook the asparagus for 6 minutes, turning occasionally. Once cooked, remove and set aside. Next, place the scallops on the grill grate with the lid open. Cook the scallops for 4 to 6 minutes or until cooked to your preference. Serve the scallops on a bed of grilled asparagus spears.

Serves 2 to 4, Preparation time approx 10 mins, Cooking time approx 12 minutes

Smoked Blackened Fish

4 to 6 thick white fish fillets with skin on one side (cod, haddock, snapper, etc.)			
Blackening seasoning or use our recipe below			2 tbsp

Blackening Seasoning

Paprika	2 tsp	Ground black pepper	1/2 tsp
Dried oregano	2 tsp	White pepper	1/2 tsp
Dried thyme	2 tsp	Garlic powder	1/2 tsp
Cayenne pepper	2 tsp	Sea salt	1/2 tsp

Mix the blackening seasoning ingredients in a wide bowl and rub it onto each fillet, covering them all over. Add pellets of your choice to the smoke box, turn the Woodfire dial to GRILL, press WOODFIRE FLAVOUR, set the temperature to HI, and the timer for 10 minutes. Press START/STOP to begin preheating.

Once the ADD FOOD message appears, open the lid and carefully transfer the fish to the grill grate, with the skin side down if there is any. Close the lid to start cooking. Check on the fish after 6 minutes. Aim for an internal temperature between 62 and 68 degrees Celsius. Once the fish is cooked to your liking, remove it from the Woodfire and serve.

Serves 2 to 3, Preparation time approx 15 minutes, Cooking time approx 10 minutes

Smoked Herb Stuffed Rainbow Trout

Coarse sea salt	1 tsp	Olive oil	15 ml	1 tbsp
2 to 4 whole rainbow trout, gutted and descaled				
Seasoning for Stuffing				
2 small sweet onions, thinly sliced		1 tbsp fresh thyme, chopped		1 tbsp
2 garlic cloves, finely grated		Zest and juice of 1 lemon		
Fresh rosemary, chopped	1 tbsp			

In a small bowl, combine the stuffing ingredients and place the mixture into each trout's cavity. Coat both sides of the trout with olive oil and sprinkle with sea salt. Add pellets of choice to the smoke box. Turn the Woodfire dial to GRILL and press the WOODFIRE FLAVOUR button. Adjust the temperature to HI and the timer to 15 minutes, then press START/STOP to start preheating.

Once preheating is complete and the ADD FOOD message appears, open the lid, place the trout on the grill grate, and close the lid. After 5 minutes, gently turn the trout over, close the lid, and continue cooking until they are cooked to your liking or until a thermometer reads an internal temperature between 63 to 68C.

Serves 2 to 4, Preparation time approx 15 minutes, Cooking time approx 15 minutes

Smoked Mussels

Mussels, scrubbed, debearded, and discard any that are open				900 g to 1.8 kg	2 to 4 lb
Ground black pepper		1/2 tsp	A handful of fresh parsley, torn apart		
Sea salt	20 g	2 tbsp	1 lemon, cut into wedges		

To prepare the mussels, cover them in a bowl with cold water and 1 tbsp of salt for 15 minutes, then repeat the process once more. Since they have a short cooking time, use robust and strongly scented pellets in the smoke box. Set the Woodfire to GRILL and press the WOODFIRE FLAVOUR button. Adjust the temperature to HI and set the timer for 10 minutes. Press START/STOP to begin preheating.

Once the ADD FOOD message appears, scatter the mussels across the grill grate or BBQ heat-proof mat and close the lid (discard any already opened mussels). Although the grill setting is 10 minutes, the mussels only take a few minutes to cook. Check them frequently until they open and absorb some of the smoke flavours. Once done, turn off the Woodfire, add a little lemon juice, and place on the remaining wedges and parsley. Serve the mussels on the grill grate or mat, and let everyone help themselves.

Serves 2 to 4, Preparation time approx 30 mins, Cooking time approx 10 minutes

Spicy Salmon Jerky

Fresh salmon fillets, skin and bones removed, approx weight					900 g	2 lb
Spicy Marinade						
Soy sauce	250 ml	1 cup	Hot sauce of choice		10 ml	2 tsp
Molasses or dark treacle	30 ml	2 tbsp	Lemon juice		30 ml	2 tbsp
Sugar		2 tbsp	Ground black pepper			1 tsp
Worcestershire sauce	30 ml	2 tbsp	Red chilli flakes			2 tsp
Sesame seeds		2 tsp				

Cut the salmon fillets into approximately 12 cm slabs. Unlike some meats cut across the grain for tenderness, cut the salmon into strips about 0.5 cm thick (or slightly thicker) and start cutting from the tail end towards the head.

Combine the marinade ingredients in a large bowl, then add the salmon strips and coat them well. Leave the strips in the bowl with the marinade and place them in the fridge for no more than 4 hours. Empty the bowl into a colander, drain off the marinade, and dispose of it.

Place the slices evenly in a single layer in the air fryer basket, on the grill grate, or racks on the grill grate, and close the lid. Add pellets of your choice to the smoke box. Set the dial to DEHYDRATE, press the WOODFIRE FLAVOUR button, set the temperature to 70C, and the timer for 4 hours. Press START/STOP to begin cooking. Check on the jerky after 2 hours and every half-hour thereafter until the jerky is done to your liking.

Serves 4 to 6, Preparation time approx 4 1/2 hours, Cooking time approx 4 hours

Spicy Prawn Skewers

12 to 24 large whole prawns, shells intact to help retain the juices				
Lemon or orange slices, for placing 1 or 2 slices on each skewer after grilling				
4 to 8 long wooden skewers, soaked in water for 30 minutes before grilling				
3 garlic cloves, finely grated		Smoked paprika		1 tbsp
1 red chilli, finely chopped		Olive oil	60 ml	1/4 cup
Fresh parsley, chopped	1 tbsp			

Combine the garlic, chilli, parsley, paprika, and olive oil. Add the fruit slices and prawns, gently stirring to season them well. Cover with cling film and refrigerate for 1 hour. Afterwards, thread the prawns onto the skewers, placing approximately 3 on each skewer, depending on their size.

When you're ready to cook, set the Woodfire dial to GRILL, adjust the temperature to HI, set the timer for 10 minutes, and press START/STOP to start preheating. Once the ADD FOOD message appears, lift the lid and place each prawn-filled skewer on the grill grate. Close the lid to continue cooking. After 3 minutes, open the lid and gently flip the skewers and prawns over. Place all fruit slices on any available space on the grill grate. Close the lid and continue cooking. Check on them periodically until they reach your desired level of doneness without being overcooked. Then, remove from the grill and add fruit slices to each skewer before serving.

Serves 2 to 4, Preparation time approx 1 hour, Cooking time approx 10 minutes

Sweet Salmon Steaks

4 to 6 salmon fillet slices 5 cm / 2 inches wide and a good depth (you can also use salmon steak cross-cuts)

Sea salt	10 g	1 tbsp	Ground ginger		1/4 tsp
Brown sugar	10 g	1 tbsp	Ground cayenne pepper		1/4 tsp
Ground black pepper		2 tsp	Olive oil	30 ml	2 tbsp
Garlic powder		1/2 tsp			

Prepare the dry seasoning by mixing the spices in a small bowl (or see our seasoning recipes for alternatives). Coat all sides of the salmon with olive oil and evenly apply the seasoning. Add pellets of choice to the smoke box. Turn the Woodfire dial to GRILL and press the WOODFIRE FLAVOUR button. Adjust the temperature to HI and the timer to 10 minutes, then press START/STOP to start preheating.

Once preheating is complete and the ADD FOOD message appears, open the lid, place the salmon on the grill grate skin-side up, and close the lid. After 5 or 6 minutes, flip the salmon and continue cooking, or until a thermometer reads an internal temperature between 63 to 65C and the salmon becomes flaky. Serve the cooked salmon to your preference.

Serves 4 to 6, Preparation time approx 15 mins, Cooking time approx 10 minutes

Sausage & Burger Making

Ground and Minced Meat

"Ground meat" and "minced meat" are often used interchangeably. But they indicate two techniques for processing raw meat: ground meat is an emulsion of lean meat and fat, whereas minced meat is often thought of as finely chopped muscle meat. Ground meat is consistent and smooth; minced meat is choppy and textured. Or at least that is how many see it. Most in the UK have just one word for these two processes: minced. In the US, either of these processes is more commonly referred to as ground. As this is a UK edition, we refer to all minced or ground meat items as minced.

Woodfire Cooking and Trimmings

Woodfire cooking can inspire many of us to venture into new culinary territories, experimenting with different meats and recipes. In addition, it may lead us to tackle significant cuts like briskets or pork shoulders that require a bit of trimming. This could involve removing thinner or fattier sections to achieve a more streamlined shape, ensuring the meat receives even smoking and cooking.

This often results in trimmings we're hesitant to discard. We may opt to fry them or incorporate them into a stew. Considering these trimmings cost just as much as leaner parts at the butcher's or supermarket, it's no surprise BBQ restaurants cleverly use nearly every bit of meat, transforming them into delicious sausages and burgers.

Knowing precisely what's in our sausages and burgers is genuinely satisfying. We've all heard unsettling stories about less desirable animal parts in these foods, causing some hesitance. Our recipes will be easy to follow for those equipped with mincing and sausage-stuffing machines. Those without these tools may need more elbow grease, but the result is well worth it, and we'll show you how.

Rusk & Breadcrumbs "fillers"

Rusk, a dried cereal product of wheat flour, salt, and a raising agent, is often used in sausage production. It's offered in several varieties: pinhead, medium, and coarse. While pinhead and medium rusk are generally used for sausages, coarser is preferred for dishes requiring a more rustic texture, such as haggis and some burgers. The critical distinction, beyond granularity, is the absorption rate - finer variants soak up liquid faster. Nutritionally, rusk is limited, but it's excellent at expanding 2 to 3 times its original size when soaking up juices and fats, filling gaps and adding volume.

Breadcrumbs, made by processing leftover dried bread in a blender or grater, have long been used as fillers in sausage and burger making. This practice originated from the necessity of reducing waste and optimising resources, especially during war rationing. Today, breadcrumbs and rusk (or base mixes) are readily available, allowing you to customise your seasonings. In addition, there are alternative fillers for those with specific dietary needs, such as gluten or lactose intolerance. These include polenta, gluten-free bread, rice, couscous, or bulgur wheat.

Sausage Skins

There are several edible casings or skins available for use in sausage making.

Natural Casings: These casings are derived from the intestines of animals, usually pigs, sheep, or cows. Natural casings provide an authentic and traditional texture to sausages. They are available in various diameters, including hog casings (used for traditional bratwurst and Italian sausages), sheep casings (used for smaller sausages like breakfast links), and beef casings (used for larger sausages like polony).

Collagen Casings: Collagen casings are made from the collagen found in the hides of animals, typically cattle. They are manufactured to have consistent sizes and are uniform in appearance. Collagen casings are versatile, easy to use, and provide a good bite to sausages. They are available in various sizes for various types of sausages.

Plant-Based Casings: Plant-based casings are made from cellulose, vegetable protein, or other plant-based polymers. They are designed to mimic the texture and appearance of traditional casings. These casings are typically edible and can be consumed along with the sausage. They are suitable for various types of sausages, including both fresh and cooked varieties.

Vegetarian Collagen Casings: Like traditional collagen casings, vegetarian collagen casings are made from plant-based collagen substitutes. They provide a similar texture and bite as animal-based collagen casings. Vegetarian collagen casings are often used in vegetarian or vegan sausages and offer a convenient and easy-to-use option.

Alginate Casings: Alginate casings are derived from seaweed and provide a natural alternative for vegetarian sausages. They are biodegradable and have a slightly elastic texture. Alginate casings are often used for cooked or smoked sausages and can be consumed with the sausage.

These sausage casings can be found in several popular shops, specialty shops, or online retailers. It's important to carefully read the product labels to ensure they suit your dietary preferences and needs.

Mincing the Meat

BBQ professionals are masters at reducing waste, making good use of nearly every part of the meat. After trimming cuts of meat, it's advisable to keep the trimmings, ideally maintaining a ratio of 70% to 80% lean meat to 20% to 30% fat. Place these trimmings in zip lock or freezer bags and store them in the freezer until you've collected enough to make roughly 20 average-sized sausages or burgers. If you have a large chunk of fat that could be reduced, save it. It can be mixed into excessively lean meat to enhance flavour and juiciness.

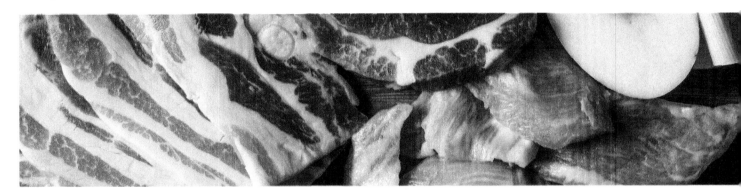

We recommend freezing different types of meat in separate freezer bags, preferably at most 500 g per bag. Ensure each bag is labelled with the contents and date. If the meat has already been frozen once, avoid refreezing it. For partially frozen meat, place the meat in the fridge at a stable and consistent temperature until ready. Alternatively, you can immerse the meat bags from the freezer into iced water and wait until the ice melts and the meat is partially frozen. Partially frozen meat tends to be easier to mince, whether using a blender, knife, meat cleaver or mincing machine.

Using Mechanical Mincers and Sausage Stuffers

You're good to go regarding mincing, but continue reading for more information.

Blenders or Food Processors

Prepare the Meat: Chop the meat into roughly 2.5 cm cubes. Make sure the meat is partially frozen but not rock solid. This makes it easier to mince and helps prevent it from becoming a mushy texture.

Prepare the Blender or Food Processor: Before starting, ensure your blender or food processor is clean and dry.

Add the Meat: Put a handful of meat cubes into your blender or food processor. Avoid filling it - you want the blades to be able to move freely and evenly to mince the meat.

Pulse the Meat: With your blender or food processor, it's best to use a pulsing motion rather than just letting it run. This will give you more control over the texture of the mince. Pulse several times until you achieve your desired consistency.

Empty and Repeat: Once you've achieved the desired mince, empty the contents into a bowl, and repeat the process with the next batch of meat.

Safety First: Always remember never to put your fingers or utensils near the blades while the machine runs.

Clean Up: Once finished, clean your blender or food processor thoroughly to avoid bacterial build-up.

Mincing Using a Knife or Meat Cleaver

Mincing meat at home doesn't necessarily require special kitchen appliances. Even with a knife or a meat cleaver, you can prepare minced meat.

Choose the meat: Select meat suitable for mincing, such as beef, pork, turkey, and lamb. Ensure the meat is partly defrosted so you can cut through it with a heavy knife or meat cleaver.

Set up your work area: Find a sturdy chopping board or surface. Ensure it's clean and sanitised to maintain food safety.

Prepare the meat: Trim away any excess fat, sinew, or gristle from the meat. Then, slice through the meat like you would if serving a Sunday roast. If the meat is too frozen to cut through, allow it to thaw just enough to slice with a little effort.

Chill the meat and equipment: If the meat is already thawed, place the meat in the freezer for 15 to 30 minutes before slicing and mincing. This helps firm up the meat and makes it easier to work with. Chilling your knife or cleaver can also help keep the meat cold during mincing.

Chop the meat: Begin chopping the meat with a knife or cleaver. Apply downward pressure to crush the meat and create a coarse mince. Continue chopping and rocking the knife or cleaver through the meat, repositioning and folding the meat into a tight ball or small area before chopping or rocking again.

Repeat the process: Continue mincing the meat until you achieve the desired texture. You may need to fold the meat and mince it multiple times to achieve a consistent mince. Take breaks as necessary to prevent your hand from tiring and losing focus.

Handle the ground meat: Once it is minced, transfer it to a clean bowl and inspect for unwanted bits, such as gristle or bone fragments. Remove any that you find. If you plan to store the minced meat, refrigerate or freeze it promptly to maintain freshness and food safety. If you plan to use it immediately, add seasoning and other ingredients as required before making sausages or burgers.

Remember that mincing meat by hand using a knife or cleaver requires practice, patience, and caution. Avoid injuring yourself while handling the sharp blade, and always follow proper food handling and safety practices.

Manual Sausage Stuffing

Prepare the sausage casings as instructed on the packaging, which usually involves soaking the casings in water for up to 30 minutes before use. It might also include tying a knot at one end to start the links.

Stuffing sausages by hand can be a fun and fulfilling process, even if you don't have a sausage stuffing machine. All you need are a few basic tools.

Prepare Your Ingredients: Start with your freshly minced meat mixture. The meat should be cold and well-seasoned according to your recipe. You'll also need sausage casings.

Open the Casing: Once your casings are ready, run some warm water inside to ensure they are fully open and easy to work with if the casing instructions permit.

Start Stuffing: Take one end of the casing and push it onto the tube of a wide-mouthed funnel, then push the entire casing onto the tube, leaving about 15 cm hanging off the end. Hold the end of the casing shut and push your sausage mix into the funnel and down into the casing.

Pace Yourself: The key here is patience and consistency. Go slow and steady, filling the casing evenly and firmly but not too tight to prevent the casing from bursting. This process is easier with two people: one to push the meat through and another to control the speed at which the casing fills.

Twist the Sausages: Once the casing is filled, twist the sausage into links. Twist each link in an alternating direction to prevent them from unravelling.

Store Properly: After stuffing and twisting, your sausages should be placed in the fridge to rest. This allows the flavours to meld together.

Cook and Enjoy: You are ready to cook your sausages with your favourite recipe. Remember, making sausages at home can be a labour of love. It's a great activity to share with family or friends and makes for a fantastic culinary experience.

We have provided sausage recipes, including skinless and vegetarian options, throughout this publication, so please be sure to check them out and refer back to this section when needed. The information here will help you achieve the perfect texture for your burgers, as the same technique can be used to prepare and mince the meat before adding seasoning and other ingredients.

Air-Fried Chicken

8 chicken pieces of choice, bone-in			Onion powder		2 tsp
Buttermilk	500 ml	2 cups	Garlic powder		2 tsp
Sea salt		1/4 tsp	Paprika		1 tsp
Ground black pepper		1/4 tsp	Chilli powder		1/2 tsp
Cornflour	240 g	2 cups	Cayenne pepper		1/2 tsp
Plain flour	120 g	1 cup	Dried thyme		1 tsp

Position the air fryer basket on the grill grate and close the lid. Add your choice of pellets to the smoke box. Turn the dial to AIR FRY and press the WOODFIRE FLAVOUR button. Set the temperature to 180C and the timer for 30 minutes, then press START/STOP to begin preheating. You might only need part of the 30 minutes, so check the chicken occasionally as it cooks.

In a bowl, lightly whisk the buttermilk, salt, and pepper to combine. Whisk together all remaining ingredients in a separate bowl, excluding the chicken. Dip the chicken pieces into the buttermilk mixture, then coat them in the seasoned flour mixture, pressing firmly. Spray each coated chicken piece with cooking spray to help hold the flour mixture onto the chicken. Once the ADD FOOD message appears, open the lid, place the chicken pieces in the air fryer basket, and close the lid to continue. Once cooked, serve the air-fried chicken.

"Batter Splatter"

Our air fryer recipe book, "**Air Fryer UK Recipes - Ultimate UK Cookbook**", is compatible with the Woodfire and offers tips on preventing batter detachment during air frying. In that book, we coined this "Batter Splatter." In brief, ensure your batter or wet coatings are as thick as possible. If you find the batter too thin for this recipe, add more flour to thicken it, but not too thick so that you can't coat the chicken easily with it. You could cover the air fryer basket with foil for a few minutes to allow the batter to firm up before removing the foil and continuing the cooking process.

Serves 2 to 4, Preparation time approx 10 mins, Cooking time approx 30 minutes

Air-Fried Smoked Wings

20 chicken wing sections (aka: drumettes and wingettes)	
Seasoning of choice (or refer to our sseasoning recipes)	1 tbsp

Place the air fryer basket in the Woodfire. Add your preferred pellets to the smoke box and select AIR FRY, followed by WOODFIRE FLAVOUR. Set the temperature to 200C and the timer to 25 minutes. Next, press START/STOP to initiate preheating. Place the wings in a large bowl, add the seasoning, and mix well.

When the ADD FOOD message appears, open the lid and place the wings in the air fryer basket. Close the lid to start cooking. Flip the wings halfway through and close the lid again to continue cooking. Once the cooking is complete, remove and serve them a dip or sauce.

Serves 2 to 4, Preparation time approx 5 mins, Cooking time approx 25 minutes

Bacon-Wrapped Chicken Breasts

4 to 6 chicken breasts, skinless, boneless		Sea salt	1/4 tsp
Garlic powder	2 tsp	Ground black pepper	1/4 tsp
Brown sugar	2 tsp	8 to 12 rashers of bacon, medium thickness	
Paprika	1/4 tsp		

12 to 18 toothpicks, soaked in water for 15 minutes before use

Combine garlic, sugar, paprika, salt, and pepper in a large bowl. Add the chicken breasts to the bowl and coat each with the mixture. Wrap two slices of bacon around each breast, starting from one end and winding to the other, aiming to cover most, if not all, of the breasts. Use toothpicks to secure the bacon as needed. Sprinkle any remaining seasoning mix onto the bacon surrounding the breasts. The bacon will help keep the breasts moist.

Set the Woodfire dial to GRILL, adjust the temperature to HI, set the timer for 20 minutes, and press the START/STOP button to initiate preheating. When the ADD FOOD message appears, gently lift the lid, place the breasts on the grill grate, and close the lid to begin cooking.

After 10 minutes, check the breasts and carefully flip them over. Continue cooking until they are done to your liking and the internal temperature reads 74 to 80C, ensuring the breasts are cooked. Once cooked, remove the toothpicks and serve.

Serves 4 to 6, Preparation time approx 30 minutes, Cooking time approx 20 minutes

Baked Turkey Meatballs

Lean turkey mince	900 g	2 lb	Dried basil	1/2 tsp
Panko or coarse breadcrumbs	100 g	1 cup	Dried oregano	1/2 tsp
1 onion, peeled, finely chopped			Sea salt	1/2 tsp
Fresh parsley, finely chopped	30 g	1 oz	Ground black pepper	1/2 tsp
2 large eggs			Oil spray	
3 garlic cloves, finely grated			Garnish of choice	
Worcestershire sauce	15 ml	1 tbsp		

Combine all the ingredients except the oil and garnish in a large bowl. Mix thoroughly using your hands, preferably while wearing thin kitchen gloves. Shape the mixture into 4 cm-sized balls.

Set the Woodfire dial to BAKE, adjust the temperature to 190C, set the timer for 40 minutes, and press START/STOP to initiate preheating. When the ADD FOOD message appears, lift the lid and lightly spray the grill grate with oil (not to prevent sticking, but to provide a light, even layer of oil on the balls). Place the balls on the grill grate and lightly spray them with oil. Close the lid to begin cooking.

After approximately 10 minutes, lift the lid, flip the balls, and close the lid to continue cooking. Continue cooking until they are cooked to your liking, and the internal temperature reaches 74C or higher. Serve the balls with your choice of garnish.

Serves 2 to 4, Preparation time approx 30 minutes, Cooking time approx 40 minutes

BBQ Smoked Tandoori Chicken

One medium-sized whole chicken cut down to drumsticks, thighs, wings, and each breast into 3 pieces, skin off or on if you like it with skin.

Chaat masala		1/4 tsp			
Tandoori marinade					
Freshly squeezed lemon juice	30 ml	2 tbsp	Fresh ginger, grated	30 g	1 oz
Kashmiri chilli powder	10 g	2 tbsp	Garam masala		1 tsp
Sea salt		1 tsp	Ground turmeric		1 tsp
Plain yoghurt	80 ml	1/3 cup	Ground cumin		1 tsp
4 garlic cloves, grated					

Marinade:

Combine all marinade ingredients in a large bowl and mix thoroughly. Add the chicken pieces and firmly massage the marinade into them. Cover the bowl with cling film and refrigerate for at least 4 hours, ideally overnight.

Cooking:

When ready to cook, set the Woodfire to GRILL and press the WOODFIRE FLAVOUR button with the temperature on HI and the timer for 30 minutes. Press START/STOP to begin. Once preheated, place drumsticks and thighs on the grill grate and close the lid. After ten minutes, add wings and breast pieces. Cook the chicken until its internal temperature reaches 75 to 80C on a thermometer, removing it before the full 30 minutes if necessary. No red colouring is included, so it is a more subtle colour. Add a light sprinkle of chaat masala before serving.

Serves 4 to 6, Preparation time approx 4.5 hours, Cooking time approx 20 minutes

Buffalo Drumsticks

10 chicken drumsticks (or 20 to 30 wing joints)			Sea salt		1 tsp
Onion powder		2 tsp	Olive oil	30 ml	2 tbsp
Easy buffalo sauce					
Unsalted butter, melted	90 g	3 oz	Hot sauce of choice	15 ml	1 tbsp
Blue cheese dipping sauce					
Crumbled blue cheese	60 g	2 oz	Mayonnaise	45 ml	3 tbsp
Onion powder		1 tsp	Freshly squeezed lime juice	15 ml	1 tbsp
Fresh parsly, finely chopped		2 tbsp	Onion powder		1 tsp
Soured cream	45 ml	3 tbsp			

Blue cheese sauce: Blend the blue cheese sauce ingredients in a bowl and refridgerate until ready to serve the chicken.

Easy buffalo sauce: Combine the melted butter and hot sauce.

Toss the drumsticks or chicken wings in a large bowl with 2 tsp garlic powder, 1 tsp sea salt, and 2 tbsp olive oil. Mix well to coat the chicken.

Set the Woodfire to AIR FRY at 200C and the timer to 25 minutes, and press START/STOP for preheating. When prompted to ADD FOOD, place the chicken in the preheated air fryer basket inside the Woodfire, ensuring it's not overcrowded. Close the lid to cook, flipping the chicken halfway through and coating it with buffalo sauce. Check that the internal temperature of the chicken exceeds 75C with a thermometer. Once done to your liking, serve the chicken with blue cheese dip and any remaining buffalo sauce.

Serves 2 to 5, Preparation time approx 30 mins, Cooking time approx 25 minutes

Garlic Lemon Brined Chicken Portions

10 to 15 chicken portions (not quarters or halves) skin on, bones in

Garlic Lemon Brine (page 47) or brine of your choice

You can follow the brining recipe (refer to page 47) or create a brine. Once the chicken has finished brining, according to the brine recipe instructions, place the air fryer basket on the grill grate and close the lid. Set the Woodfire dial to AIR FRY, adjust the temperature to HI, set the timer for 30 minutes, and press START/STOP to start preheating.

When the ADD FOOD message appears, lift the lid, place the chicken in the air fryer basket and close the lid to begin cooking. Check on the chicken after 10 minutes and give them a flip. Check on them and flip them again after 10 minutes more. Check on the chicken every few minutes after that until the portions reach an internal temperature of 74 to 80C. Remove the chicken when cooked to your liking.

Serves 4 to 6, Preparation time approx 4 to 6 hours, Cooking time approx 30 minutes

Grilled Chicken Breasts

Seasoning of choice (refer to our seasoning recipes)				10 g	2 tbsp
Olive oil	30 ml	2 tbsp	4 to 6 boneless, skinless chicken breasts		

Turn the Woodfire dial to GRILL, set the temperature to HI, and the timer for 15 minutes —press START/STOP to start the preheating.

While the Woodfire preheats, season the chicken on all sides with oil, then your seasoning of choice. When the ADD FOOD message appears, open the lid, place the chicken on the grill grate, and close the lid to begin cooking. After 5 minutes, open the lid, flip the breasts, and close the lid again to continue cooking. Once the chicken is cooked to your liking, remove it and serve.

If the breasts are particularly large or small, use the timer arrows to add or subtract minutes as needed, or stop cooking once the chicken is cooked to your liking with internal temperatures of 74C or higher.

Serves 4 to 6, Preparation time approx 10 mins, Cooking time approx 15 minutes

Mediterranean Crispy Chicken

20 chicken wings or 10 drumsticks, (wingettes or drumettes) or a mix of both

2 tbsp of Mediterranean seasoning (page 10)   Olive oil to drizzle

Sesame seeds   1 tbsp

Towel dry the chicken portions and leave uncovered in the fridge for about 2 hours to dry out further. When ready to cook, place the chicken in a large bowl, drizzle a little olive oil over it, and spoon enough Mediterranean seasoning to lightly coat the chicken portions when mixed thoroughly.

Add your preferred pellets to the smoke box, place the air fryer basket on the grill grate, and close the lid. Select AIR FRY, press the WOODFIRE FLAVOUR button, set the temperature to 200C and the timer to 25 minutes, and press START/STOP to initiate preheating.

When the ADD FOOD message appears, open the lid, place the wings in the air fryer basket, and sprinkle the chicken with sesame seeds. Close the lid to start cooking. Flip the wings halfway through and close the lid again to continue cooking. Check on the chicken regularly, and once the cooking is complete to your liking and the internal temperature of the chicken is at least 74C, remove them and serve.

Serves 2 to 4, Preparation time approx 2 1/2 hours, Cooking time approx 25 minutes

Peri-Peri Chicken Salad

4 to 6 chicken breasts and salad items of choice			Peri-Peri sauce	80 ml	1/3 cup
Peri-Peri sauce					
2 large fresh fire-roasted peppers/bell peppers			6 red chilies, finely chopped and seeds removed		
Olive oil	30 ml	2 tbsp	Zest of 1 lemon		
4 garlic cloves, crushed			Brown sugar	10 g	1 tbsp
1 medium diced red onion			Dried oregano		1 tbsp
Sweet paprika	10 g	2 tbsp	Sea salt		1 tsp
Red wine vinegar	250 ml	1 cup	Ground black pepper		1 tsp
Freshly squeezed lemon juice	45 ml	3 tbsp			

First, assemble your chosen ingredients in a large bowl for the salad, cover it with cling film, and refrigerate until needed.

Peri-Peri sauce, if using the above recipe:

Heat the oil and sauté onions, garlic, and paprika in a saucepan until soft. Blend all sauce ingredients, including from the saucepan, until almost smooth.

Chicken:

Add your choice of pellets to the smoke box. Set the Woodfire to GRILL and press WOODFIRE FLAVOUR with the temperature on HI and the timer for 20 minutes. Press START/STOP to preheat. During preheating, coat the chicken in 100 ml peri-peri sauce in a large bowl. Once preheating is done and the ADD FOOD message appears, gently press the chicken on the grill grate. Close the lid to cook. Flip the chicken after 5 minutes, baste with extra sauce, and continue cooking. The chicken is done when its internal temperature is 75 to 80C on a thermometer. Let the chicken rest for 5 minutes before slicing and serving atop the prepared salads.

Serves 4 to 6, Preparation time approx 15 mins, Cooking time approx 20 minutes

Roasted Whole Duck

1 medium-sized fresh duck	Coarse sea salt	1 tbsp

Position the duck on a chopping board and place another board on top. Apply pressure to gently flatten the duck a little if it is too pronounced, reducing its height slightly, as the overhead element of the Woodfire is quite low for a plump duck. If the legs are tied, and the wings are tucked, untie the legs and untuck the wings. Using a sharp knife, score the breast area just below the skin, and do the same on the underside of the duck.

Facing the rear of the duck, lift each leg and make a 2.5 cm deep incision through the skin between the legs and thighs. This ensures even cooking of the breast, legs, and thighs. Rub the salt all over the duck.

Set the Woodfire dial to ROAST, adjust the temperature to 180C, set the timer for 2 hours, and press START/STOP to initiate preheating. Ensure you have a new fat tray underneath the Woodfire, as the duck will release a significant amount of fat and juices. If you have a clean tray, you can use the contents to roast potatoes. It's important to note that cooked duck has a pink or brown hue compared to chicken.

When the ADD FOOD message appears, open the lid and place the duck on the grill grate, breast side down. Close the lid to begin cooking. After approximately 45 minutes, open the lid, carefully turn the duck over, and close the lid to continue cooking. Cook until the skin is crispy and the internal temperature of the duck reaches 74 to 80C. Remove the duck from the Woodfire and let it rest for 15 minutes.

Serves 4, Preparation time approx 30 mins, Cooking time approx 2 hours

Salt & Pepper Chicken Wings

20 chicken wing sections (aka drumettes and wingettes)				
salt and pepper seasoning mix	2 tbsp			
Salt and Pepper Seasoning Recipe				
Sea salt	1 tsp	Garlic powder	1/2 tsp
Ground black pepper	1 tsp	Ground ginger	1/2 tsp
Chilli flakes	1 tsp	Sugar	1 tsp
Chinese five spice	1/2 tsp		

Place the air fryer basket on the grill grate, turn the Woodfire dial to AIR FRY, set the temperature to HI, and the timer for 25 minutes, then press START/STOP to start preheating. Combine the salt and pepper seasoning ingredients in a large bowl, mix well and add the wings, pressing the seasoning onto the wings.

When the ADD FOOD message appears, open the lid and place the wings in the air fryer basket, which has been heating up during preheating. Close the lid to start cooking. Flip the wings halfway through and close the lid again to continue cooking. Once the wings are cooked to your liking, remove them and serve with a dip or sauce.

Serves 2 to 4, Preparation time approx 10 mins, Cooking time approx 25 minutes

Santa Maria-Style Chicken Leg Quarters

1 tbsp Santa Maria-style seasoning (see page 9), or your seasoning of choice

| 4 to 6 chicken leg quarters | Olive oil | 15 ml | 1 tbsp |

Toss the chicken leg quarters in a large bowl with the Santa Maria seasoning and olive oil. Mix well to coat the chicken. Leave uncovered in the fridge for 30 minutes to 1 hour before cooking.

Place the air fryer basket into the Woodfire, turn the dial to AIR FRY, set the temperature to 200C, and the timer for 30 minutes, and press START/STOP to start preheating. When prompted to ADD FOOD, place the chicken in the preheated air fryer basket inside the Woodfire, but ensure it's not overcrowded. Close the lid to cook, flipping the chicken halfway through.

Cook until the chicken is cooked to your liking and the internal temperature of the chicken exceeds 74C with a thermometer. Once cooked, remove and serve.

Serves 2 to 3, Preparation time approx 1 hour, Cooking time approx 30 minutes

6 to 10 wooden skewers soaked in water for 15 minutes			8 boneless, skinless thighs cut to 2.5 cm / 1-inch pieces		
Canned/tinned coconut milk	60 ml	1/2 cup	Brown sugar	30 g	3 tbsp
Reduced-sodium soy sauce	60 ml	1/4 cup	Fish sauce	5 ml	1 tsp
2 garlic cloves, grated			Freshly squeezed lime juice	5 ml	1 tsp
Peanut dipping sauce					
Peanut butter	125 g	1/2 cup	Sesame oil	5 ml	1 tsp
Rice wine vinegar	30 ml	2 tbsp	Fresh ginger, grated		2 tsp
Reduced-sodium soy sauce	30 ml	2 tbsp	2 garlic cloves, grated		
Honey	45 ml	3 tbsp	Water	30 ml	2 tbsp

Whisk together coconut milk, soy sauce, garlic, sugar, fish sauce, and lime juice in a bowl. Place the marinade and chicken in a large resealable plastic bag. Massage the bag to ensure the marinade coats the chicken evenly, then refrigerate for 3 to 8 hours. After marinating, remove the chicken and thread it onto skewers.

Load your choice of pellets into the smoke box, turn the dial to GRILL, set the temperature to MED, and the timer for 20 minutes. Press the WOODFIRE FLAVOUR button and START/STOP to begin preheating. Once the ADD FOOD message appears, open the lid, place the skewered chicken on the grill grate, and close the lid to start cooking. Flip the chicken every 5 minutes until cooked to your preference.

Peanut dipping sauce:

Meanwhile, whisk together all peanut dipping sauce ingredients, excluding water. Gradually add water to achieve the desired consistency. Once the chicken is cooked, serve it with the dipping sauce.

Serves 4 to 6, Preparation time approx 3 hours, Cooking time approx 20 minutes

Smoked Crispy Chicken Sandwich

Sea salt		1/2 tsp	Paprika	1 tsp
Ground black pepper		1/2 tsp	Chilli powder	1/2 tsp
Buttermilk	500 ml	2 cups	Cayenne pepper	1/2 tsp
Cornflour	60 g	1/2 cup	Dried thyme	1 tsp
Panko or coarse breadcrumbs	100 g	1 cup	4 burger buns	
450 g / 1 lb chicken breast strips, 1.5 cm / 1/2 inch thick			1/2 iceberg lettuce, shredded	
Onion powder		2 tsp	Sauce and relish of choice	
Garlic powder		2 tsp		

Place the air fryer basket on the grill grate and close the lid. Add your chosen pellets to the smoke box, turn the dial to AIR FRY, and press WOODFIRE FLAVOUR. Set the temperature to 180C and the timer for 20 minutes. Press START/STOP to preheat.

Whisk together buttermilk, onion powder, garlic powder, paprika, chilli powder, cayenne pepper, and dried thyme in a medium bowl. In another bowl, mix cornflour, breadcrumbs, salt, and pepper. Dip chicken strips into the buttermilk mixture, then coat with seasoned breadcrumbs, pressing to ensure they stick. Spray each breaded strip with cooking spray.

When the ADD FOOD message appears, open the lid, place the strips in the air fryer basket, and close the lid to cook. After 5 minutes, flip the strips and continue cooking. Check on the strips every 5 minutes until cooked to your liking. At any point, slice the buns in half, open the lid and put the cut side down on the grill grate for 15 to 30 seconds after closing the lid to toast but not burn the buns. Then, remove them and close the lid to continue.

Once cooked, remove the strips from the basket and set aside. Assemble your buns with lettuce and your choice of sauce or relish (see our sauce recipes).

Serves 4, Preparation time approx 15 mins, Cooking time approx 20 minutes

Smoked Sausage & Chicken Kebabs

2 large chicken breasts, skinless, cut into 2.5 / 1 inch squares (or as near to squares as you can, as we appreciate that chicken breasts are not cubes)				
1 large Italian sausage or firm sausage of choice, cut into 2.5 cm / 1 inch thick slices				
Olive oil	30 ml	2 tbsp	Sea salt	1/2 tsp
2 garlic cloves, grated			Ground black pepper	1/2 tsp
Juice of 1 lemon			Freshly chopped parsley to garnish (optional)	

Mix chicken, oil, garlic, lemon juice, salt, and pepper in a bowl until evenly combined. Thread chicken and sausage alternately onto each skewer. Add your chosen pellets to the smoke box and set the dial to GRILL. Press WOODFIRE FLAVOUR, select HI temperature and set the timer for 10 minutes. Press START/STOP to start preheating.

Once the ADD FOOD message appears, open the lid and place the kebabs horizontally across the grill grate lines, ensuring the skewers don't sit in the grooves. Close the lid to begin cooking. Flip the kebabs halfway through and close the lid to continue cooking. After 8 minutes, check if the meats are cooked, extending the cooking time if needed. When cooked, remove the kebabs and serve. Optionally, garnish with chopped parsley.

Serves 2, Preparation time approx 10 mins, Cooking time approx 10 minutes

Smoked Spatchcock Chicken

Seasoning or rub of choice (or refer to our seasoning and rub recipes)	20 g	1/4 cup
Whole chicken	1.8 to 2.7 kg	4 to 6 lb

Turn the chicken over so that it's back-side up. Cut through each side of the backbone and remove it. Gently open the chicken from the cut and lay it flat on a board, back-side down, then press the breast until it flattens out. Season the chicken with the dry mixture into all the nooks and crannies.

Add pellets of choice to the smoke box. Turn the dial to ROAST, press the WOODFIRE FLAVOUR button, and set the temp to 180C and the timer for 40 mins. Press START/STOP to preheat.

Once the ADD FOOD message appears, place the chicken on the grill grate and close the lid to start cooking. With 10 minutes remaining, check whether the chicken is cooked with an internal temp of 75 to 80C. Remove the chicken from the Woodfire, wrap it in foil, and let it rest for 15 minutes.

Serves 4 to 6, Preparation time approx 20 mins, Cooking time approx 40 minutes

Spicy Breaded Chicken Cutlets

2 large chicken breasts, boneless and skinless, sliced into 1.25 cm thick cutlets					
Olive oil	15 ml	1 tbsp	Garlic powder		1/4 tsp
Dried breadcrumbs	50 g	1/2 cup	Onion powder		1/4 tsp
Paprika		1/2 tsp	Cayenne pepper		1/4 tsp
Dried chilli powder		1/2 tsp	Sea salt		1/4 tsp
Ground black pepper		1/4 tsp			

Place the chicken breasts in a bowl and drizzle them with oil, ensuring they are evenly coated. In a shallow dish, combine the dried bread crumbs with the spices. Coat each chicken breast with the breadcrumb mixture.

Place the air fryer basket on the grill grate, close the lid, and set the dial to AIR FRY. Adjust the temperature to 200C, set the timer for 15 minutes, and press the START/STOP button to start preheating.

Once the ADD FOOD message appears, open the lid and arrange the chicken cutlets in a single layer in the air fryer basket. Close the lid to resume cooking. Check the cutlets after 8 minutes and periodically until they turn golden brown and are cooked.

Turkey Legs

Seasoning of choice (or refer to our seasoning recipes)	10 to 20 g	2 to 4 tbsp
2 to 4 turkey legs		

Coat the legs evenly with the seasoning of choice or just salt and pepper.

Place the turkey legs on the grill grate. Add your choice of pellets to the smoke box and close the Woodfire lid. Turn the dial to SMOKER, set the temperature to 120C and the timer for 3 hours—press START/STOP to start cooking.

Check the legs after 1 hour and flip them over. If some areas appear dry, lightly spray them with water. Keep checking, and when cooked to your liking, the internal temp reaches 75 to 80C, and the probe should go in with minimal resistance. Keep cooking if you need to. Once satisfied with the tenderness, remove and serve them warm or wrap them in foil and leave them to rest for an hour.

Serves 2 to 4, Preparation time approx 15 mins, Cooking time approx 4 hours

Intro to Seasonings, Rubs, Sauces & Marinades

Barbecue (BBQ) is a fundamental element of Woodfire cooking. Here we focus on seasonings, rubs, sauces, and marinades. These terms denote distinct techniques for enhancing flavours in various dishes, each serving a particular purpose and unique characteristics. Teaspoons (tsp) or tablespoons (tbsp) are level spoons, not heaped.

Seasonings

Seasoning refers to adding herbs, spices, salt, or other flavour-enhancing ingredients to a dish during or after cooking. The primary goal is to complement and accentuate the ingredients' natural flavours without overpowering them. Seasonings can range from simple salt and pepper to more complex blends of herbs and spices.

Rubs

A rub is a dry mixture of spices, herbs, and sometimes sugar or salt applied to the meat surface before cooking. Rubs are popular in grilling and barbecuing, forming a flavourful and often crispy crust. They can be mild, spicy, sweet, or savoury and are also used in slow-cooking methods like smoking to develop rich, complex flavours over time.

Sauces

Sauce is a liquid or semi-liquid mixture that adds flavour, moisture, and visual appeal to a dish. Sauces can be served on the side, drizzled over the dish, or used as a base on which the main ingredient is cooked. Made from various ingredients, including vegetables, fruits, dairy products, and stock, sauces can be savoury, sweet, spicy, or tangy. They often serve to balance and harmonise the flavours of a dish. Examples include gravy, béarnaise, tomato sauce, and hollandaise.

Marinades

A marinade is a seasoned liquid mixture used to marinate or soak food, typically meat, poultry, or fish, for a period of time before cooking. Marinades can be made with a variety of ingredients, such as oil, vinegar, citrus juice, herbs, spices, and aromatics. The purpose of a marinade is to add flavor, tenderize the meat, and in some cases, help preserve it. The length of time that food should be marinated varies depending on the type of food and the recipe, but it generally ranges from a few hours to overnight.

Popular Rub Recipes

"The Woodfire Way - For Beginners" introduces dozens of seasonings, rubs, sauces, and marinade recipes. "The Woodfire Way 2 NEXT LEVEL" showcases some of the most popular and renowned favourites.

Like most rubs, it's advisable to let the meat rest for at least 30 minutes after application. A minimum of a few hours is recommended for wet rubs and marinades. Moreover, many marinades and brines yield optimal results with overnight rests in the fridge or cool area.

The amount of rub or seasoning required largely depends on the cut size and your taste. Some recommend approximately 1 tbsp per half kilogram of meat, while others advocate for 1/2 to 1 tbsp per 15 x 15 cm surface area. Alternatively, some add what they think is best or what they have available. While going overboard is hard, it's always wise to exercise restraint. When more seasoning is required, often the salt is reduced.

Each pitmaster has their unique perspective on how rubs and preparation should be executed, just as professionals in other fields have their methods. Stories of secret recipes being passed down from generation to generation abound. However, a "secret recipe" alone will not yield the perfect BBQ; that achievement is anchored in mastering the right technique. While rubs, seasonings, and marinades are often deemed as essential as gravy on roast beef, the quality of the meat is paramount. If the meat doesn't hit the mark, even the best rub or seasoning won't redeem it. That's why we emphasise all facets of Woodfire cooking and preparation.

The ingredients that form the basis of beef brisket rubs are identical to those you'd sprinkle on a plump, juicy steak—garlic powder, onion powder, top-notch salt, and coarse black pepper. The cornerstone of any superior rub invariably rests on salt and pepper. Following this, extra ingredients are added to amplify flavours that accentuate the meat for which the rub is designed. The choice of salt boils down to personal preference. Kosher, sea, and seasoning salts are suitable and can often be used interchangeably. However, when a recipe calls for substantial amounts of salt, it's better to rely on kosher or sea salt, rather than seasoning salts.

Numerous pitmasters and people who barbecue at home often apply yellow or Dijon mustard or other adhesive substances to the meat before adding the seasoning to ensure it adheres well. However, many choose to forgo any liquid application, no matter how sticky, as it introduces additional moisture. If you consistently encounter issues with your rub or seasoning not adhering sufficiently, consider adding a very thin layer of Dijon mustard, then pat dry any excessively wet areas before applying your rubs or seasonings. Seasonings and rubs can last in sealed jars or containers for many weeks.

Argentine Chimichurri Rub

Argentine Chimichurri rub is a dry version of the famous Argentinean sauce, Chimichurri, typically used as a marinade or a garnish for barbecued meats. The rub incorporates the key flavours of the sauce, delivering a vibrant and tangy flavour profile. This rub is most commonly used on beef, particularly steak, in line with Argentina's renowned beef barbecue tradition. However, its bright and savoury flavours can enhance other foods.

Ingredients:

- 2 tbsp dried oregano
- 2 tbsp dried basil
- 1 tbsp dried parsley
- 1 tbsp dried thyme
- 1 tbsp garlic powder
- 1 tbsp onion powder
- 1 tbsp ground black pepper

- 1 tbsp paprika
- 1 tbsp red pepper flakes

Asian Five-Spice

Asian Five-Spice rubs are a distinctive blend of five essential spices traditionally used at the heart of Chinese and other Asian cuisines. This rub offers a balance of flavours that is simultaneously sweet, savoury, bitter, and spicy, which enhances a wide variety of dishes. It's traditionally used with fatty meats like pork or duck but can also be used to season chicken, beef, or seafood. It can penetrate into the meat, infusing it with flavour.

Ingredients:

- 2 tbsp five-spice powder
- 2 tbsp garlic powder
- 2 tbsp onion powder
- 1 tbsp ginger powder
- 1 tbsp brown sugar
- 1/2 tbsp sea salt
- 1 tbsp ground black pepper

Cajun Blackening Spice

Cajun blackening spice, or blackened seasoning, is a flavourful blend of spices that originated in Louisiana, particularly Cajun cuisine. It's typically used in the blackening process of cooking, where meat or fish is coated in melted butter, dredged in the spice mixture, and seared in a hot frying pan. This process results in a characteristic black, crusty layer on the outside of the food. Hence the term "blackened." Blackened dishes are not burnt but intensely flavoured and deliciously spicy despite the dark colour. The blackening technique and its associated spice blend are commonly used on fish (like catfish or redfish), chicken, steak, and even vegetables. Here is a delicious recipe.

Ingredients:

- 2 tbsp paprika
- 1 tbsp cayenne pepper
- 1 tbsp onion powder
- 1 tbsp garlic powder
- 1 tbsp dried thyme
- 1 tbsp dried oregano

- 1 tbsp ground black pepper
- 1 tbsp sea salt

Classic Carolina

Carolina, particularly North Carolina, is famous for its unique barbecue and ruby style due to its rich history and tradition in slow-cooked, smoked meats. In Carolina barbecue, the emphasis is often on pork, and it's typically prepared in one of two ways: "Eastern Style," where the whole hog is smoked and chopped, and "Western Style" (or "Lexington Style"), where only the pork shoulder is used. These regional variations in rubs and sauces and a deep-rooted tradition of slow-smoking pork have made Carolina famous in the barbecue world. Here's a simple Carolina rub.

Ingredients:

- 1 tbsp paprika
- 1 tbsp sea salt
- 1 tbsp white sugar
- 1 tbsp brown sugar
- 1 tbsp ground cumin
- 1 tsp chilli powder

- 1/2 tsp oregano
- 1/2 tsp celery seeds
- 1/2 tsp mustard powder

Kansas City

Kansas City BBQ rubs are known for their unique balance of sweet and spicy flavours, typically featuring a blend of brown sugar for sweetness, chilli powder for heat, and various other spices like paprika, garlic powder, onion powder, and black pepper for a rich, complex flavour profile. The combination of sweet and spicy helps create a caramelised crust on the meat when it's cooked, adding a layer of texture and flavour characteristic of Kansas City BBQ. Try this:

Ingredients:

- 3 tbsp brown sugar
- 1 tbsp paprika
- 1 tbsp ground black pepper
- 1 tbsp sea salt
- 1 tbsp chilli powder
- 1 tbsp garlic powder

- 1 tbsp onion powder
- 1 tsp cayenne pepper

Memphis-Style

The Memphis rub is a versatile seasoning, most commonly enhancing foods during smoking. Thanks to the city's profound barbecue legacy and unique regional cooking style, Memphis, Tennessee, is synonymous with dry barbecue rubs. The blend of historical influences, the significant contributions of African-American pitmasters, the emphasis on richly flavoured seasonings, the use of slow smoking techniques, and the preference for dry ribs have all solidified Memphis's reputation. There are hundreds of Memphis rubs, but here's a good start.

Ingredients:

- 3 tbsp smoked paprika
- 3 tbsp sea salt
- 1 tbsp ground black pepper
- 2 tbsp brown sugar
- 2 tsp garlic powder
- 2 tsp onion powder

- 1 tsp oregano
- 1 tsp celery seeds
- 1 tsp mustard powder

Mediterranean Herbs

The flavours of fish can often be delicate and lack the robust juices characteristic of red meats. As a result, it's crucial to ensure that rubs or seasonings do not overwhelm the taste of the fish.

To use it as a rub, apply it before cooking, gently massaging it into the fish, paying attention to any crevices or cuts. Conversely, to use it as a seasoning, lightly sprinkle it over the fish during the cooking process without rubbing it in, or add a dash during serving. The method you choose depends on the level of flavour intensity you wish. Here is a great all-rounder.

Ingredients:

- 1 tsp dried rosemary
- 1 tsp ground black pepper
- 1 tsp dried basil
- 1 tsp dried tarragon
- 1 tsp garlic powder
- 1 tsp dried grated lemon peel

Here is another great all-rounder for those wanting a little more spice.

Ingredients:

- 1 tsp celery salt (or 1/2 tsp sea salt]
- 1/2 tsp ground black pepper
- 2 tsp smoked paprika
- 1/2 tsp mustard powder
- 1/2 tsp ground mace
- 1/2 tsp allspice
- 1/4 tsp ground cloves
- 1/4 tsp ginger powder
- 1/4 tsp cayenne pepper (or chilli powder)
- 1/4 tsp ground cardamom

Middle-Eastern Lamb

This exquisite wet rub, featuring an impeccable blend of aromatic and flavourful ingredients, is ideal for any cut of lamb. Though originally formulated for larger cuts like the shoulder or whole leg, it is versatile and adaptable. We also recommend trying it on larger cuts of mutton. Adding olive oil, lemon juice, and apple cider vinegar to many of these rub recipes allows you to create ample liquid to cover the food, transforming them into delectable marinades. Give it a try and savour the enriched flavours.

Ingredients:

- 1 small onion, finely chopped
- 4 garlic cloves, finely grated
- 30 ml (2 tbsp) freshly squeezed lemon juice
- 15 ml (1 tbsp) apple cider vinegar
- 15 ml (1 tbsp) olive oil
- 1 tbsp sea salt
- 1 tsp ground cumin
- 1/2 tsp ground black pepper
- 1/2 tsp cayenne pepper
- 1/2 tsp ground cinnamon
- 1/2 tsp ground nutmeg
- 1/2 tsp ground cloves

Santa Maria-Style

Santa Maria-style BBQ rub is a simple and traditional seasoning blend from the Santa Maria Valley in California. This rub is primarily known for its use in Santa Maria-style barbecue, which traditionally involves grilling tri-tip steak over an open fire made from red oak wood. The simplicity of this rub allows the meat's natural flavours to shine through while adding just the right touch of seasoning.

Ingredients:

- 2 tbsp garlic powder
- 2 tbsp dried rosemary
- 2 tbsp coarse sea salt
- 1 tbsp ground black pepper
- 1 tbsp dried sage
- 1 tbsp dried oregano

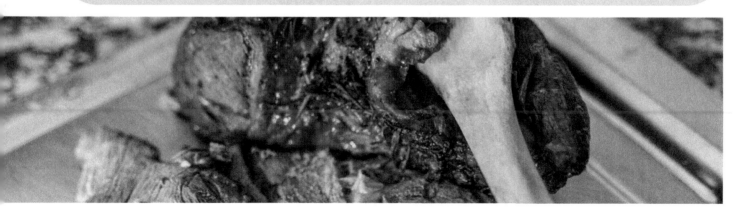

Texas-Style

Crafting a special rub or seasoning can be as straightforward as combining two fundamental ingredients. Often used independently, these two components can also serve as a robust base to enhance further.

Ingredients:

- 2 tbsp coarse ground black pepper
- 2 tbsp coarse sea salt

The fundamental ingredients mentioned above can be effortlessly enriched by integrating your preferred flavours, paving the way for innovative and personalised rub creations. For instance, consider the following delightful spicy blend:

Add to the above ingredients:

- 1 tsp chilli powder
- 1 tsp garlic powder
- 1 tsp cayenne pepper
- 1 tsp onion powder
- 1/2 tsp paprika
- 1/2 tsp English mustard powder

Hold on; we're still going. The rub above is an excellent choice for a lengthy cook, like brisket or pork shoulder. However, if you opt for a shorter cook, like chicken, you could include 1 tbsp of brown sugar in the blend. This will give it an added layer of flavour.

Seasonings

Instructions for seasonings:

1. Combine all of the ingredients in a small bowl and mix well.
2. Sprinkle the seasoning generously over the meat, rubbing it in with your hands.

Allow the meat to sit for at least 15 minutes before cooking to allow the flavours to penetrate. Overnight in the fridge is also a good option if you have the time.

It is possible to store dry seasonings and dry rubs in airtight containers in a cupboard out of sunlight and heat for three months or more if you are multiplying the ingredients.

Best of British - Meat

Ingredients:

- 2 tsp dried dill (if no dill, skip this)
- 2 tsp dried parsley
- 1 tsp dried oregano
- 1 tsp dried chives
- 1 tsp garlic granules
- 1 tsp onion granules
- 1 tsp ground black pepper
- 1 tsp sea salt
- 1 tsp lemon zest (dried or freshly grated)
- 1 tsp ground coriander
- 1/2 tsp ground paprika
- 1/4 tsp cayenne pepper (optional)

Best of British - Fish

Ingredients:

- 2 tsp dried rosemary
- 2 tsp dried thyme
- 2 tsp dried sage
- 1 tsp dried oregano
- 1 tsp dried parsley
- 1 tsp garlic powder
- 1 tsp onion powder
- 1 tsp paprika (preferably smoked)
- 1 tsp ground black pepper
- 1 tsp sea salt
- 1 tsp ground coriander
- 1 tsp ground cumin
- 1/2 tsp ground nutmeg

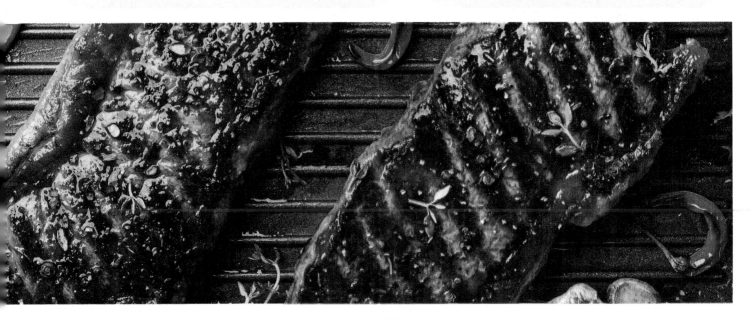

Salt & Pepper

By far, one of the most popular simple seasonings in the UK is Salt & Pepper, and here are two great versions.

Ingredients:

- 2 tsp sea salt
- 1 tsp freshly ground black pepper
- 1/2 tsp garlic powder
- 1/2 tsp onion powder
- 1/4 tsp paprika

Ingredients:

- 1 tsp sea salt
- 1 tsp of black pepper crushed
- 1 tsp chilli flakes
- 1/2 tsp Chinese 5-spice
- 1/2 tsp garlic powder
- 1/2 tsp ground ginger
- 1 tsp caster sugar

Indian

Ingredients:

- 1 tsp cumin powder
- 1 tsp coriander powder
- 1 tsp garam masala
- 1 tsp paprika
- 1 tsp turmeric
- 1 tsp garlic powder
- 1 tsp sea salt
- 1/2 tsp ground black pepper
- 1/2 tsp cayenne pepper
- 1/2 tsp cinnamon

Chinese

Ingredients:

- 2 tsp brown sugar
- 1 tsp Chinese 5-spice powder
- 1 tsp garlic powder
- 1 tsp onion powder
- 1 tsp ground ginger
- 1 tsp sea salt
- 1/2 tsp ground black pepper

Thai

Ingredients:

- 2 tsp paprika
- 1 tsp turmeric
- 1 tsp ground black pepper
- 1 tsp ground coriander
- 1 tsp ground fenugreek or garam masala
- 1/2 tsp dry mustard
- 1/2 tsp ground cumin
- 1/2 tsp ground ginger
- 1/4 tsp cayenne powder

Cajun

Ingredients:

- 1 tsp coarse sea salt
- 1 tsp paprika
- 1 tsp cayenne pepper
- 1 tsp ground cumin
- 1 tsp garlic granules
- 1 tsp dried thyme
- 1 tsp dried oregano

Rubs

Instructions for applying rubs: As with volumes, sugar plays a large part.

1. Prepare your meat by removing excess fat and patting it dry with paper towels.
2. Sprinkle the rub generously over the entire surface of the meat, using your hands to massage it in and ensure that it sticks to the meat. Be sure to coat all sides evenly.
3. Once the meat is fully coated in the rub, wrap it in plastic wrap and refrigerate it for at least 30 minutes, up to several hours or overnight. This will allow the flavours of the rub to penetrate the meat.
4. When you're ready to cook, remove the meat from the fridge and let it come to room temperature for about 30 minutes before cooking.

Cook the meat according to your preferred method. After cooking, leave to sit for at least 15 minutes before slicing or serving.

Nice'n Spicy

Ingredients:

- 1/2 tsp ground coriander
- 2 tsp garlic powder
- 1 tbsp sea salt
- 2 tbsp caster sugar
- 1 tbsp smoked paprika
- 1 tbsp garlic powder
- 1 tbsp onion powder
- 1 tsp English mustard powder
- 1 tsp cayenne pepper
- 1 tsp dried thyme

The Jerk

Ingredients:

- 1 tbsp garlic powder
- 1 tbsp onion powder
- 1 tbsp brown sugar
- 1 tbsp dried parsley
- 2 tsp cayenne pepper
- 1 tsp ground cinnamon
- 1 tsp sea salt
- 1/2 tsp ground black pepper
- 1/2 tsp ground allspice
- 1/2 tsp ground clove
- 1/2 tsp chilli flakes
- 1/2 tsp chilli powder
- 1/2 tsp paprika
- 1/2 tsp ground nutmeg

Cheeky Monkey

Ingredients:

- 2 tbsp brown sugar
- 1 tbsp smoked paprika
- 1 tbsp ground black pepper
- 1 tbsp sea salt
- 1 tsp garlic powder
- 1 tsp onion powder

CAFÉ

Ingredients:

- 2 tbsp brown sugar
- 1 tsp cayenne pepper
- 1 tsp sea salt
- 1 tbsp smoked paprika
- 1 tbsp coffee granules
- 1 tbsp cocoa powder

Texan

Ingredients:

- 1/2 tsp celery ground seeds
- 1/2 tsp ground cumin
- 1 tsp ground mustard seeds
- 1 tsp ground coriander seeds
- 4 tbsp demerara sugar
- 4 tbsp dark brown sugar
- 2 tbsp paprika
- 1 tbsp sea salt
- 2 tsp onion powder
- 2 tsp garlic powder
- 3 tsp chilli powder
- 1 tsp dried oregano
- 1 tsp ground black pepper

Baby Spice

Ingredients:

- 1 tbsp sea salt
- 2 tbsp packed brown sugar
- 1 tsp ground black pepper
- 1 tsp ground coriander
- 1 tsp ground cumin
- 1 tsp ground cinnamon
- 1 tsp dried thyme, crushed
- 1 tsp garlic powder
- 1 tsp ground cardamom
- 1 tsp ground ginger
- 1 tsp ground nutmeg
- 1 small bay leaf, finely crumbled

Smoky

Ingredients:

- 1 tbsp smoked paprika
- 1 tbsp onion powder
- 1 tsp garlic powder
- 1 tsp sea salt
- 1 tsp mustard powder
- 1 tsp ground ginger

Mexican

Ingredients:

- 2 tsp ground cumin
- 1 tsp ground coriander
- 2 tsp sea salt
- 2 tsp chilli powder
- 2 tsp onion powder
- 2 tsp garlic powder
- 1 tsp dried oregano
- 1/2 tsp chilli powder (optional)

Memphis Bell

Ingredients:

- 2 tbsp dark brown sugar
- 2 tbsp white sugar
- 1 tbsp paprika
- 2 tsp garlic powder
- 2 tsp ground black pepper
- 2 tsp ground ginger
- 2 tsp onion powder
- 2 tsp ground rosemary

Smooth Cajun

Ingredients:

- 1 tbsp garlic powder
- 1 tbsp onion powder
- 1 tbsp white pepper
- 1 tbsp cayenne pepper
- 1 tbsp sea salt
- 1 tbsp paprika
- 2 tsp dried thyme
- 2 tsp dried oregano

Sauces

Instructions for preparing uncooked sauces can be either applied to the meat before cooking on the Woodfire or heated and drizzled over the cooked food. You can store it in the fridge for up to two weeks. If using the sauce before cooking, leave the meat in the sauce to marinate for at least 2 hours in the fridge.

1. Combine all ingredients in a bowl.
2. Whisk or blend until a smooth consistency.

BBQ

Ingredients:

- 250 ml tomato ketchup
- 4 tbsp brown sugar
- 90 ml apple cider vinegar
- 30 ml (2 tbsp) Dijon mustard
- 15 ml (1 tbsp) Worcestershire sauce
- 15 ml (1 tbsp) honey
- 2 tsp chilli powder
- 1/2 tsp sea salt
- 1/2 tsp ground black pepper

Herb Butter

Ingredients:

- 120 ml melted unsalted butter
- 2 tbsp fresh parsley, chopped
- 2 tbsp chives, chopped
- 1 tbsp fresh thyme, chopped
- 1/2 tsp garlic powder
- 1/4 tsp sea salt
- 1/4 tsp ground black pepper

Mustard Maple

Ingredients:

- 60 ml (4 tbsp) Dijon mustard
- 30 ml (2 tbsp)maple syrup
- 30 ml apple cider vinegar
- 15 ml soy sauce
- 1 tbsp garlic powder
- 1/2 tsp black pepper

Kansas City

Ingredients:

- 250 ml tomato ketchup
- 2 tbsp dark brown sugar
- 120 ml water
- 120 ml white wine vinegar
- 120 ml tomato paste
- 30 ml (2 tbsp) Dijon mustard
- 2 tbsp chilli powder
- 1 tbsp ground black pepper
- 1 tsp sea salt
- 1 tsp onion powder
- 1 tsp garlic powder
- 1 tsp ground ginger

Lemon Herb

Ingredients:

- 60 ml (4 tbsp) olive oil
- 30 ml (2 tbsp) lemon juice
- 1 tbsp fresh thyme, chopped
- 1 tbsp fresh rosemary, chopped
- 1 tbsp fresh parsley, chopped
- 1 tsp garlic powder
- 1 tsp sea salt
- 1/2 tsp ground black pepper

Horseradish

Ingredients:

- 250 ml mayonnaise
- 60 ml (4 tbsp) apple cider vinegar
- 2 tbsp dark brown sugar
- 15 ml (1 tbsp) brown mustard
- 2 tbsp finely grated fresh horseradish
- 5 ml (1 tsp) lemon juice
- 5 ml (1 tsp) hot sauce
- 1/4 tsp sea salt
- 1/4 tsp ground black pepper

3 Ingredient BBQ

Ingredients:

- 250 ml tomato ketchup
- 120 ml warmed honey
- 45 ml (3 tbsp) Worcestershire Sauce

Extra Spicy

Ingredients:

- 250 ml mayonnaise
- 120 ml sweet chilli sauce
- 60 ml (4 tbsp) olive oil
- 60 ml (4 tbsp) tomato ketchup
- 30 ml (2 tbsp) lemon juice
- 15 ml (1 tbsp) Worcestershire sauce
- 15 ml (1 tbsp) Dijon mustard
- 2 tsp garlic powder
- 1 tsp onion powder

Honey Mustard

Ingredients:

- 250 ml whole-grain mustard
- 60 ml (4 tbsp) apple cider vinegar
- 60 ml (4 tbsp) honey
- 15 ml (1 tbsp) Worcestershire sauce
- 15 ml (1 tbsp) soy sauce
- 4 tsp chilli powder
- 1 tsp garlic powder
- 1/4 tsp sea salt
- 1/4 tsp ground black pepper

Sweet Vinegar Apple

Ingredients:

- 250 ml apple cider vinegar
- 1 tbsp dark brown sugar
- 15 ml (1 tbsp) tomato ketchup
- 15 ml (1 tbsp) chilli sauce
- 1/4 tsp sea salt
- 1/4 tsp ground black pepper

Marinades

Blend them in a food processor for marinades that can't be mixed easily. Rub or brush the marinade onto the meat or fish of choice, cover and refrigerate for several hours or overnight to allow the flavours to penetrate the meat or fish. Then, cook as desired.

Spicy Havana

Ingredients:

- Juice of 1 medium orange
- 1 red chilli, finely chopped
- 2 spring onions, finely chopped
- 30 ml (2 tbsp) olive oil
- 1 lime, finely grated zest

Tandoori

Ingredients:

- 100 ml Greek-style yoghurt
- 1 tbsp ginger, finely grated
- 2 tsp smoked paprika
- 1 tsp ground cumin
- 15 ml (1 tbsp) olive oil

Lemon Zest

Ingredients:

- 1 lemon, zest and juice
- 2 garlic cloves, crushed
- 3 sprigs of rosemary, finely chopped
- 60 ml (4 tbsp) olive oil

Hi Honey

Ingredients:

- 2 garlic cloves, crushed
- 1 red chilli, finely chopped
- 1 tbsp fresh parsley, finely chopped
- 45 ml (3 tbsp) pure honey
- 45 ml (3 tbsp) olive oil

Ginger Pineapple

Ingredients:

- 220 to 250 g tin of pineapple slices in juice, drained and finely chopped
- 2 tbsp ginger, finely grated
- 30 ml (2 tbsp) soy sauce
- 30 ml (2 tbsp) olive oil

Smoky BBQ

Ingredients:

- 2 garlic cloves, finely chopped
- 1 tbsp smoked paprika
- 2 tbsp brown sugar
- 60 ml (4 tbsp) golden syrup
- 15 ml (1 tbsp) white wine vinegar
- 15 ml (1 tbsp) olive oil
- 30 ml (2 tbsp) barbecue sauce

The Big Smoky

Ingredients:

- 1 red onion, peeled and roughly chopped
- 15 ml (1 tbsp) olive oil
- 1 garlic clove, peeled and sliced
- 1/2 fresh red chilli, deseeded and finely chopped
- 1 tbsp fresh, finely chopped basil leaves
- 1 tsp onion seeds
- 1/2 tsp sea salt
- 1/2 tsp ground black pepper
- 250 g tomatoes, halved
- 250 g tinned chopped tomatoes
- 15 ml (1 tbsp) soy sauce
- 30 ml (2 tbsp) Liquid Smoke
- 1 bay leaf
- 30 ml (2 tbsp) pure maple syrup
- 1 tsp smoked paprika
- 250 ml cold water
- 120 ml red wine vinegar
- 3 tbsp brown sugar

Cheeky Chicken

Ingredients:

- 1/2 onion, peeled and quartered
- 5 garlic cloves, peeled and quartered
- 2 red chillies, fresh, stalks removed
- 30 ml (2 tbsp) olive oil
- 4 tbsp soft brown sugar
- 100 ml balsamic vinegar
- 200 ml tomato ketchup
- 30 ml (2 tbsp) Worcestershire sauce
- 15 ml (1 tbsp) English mustard
- 1 tsp sea salt
- 1 tsp ground black pepper

Fish Med

Ingredients:

- 15 ml (1 tbsp) olive oil
- 4 tbsp fresh parsley, finely chopped
- 4 tbsp fresh coriander, finely chopped
- 80 ml fresh lemon juice
- Juice of 1 lime
- 3 garlic cloves, crushed
- 4 tsp paprika
- 2 tsp ground cumin
- 1 tsp ground black pepper

Spicy Fish

Ingredients:

- 2 tsp paprika
- 1/2 tsp garlic granules
- 1/2 tsp onion granules
- 1/2 tsp dried parsley
- 1/2 tsp ground black pepper
- 60 ml (4 tbsp) olive oil
- 60 ml (4 tbsp) lemon juice
- 30 ml (2 tbsp) soy sauce

Air-Fried Pork Chops

4 pork chops, ideally with a little fat throughout or on them					
Olive oil	15 ml	1 tbsp	Sea salt		1/2 tsp
Ground black pepper		1/2 tsp			
Alternatively, replace the salt and pepper with a seasoning of your choice.					

Place the air fryer basket on the grill grate, close the lid, and turn the Woodfire dial to AIR FRY. Set the temperature to 200C, the timer for 20 minutes, and press START/STOP to begin preheating.

While preheating, combine the oil, salt, and pepper in a large bowl. Add the chops and rub the mixture all over them. Once the ADD FOOD message appears, lift the lid and place the chops in the air fryer basket. Close the lid to start cooking. After 5 minutes, open the lid, flip the chops over and close the lid and continue cooking to your liking.

Serves 2 to 4, Preparation time approx 10 mins, Cooking time approx 20 minutes

Air-Fried Pork Joint

Boneless shoulder or bone-in rack with a layer fat and skin/rind for crackling	900 g to 1.2 kg	2 lb to 2 lb 9 oz
Sea salt	25 g	2 tbsp

First, pat the joint dry with a tea towel or kitchen roll and score the fat without cutting into the meat. Rub salt into the skin and sprinkle the remaining salt over it, allowing some to fall into the scored areas. Leave the joint uncovered in the fridge overnight.

When you're ready to cook, dry the joint again and place it on the grill grate (no oil needed). Optionally, arrange halved onions or sliced vegetables around the joint, but keep an eye on them as they may cook faster. If they do, remove them when cooked and let the joint continue cooking. You can return the vegetables for the last 5 minutes.

Add your chosen pellets to the smoke box, set the dial to AIR FRY, press the WOODFIRE FLAVOUR button and the temperature to 200C and set the timer for 1 hour. Press START/STOP to begin cooking. Cook until its internal temperature reaches 60 to 65C.

Once the joint reaches the desired temperature and the skin turns into crispy crackling, remove it from the grill and let it rest for 15 minutes before serving.

Serves 4 to 6, Preparation time approx 24 hours, Cooking time approx 1 hour

Bacon Jam Baby Back Ribs

2 racks of baby back ribs			Salted butter		30 g	1 oz
Drizzle of honey						
Bacon Jam						
Bacon, diced	450 g	1 lb	Balsamic vinegar		60 ml	1/4 cup
1 large white onion, peeled, diced			Apple cider vinegar		60 ml	1/4 cup
Brown sugar	45 g	1/4 cup	Strong brewed black coffee		60 ml	1/4 cup
Pure maple syrup	60 ml	1/4 cup	Water		60 ml	1/4 cup

Bacon Jam, if using the recipe above:

In a frying pan on medium heat, fry the bacon until crisp and the fat fully rendered. Remove the bacon and excess fat, leaving a bit to fry the onion. Add the onion and cook until it turns pale, then reduce the heat and simmer for 15-20 minutes, avoiding dark browning or charring. Increase the heat to medium, reintroduce the bacon, and add the remaining ingredients. Simmer for about 15 minutes until the liquid is absorbed and the mixture turns sticky. Blend the mixture in a food processor to achieve your desired texture. You can store leftover bacon jam in an airtight jar for up to 2 weeks.

Ribs:

Fill the smoke box with a robust pellet blend and place the ribs on the grill grate. Choose the SMOKER setting at 120C with a 1.5-hour timer, and press START/STOP. Check the ribs' internal temperature with a thermometer after 1 hour and continue checking every 10 minutes until they reach 70 to 75C. Lay out two foil sheets, adding the butter and a drizzle of honey. Place the ribs meat-side down on the butter and honey, wrap tightly, and return them to the Woodfire, meat-side down. Select BAKE at 150C for 1 hour, checking the ribs occasionally until their internal temperature reaches 90 to 95C, and a probe inserts easily. Unwrap the ribs, place them meat-side up on the grill gate, and cover them with bacon jam. Close the lid and cook for around 10 minutes.

Serves 2 to 4, Preparation time approx 40 minutes, Cooking time approx 2 1/2 hours

Bacon Smoked Mac & Cheese

Enough cooked elbow macaroni to 3/4-fill a 23 x 33 cm / 9 x 13-inch baking/roasting dish or a dish size close to it and any shape as long as it fits easily in the Woodfire

8 rashers of smoky bacon, cooked and diced			Swiss cheese, grated	225 g	8 oz
Mature cheddar, grated	225 g	8 oz	Panko or coarse breadcrumbs	50 g	1/2 cup
Parmesan cheese, grated	60 g	2 oz	Milk	180 ml	3/4 cup

Combine pasta, bacon, cheddar, Swiss cheese, and milk in a baking dish, then place it on the Woodfire grill grate. Add your preferred pellets to the smoke box, set the Woodfire to BAKE, press the WOODFIRE FLAVOUR button, set the temperature to 150C and the timer for 40 minutes, and press START/STOP to begin.

The food will sit in the Woodfire during preheating. Cook until the cheese has melted, then mix well. Cover with breadcrumbs and top with parmesan cheese. Close the lid and continue cooking until done, ensuring the parmesan isn't burnt. Allow it to rest for 5 minutes before serving.

Serves 4 to 6, Preparation time approx 20 mins, Cooking time approx 40 minutes

Bacon Wrapped Pork Tenderloin

Clear honey	15 ml	1 tbsp	Dijon mustard	15 ml	1 tbsp
Sea salt		1 tsp	Ground black pepper		1 tsp
Garlic powder		1 tsp			
8 bacon rashers, or enough to cover the length of the loin					

Mix the honey and Dijon mustard in a small bowl, then set aside. Pat the pork dry with kitchen towels. Combine the salt, pepper, and garlic, and rub it over the pork.

Wrap the pork with the bacon crosswise and ensure each end of the bacon is tucked under the pork with the weight of the pork holding it down. It can be an idea to partly wrap the length of the loin before then tucking all the bacon at once. The bacon will tighten and stick to the pork during cooking, so it is unnecessary to pin with toothpicks.

Brush the bacon with the honey mustard mixture and let it stand for 30 minutes. When ready to cook, set the Woodfire dial to ROAST, set the temperature to 200C, the timer for 40 minutes, and press START/STOP to begin preheating. Once the ADD FOOD message appears, place the pork on the grill grate, close the lid, and start cooking. After 20 minutes, loosely cover the pork with a flat sheet of foil to prevent the bacon from burning. Continue cooking until the internal temperature exceeds 65C. Once cooked to your liking, remove the pork and let it stand for 10 minutes before serving.

Serves 2 to 4, Preparation time approx 40 mins, Cooking time approx 40 minutes

Carolina Pulled Pork Sandwich

4 to 8 buns (brioche, potato, or other, and you could also create sliders)

250 g/1 cup coleslaw of choice (or refer to our coleslaw recipe on page 30)

1.5 kg/3 lb pork shoulder or pork butt, bone, skin, and excess fat removed

2 to 3 tbsp Carolina rub (or refer to our Classic Carolina rub on page 11)

250 ml/1 cup BBQ sauce of choice (or create the sauce with this recipe below)

Carolina Mustard BBQ Sauce

Dijon mustard	125 ml	1/2 cup	Smoked paprika		1 tsp
Tomato ketchup	60 ml	1/4 cup	Ground black pepper		1/2 tsp
Apple cider vinegar	60 ml	1/4 cup	White vinegar	15 ml	1 tbsp
Sugar		1 tbsp	Ancho chilli powder / crushed flakes		1 tsp
Worcestershire sauce	15 ml	1 tbsp			

Cover the pork in the rub and pat it firmly and evenly. Place it in a large dish and refrigerate for at least 4 hours, preferably overnight. When it's time to cook, place the pork on the grill, add pellets of your choice to the smoke box, turn the dial to SMOKER, set the temperature to 120C, and the timer for 5 hours. Press START/STOP to begin.

Cook the pork until it is fork-tender, reaching an internal temperature of 90 to 96C. This may take less than 5 hours, so check it every hour or less.

While the pork cooks, add all of the sauce ingredients to a blender and mix thoroughly. When you check on the pork, give it a light spritz of water if it appears too dry. Once the pork is cooked to your preference, remove it from the grill and wrap it with foil or butcher's paper. Allow it to rest in a cool part of the kitchen for about 30 minutes to an hour. When it's ready, pull the pork apart. Spoon some sauce onto the buns, then add the pulled pork, coleslaw, and more sauce before topping with the other bun halves.

Serves 4 to 8, Preparation time approx 24 hours, Cooking time approx 5 hours

Easy Pork Chops

4 to 6 pork chops 2.5 to 4 cm / 1 to 1 1/2 inch thick, bone-in or out				
Olive oil	30 ml	2 tbsp	Ground black pepper	1/2 tsp
Sea salt		1/2 tsp		

Turn the Woodfire dial to GRILL, set the temperature to HI, and the timer for 20 minutes. Close the lid and press the START/STOP button to begin preheating. While the unit is preheating, season the pork chops with oil, salt, and pepper.

When the ADD FOOD message appears, open the lid and place the pork chops on the grill, pressing them firmly onto the grill grate. Close the lid to start cooking. Flip the chops after 7 minutes and close the lid to continue cooking. Cook until the pork chops are done to your liking.

Serves 4 to 6, Preparation time approx 10 mins, Cooking time approx 20 minutes

Glazed Gammon/Fresh Ham

					2 to 3 kg	4 lb 4 oz to 6 lb 9 oz
Gammon (aka fresh ham), boned and rolled					2 to 3 kg	4 lb 4 oz to 6 lb 9 oz
English mustard	30 ml	2 tbsp	Garlic powder			1 tbsp
Smoked paprika		1 tbsp	Sea salt			2 tsp
Light brown sugar	25 g	2 tbsp	Dried sage			1 tsp
Onion powder		1 tbsp	Dried thyme			1 tsp
Glaze						
Juice of one tangerine/manderin/clementine			Honey		45 ml	3 tbsp
Bourbon (or Brandy)	30 ml	2 tbsp	Allspice			1/2 tsp

Combine all the ingredients except the gammon and the glaze components in a small bowl. Season the gammon generously with the dry mixture. Cover and refrigerate for 6 hours or overnight. When ready to cook, place the gammon on the grill grate, then close the lid.

Turn the Woodfire dial to SMOKER, set the temperature to 120C and the timer for 4 hours. Press START/STOP to initiate cooking. Depending on the gammon's size and shape, additional time may be required during the cooking cycle.

Combine all glaze ingredients in a small saucepan over medium heat on a stove to prepare the glaze. Cook until the honey has dissolved, then remove from heat. When 1 hour remains for the gammon, open the lid and baste the gammon with the glaze. The gammon is fully cooked when an instant-read thermometer registers 85 to 90C. When cooked to your liking, turn off the Woodfire and leave the gammon where it is, but apply more glaze, close the lid and allow the gammon to rest in the residual heat for 30 minutes. Alternatively, remove the gammon from the grill, wrap it in foil, and let it rest for 1 hour.

Serves 6 to 8, Preparation time approx 15 mins, Cooking time approx 4 hours

Hawaiian Skewers

450 g/1 lb pork loin, beef fillet, ribeye, or chicken, cut into 4 cm cubes or chunks				
Half a pineapple, peeled, cored, and cut into 4 cm cubes or chunks				
4 thin bacon rashers, cut into squares or shapes allowed by the bacon				
Enough long skewers to accommodate the meat and pineapple				
Olive oil	15 ml	1 tbsp	Ground black pepper	1/2 tsp
Sea salt		1/2 tsp	Lime or lemon juice	1/2 tsp

If using long wooden skewers, soak them in water for 30 minutes before use. Combine all ingredients in a large bowl and thoroughly coat the meat and pineapple. Thread the pork, pineapple, and bacon slices onto the skewers.

Turn the Woodfire dial to GRILL, set the temperature to HI, the timer for 15 minutes, and press the START/STOP button to start preheating. Once the ADD FOOD message appears, lift the lid and place the skewers on the grill grate, then close the lid to begin cooking. After 3 minutes, open the lid and rotate the skewers one-quarter clockwise. Close the lid and continue this rotation clockwise until the food is lightly charred but not burned, or cook it to your liking.

Serves 2 to 4, Preparation time approx 30 mins, Cooking time approx 15 minutes

Skinless Pork Sausages

Pork mince, room temperature	450 g	1 lb	Dried parsley			1 tsp
Fresh breadcrumbs	50 g	1/2 cup	Sea salt			1/2 tsp
2 large spring onions, finely diced			Dried thyme			1/2 tsp
1 egg, beaten			Ground black pepper			1/2 tsp
Garlic clove, finely grated			Fennel seeds, crushed			1/2 tsp
Dried sage		1 tsp	Olive oil		30 ml	2 tsp

In a medium-sized bowl, combine all ingredients except the olive oil. Avoid overworking the meat; mix only until the ingredients are evenly distributed. If the mixture is too moist, add more breadcrumbs until it reaches a firm rollable consistency. Divide the mixture into 6 portions and gently shape them into 6-inch sausages. Refrigerate the sausages for 30 minutes before use.

When ready to cook, set the Woodfire dial to GRILL, set the temperature to HI, the timer for 15 minutes, and press START/STOP to start preheating. Once the ADD FOOD message appears, place the sausages on the grill grate or flat plate, and close the lid to start cooking. Check the sausages after 5 minutes and gently flip them over. Close the lid to continue cooking. Check on them periodically until they are cooked to your liking.

Alternatively, mince the pork yourself using the instructions in this book on sausage and burger making, and follow the same ingredients for combining the mixture. If you like, you can fill sausage skins with the mix according to our included instructions.

Serves 1 to 2, Preparation time approx 45 mins, Cooking time approx 15 minutes

Smoked Burnt Ends

Belly pork, rindless, whole or in strips. If whole, cut into 4 cm thick strips and then cut all pork into about 4 to 5 cm cubes					900 g	2 lb
Dijon mustard	15 ml	1 tbsp	Worcestershire sauce		15 ml	1 tbsp
Clear honey	30 ml	2 tbsp	Pure apple juice		30 ml	2 tbsp
Butter, softened	60 g	2 oz	Tomato ketchup		15 ml	1 tbsp
BBQ rub of choice (or our Classic Carolina rub on page 9)						2 tbsp

Combine the butter, honey, ketchup, apple juice, and Worcestershire sauce in a bowl.

Place the pork cubes in a large bowl, add the mustard, and rub it all over the pork. Then, sprinkle the rub and lightly pat or rub it onto each pork cube. Arrange the cubes on the Woodfire grill grate, leaving some space between each cube, and close the lid.

Add your choice of pellets to the smoke box. Set the Woodfire dial to SMOKER, set the temperature to 140C, the timer for 2 hours, and press START/STOP to begin cooking.

After the first hour, open the lid and transfer the cubes from the grill grate to a thick foil or two thinner sheets of cling film. Drizzle the butter mixture over the cubes, then seal them into the foil. Place the wrapped cubes back on the grill grate and close the lid to continue cooking for the remaining hour.

When the time is up, remove the cubes and serve. Pour the sauce and juices into a bowl if you wish, and place the cubes back on the grill grate without the foil for drier cubes or for a little longer cooking. For this, set the dial to BAKE, set the temperature to HI, the timer for 10 minutes, and close the lid. Click START/STOP to begin preheating. The cubes will continue to cook during preheating. Once the ADD FOOD message appears, open the lid, flip the cubes, close the lid, and continue cooking until they are cooked.

Serves 2 to 4, Preparation time approx 20 mins, Cooking time approx 2 hours

Smoked Pork Belly

Belly pork, about 2.5 cm thick	900 g	2 lb	Ground black pepper		1/2 tsp
Coarse sea salt	20 g	2 tbsp			

Alternatively, if you have it, you can use a seasoning instead of salt and pepper and a sauce from our first "The Woodfire Way" book.

Place the belly pork on a cutting board, skin side down, and cut through the meat until you are about 1 cm from the skin. The idea is to make these cuts about 8 cm apart and in 8 x 8 cm square blocks, still attached to the fat and skin. Rub salt, pepper, or seasoning into the cuts and outer edges, avoiding the skin. Flip the pork over, skin side up, and perforate the skin without scoring it. Create as many small prick holes as possible, approximately 5 to 10 per 2.5 cm square. Use a toothpick or something fine-pointed to break the skin. Leave the pork uncovered in the fridge for 8 to 12 hours.

When ready to cook, place the pork in a roasting tin on the Woodfire grill grate, ensuring the skin side is facing down to allow the meat and fat to absorb the smoke flavour. Add your choice of pellets to the smoke box, then set the dial to SMOKER. Set the temperature to 130C, the timer for 3 hours, and press the START/STOP button to cook.

After 20 minutes, flip the pork to the skin side up and close the lid to resume cooking. Check on the pork after 1 hour and 20 minutes and adjust the temperature to 200C. Close the lid and continue cooking. Periodically check on the pork until the skin reaches your desired crackling level or becomes solid when tapped. The smoking process may darken the skin's appearance. Remove the pork and allow it to rest for 10 minutes.

Serves 2 to 4, Preparation time approx 12 hours, Cooking time approx 3 hours

Smoked Pulled Pork

Dijon mustard	30 ml	2 tbsp	Pork shoulder, boned	2.5 to 3 kg	5 1/2 to 6 1/2 lb
Rub of choice (or refer to our rubs)	15 g	3 tbsp			
BBQ sauce (or refer to our sauces)	200 ml	3/4 cup			

Ensure the shoulder is patted dry, then coat it with mustard. Next, generously sprinkle your choice of rub over the surface. Place the pork on the grill grate. Add your preferred pellets to the smoke box and set the Woodfire to SMOKER. Set the temperature to 120C and the timer for 8 hours.

Cook until it is fork-tender, with an internal temperature of 90 to 95C; this might take less than 8 hours. Then, remove the pork from the grill, wrap it in foil, and let it rest for an hour.

Shred the meat with your hands or forks, and mix it with a touch more rub and some BBQ sauce. Serve in bread rolls, on its own, or as a complement to other dishes.

Serves 4 to 6, Preparation time approx 10 mins, Cooking time up to 8 hours

Sweet Hickory Smoked Baby Back Ribs

2 racks of baby back ribs		Dijon mustard	30 ml	2 tbsp
Hickory rub of choice, or use the recipe below			50 g	6 tbsp

Sweet Hickory Rub

Chilli powder	2 tbsp	Sea salt	1 tsp
Garlic powder	1 tbsp	Rosemary, ground	1/4 tsp
Paprika	1 tbsp	Mustard powder	1/2 tsp
Ground cumin	1/2 tsp	Hickory powder	1 tsp
Ground black pepper	1/2 tsp	Turbinado or demerara sugar	2 tsp

Thinly brush the mustard over the ribs. If using the Sweet Hickory Rub recipe, combine all the rub ingredients and gently pat the mixture onto the mustard-covered ribs, covering them as much as possible. Allow the ribs to stand in the fridge for 1 hour.

When ready to cook, place the ribs on the Woodfire grill grate with the rib side down and close the lid. Add your choice of pellets to the smoke box, preferably hickory or sweet-scented. Set the dial to SMOKER, set the temperature to 120C, the timer for 3 hours, and press START/STOP to begin cooking.

After 1 hour, lift the lid and loosely cover the ribs with a flat sheet of foil, ensuring hot air can still circulate while preventing direct heat from drying out the top of the ribs. Close the lid to resume cooking. Check on them periodically until they are cooked to your liking. Pour over a favourite BBQ sauce if desired.

Serves 2, Preparation time approx 1 hour, Cooking time approx 3 hours

Toasted Cheese Dogs

4 to 6 long sausages to fill out the buns (ideally, German hot dogs like Bratwurst or Frankfurters or sausages which are a little firmer and not too watery)					
4 to 6 hot dog buns			8 to 12 cheese slices of choice		
2 onions, peeled, sliced			Chives, finely chopped		1 tbsp
Olive oil	30 ml	2 tbsp	Olives, sliced (optional)		1 tbsp
Unsalted butter, melted	30 g	1 oz			

Mix butter, chives, and olives (optional) in a small bowl. In another bowl, toss the onions with 15 ml of oil. Brush the sausages with the remaining 15 ml of oil. Set the dial to GRILL, choose MED temperature, and set the timer for 15 minutes. Press START/STOP to begin preheating.

When the ADD FOOD message appears, open the lid and place the sausages in the grooves on one side of the grill grate and the sliced onions on the other. Close the lid to start cooking. Flip the sausages and onions halfway through and drizzle the butter mixture over the onions. Close the lid and check the progress after 7 minutes. Remove everything if cooked or continue cooking if needed.

Once cooked, remove the items and close the lid to retain heat. Quickly place 2 cheese slices on each bun, allowing them to overhang the edges. Spoon some onions between the cheese slices at the bottom of the bun and add the sausage on top of the onions and a few olive slices if desired. Return the hot dogs to the Woodfire for a few minutes, letting the residual heat melt the cheese and slightly toast the buns. Remove and serve with your favourite relishes.

Serves 4 to 6, Preparation time approx 20 mins, Cooking time approx 17 minutes

Best Meats for Smoking

Smoking is a low-temperature, slow-cooking method that often lasts for over 30 minutes per half a kilogram, and in some cases, meat can remain in the smoker for many hours. While many lean cuts of meat would become inedible after such a lengthy cooking process, tougher cuts require this extended time to tenderise.

Typically, cuts of meat that are often cheaper or not considered tender enough in conventional cooking can withstand extended heat exposure. Meat rich in fat and connective tissue (collagen) thrives in the smoker. The final result is tender, flavourful, and delectable meat. This transformation occurs as collagen gradually breaks down into gelatin, which helps the meat become tender and moist while the smoke infuses it with a smoky taste.

When identifying the best cuts for the smoker, classic smoking meats usually include beef brisket, pork shoulder, and ribs. These can be tough, chewy cuts if not cooked correctly and are often deemed low-quality in conventional cooking.

For those new to smoking foods, starting with a cheap cut of meat is recommended. A small pork shoulder cut is a forgiving and relatively inexpensive choice. Ideal for learning about your equipment, refining your smoking technique, and experimenting with various pellets, temperatures, times, and seasonings.

Generally, the pros often avoid smoking high-quality cuts of meat, such as pork tenderloin or lean roasts. Steaks, for example, are better suited for grilling. There is no need to invest time and money on cuts of meat that are already delicious when cooked quickly over high heat. Furthermore, smoking high-quality meats will yield few taste benefits, as the meat will likely be too dried out to enjoy.

Think of prolonged smoking as turning cheap or often tough cuts into tender dishes. So don't pass it up when you spot big gnarly chunks going cheap.

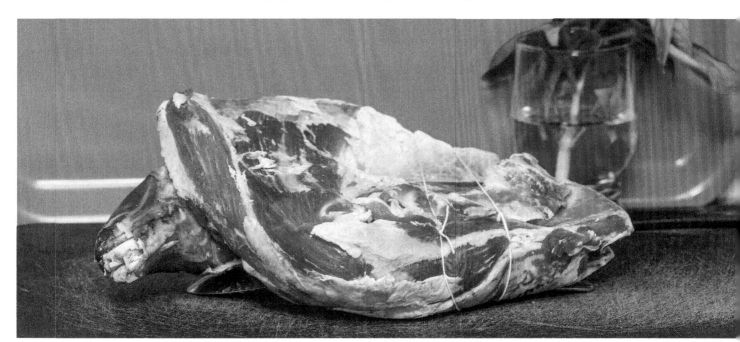

Popular Smoking Cuts:

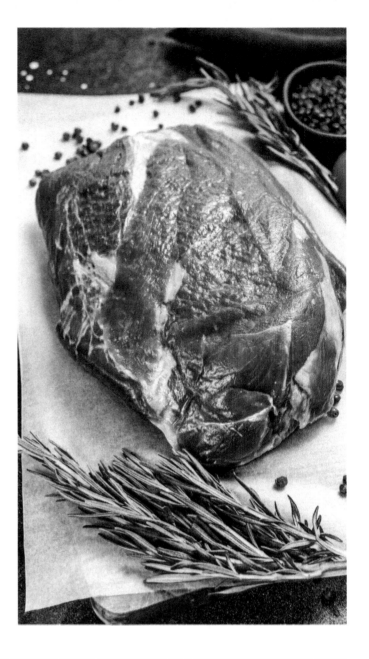

Best Beef for Smoking
- o Brisket
- o Beef Ribs
- o Braising
- o Standing Rib Roast
- o Rump Tail
- o Ox or Beef Cheeks

Best Pork for Smoking
- o Shoulder or Boston Butt
- o Spare, St. Louis, Baby Back Ribs
- o Ham

Best Lamb for Smoking
- o Leg
- o Shoulder
- o Rack of Lamb

Best Poultry for Smoking
- o Chicken
- o Turkey

Best Exotic Meats and Game for Smoking
- o Boar
- o Venison
- o Buffalo
- o Bison
- o Crocodile / Aligator
- o Ostrich

Often Preferred During Smoking On Long Cooks	Often Preferred On Shorter Cooks
Lots of fat, marbling and fat cap	Lean
Tough muscle fibers	Fine texture
Connective tissues (collagen)	Minus connective tissues
Low cost per kg	Expensive per kg

Trimming Meat For Smoking

Trimming meat for smoking is essential in preparing the perfect cut for the smoking process. Proper trimming ensures even cooking, allows the meat to absorb smoke and seasonings better, and reduces the risk of overcooked or undercooked areas. Here's a step-by-step starter guide to trimming meat for smoking:

Choose the right knife. A sharp, professional narrow-bladed boning knife is ideal for trimming meat. Ensure your blade is sharpened adequately for precise cuts and to avoid tearing the flesh.

Prepare your workspace. Clean and sanitise your chopping board and countertop. Keep a clean towel, disposable gloves, and a waste container nearby to dispose of unwanted trimmed fat and other unwanted parts.

Remove excess fat. Fat is essential for flavour and moisture, but too much fat can prevent the meat from absorbing smoke and seasonings. Trim off large, thick layers of fat, leaving a thin layer (about 3 to 6 mm) to help protect the meat during cooking. For a large brisket, try making it aerodynamic for the smoke to flow smoothly.

Remove silver skin. The silver skin is a thin, tough, almost transparent membrane found on some cuts of meat (e.g., ribs, pork tenderloin, beef brisket). It doesn't render or break down during smoking, so it's best to remove it. First, slide the tip of your knife under the silver skin, angling the blade slightly upward and away from you (always angle a knife away or down). Next, hold the loose end of the silver skin with one hand and gently cut along the surface of the meat, keeping the blade parallel to the cutting board. Once part of the silver skin is loose, the rest can often be torn off in large sections.

Trim connective tissue and unwanted parts. Remove loose or dangling pieces of meat, fat, or connective tissue, as they can dry out and become unpleasantly chewy during smoking. For cuts like pork shoulder, trim any large chunks of fat or connective tissue, but be mindful not to over-trim, as some fat is essential for flavour and moisture.

Shape the meat. For an even cook, it's crucial to have a uniform shape. Trim any uneven areas so the meat is consistent in thickness, if possible. This helps prevent thinner parts from overcooking while thicker areas remain undercooked. Whereas BBQ restaurants can turn large offcuts into other dishes, we rarely have that luxury, so trim off only what is necessary to avoid waste.

Rinse and pat dry: After trimming, rinse the meat under cold running water to remove any small particles, and then pat it dry with clean kitchen towels. A drier surface allows for better smoke absorption and improved adherence to seasoning rubs. Once the meat is trimmed, it can be seasoned and smoked. Remember that practice makes perfect, so keep going even if your first few attempts at trimming aren't perfect. As you gain experience, your trimming skills will improve.

Fragrant Smoked Shoulder of Lamb

1 whole shoulder of lamb		Fresh ginger, finely grated	1 tbsp
Coriander seeds	1 tbsp	Zest of 2 oranges, finely grated	
Cumin seeds	1/2 tbsp	Dried thyme	2 tbsp
Fennel seeds	1/2 tbsp	Coarse sea salt	2 tsp
6 garlic cloves, crushed		Ground black pepper	1 tsp

Set the Woodfire dial to GRILL, adjust the temperature to HIGH, set the timer for 15 minutes, and press START/STOP to initiate preheating. When the ADD FOOD message appears, open the lid and keep it open. Place a frying pan on the grill grate and add all the seeds without oil. Stir the seeds gently for a few minutes until they release a fragrance, but be careful not to burn them. Remove the frying pan and place the lamb on the grill for a few minutes on each side to give it a light sear. Turn off the Woodfire, remove the lamb from the grill grate, and close the lid.

Add mild or fragrant pellets to the smoke box. Set the Woodfire dial to ROAST, press the WOODFIRE FLAVOUR button, adjust the temperature to 165C, set the timer for 2 hours, and press START/STOP to initiate preheating. While preheating (which shouldn't take long), crush the seeds in a pestle and mortar or blender until they resemble a rough powder. Transfer the rough powdered seeds to a bowl, add the remaining ingredients except for the lamb, and stir to form a paste. Generously smear the paste over the lamb, ensuring no part is missed.

When the ADD FOOD message appears, lift the lid and place the lamb on the grill grate. Close the lid to begin cooking. After 45 minutes, check on the lamb and add more pellets to the smoke box if desired. For the remaining cooking time, check on the lamb every 15 minutes until it is cooked to your liking and the internal temperature reads around 63C or higher.

Serves 4 to 6, Preparation time approx 10 minutes, Cooking time approx 2 hours

Garlic & Rosemary Leg of Lamb

1 whole leg of lamb		10 garlic cloves, peeled and sliced in half
5 sprigs of fresh rosemary		15 ml (1 tbsp) olive oil

Pat dry the leg of lamb with kitchen towels. Make small, even incisions all over the lamb, just wide enough to insert half a garlic clove and some fresh rosemary, about 1.3 cm deep. Rub the lamb with olive oil.

Set the Woodfire dial to ROAST, adjust the temperature to 170C, set the timer for 2 hours, and press START/STOP to initiate preheating. When the ADD FOOD message appears, open the lid and place the lamb on the grill grate underside up. Close the lid to begin cooking. After 45 minutes, open the lid, turn the lamb over, and close the lid to continue cooking. Check on the lamb every 15 minutes after the first 45 minutes, cooking until it reaches your liking or an internal temperature of approximately 63C. Once cooked, remove the lamb and let it rest for 10 minutes before slicing.

Serves 4 to 6, Preparation time approx 20 minutes, Cooking time approx 2 hours

Honey Mustard Lamb Chops

10 to 16 lamb chops, bone-in to hold		
Honey mustard sauce of choice (or refer to our Honey Mustard sauce recipe)	30 to 60 ml	2 to 4 tbsp

To prepare honey mustard chops on the Woodfire, coat the chops in honey mustard sauce and refrigerate for at least 4 hours. When ready to start cooking, add your preferred pellets to the smoke box, set the Woodfire to GRILL, and press WOODFIRE FLAVOUR. Set the temperature to HI, the timer for 20 minutes, and press START/STOP.

Once the ADD FOOD message appears, place the chops on the grill grate and the remaining sauce in a heatproof dish. Flip the chops after 7 minutes and add the dish of remaining sauce onto the grill grate. Check the chops at the 15-minute mark, and once they're cooked to your liking, remove them from the Woodfire. Otherwise, continue cooking until they're done. Serve with preferred side dishes and a fresh drizzle of the remaining warm mustard sauce.

Serves 2 to 4, Preparation time approx 4 hours, Cooking time approx 20 minutes

Lamb Chops & Red Wine Vinegar

Lamb chops, loin, chump or leg	900 g	2 lb		
Red Wine Vinegar Marinade				
Olive oil	30 ml	2 tbsp	Sea salt	1/2 tsp
Red wine vinegar	15 ml	1 tbsp	Garlic powder	1/2 tsp
Dried rosemary		1 tsp	Ground black pepper	1/2 tsp
Dried oregano		1/2 tsp		

In a large bowl, combine the marinade ingredients, then add the lamb chops. Rub the marinade into the meat, cover with cling film, and refrigerate for 1 to 2 hours.

When cooking the chops, position the air fryer basket on the grill grate, close the lid, and choose the AIR FRY setting. Set the temperature to 190C and the timer for 15 minutes. Press START/STOP to start preheating.

When the ADD FOOD message appears, open the lid and place the chops in a single layer in the air fryer basket. Close the lid to start cooking. After 5 minutes, open the lid, flip the chops over, and close the lid to continue cooking. Check the chops periodically until they are cooked to your liking. Serve with sauce if desired.

Serves 2 to 4, Preparation time approx 2 hours, Cooking time approx 15 minutes

Leftover Crispy Lamb Pancakes

450 g/1 lb to 900 g/2 lb cooked lamb (leftover lamb, grilled or air fryer chops from our recipes, or implement one of our leg or shoulder recipes, or save up leftover lamb in the freezer until you have enough for this recipe. (Precooked meat is needed for this recipe)					
1 cucumber, peeled, with the middle removed so there are no seeds, and sliced					
20 to 40 Chinese pancakes (alternatively, instead of pancakes, use lettuce leaves)					
6 spring onions, finely sliced			1 bottle of Hoisin sauce		
Chinese 5 spice		1 tsp	Olive oil	15 ml	1 tbsp

Position a large shallow roasting tin that fits on the grill grate. Set the Woodfire dial to GRILL, set the temperature to HIGH, the timer for 30 minutes, and press START/STOP to initiate preheating.

While preheating, shred the lamb and place it in a large bowl. Add the olive oil and 5 spice, and mix thoroughly. When the ADD FOOD message appears, raise the lid and transfer the lamb mixture to the roasting tin, keeping the lid up. Stir the lamb frequently until it is hot, fully cooked, and crispy in some parts. Once cooked to your liking, turn off the Woodfire and leave the roasting tin with the lamb on the grill grate, keeping the lid up and stirring the lamb occasionally.

Prepare the other ingredients by arranging cucumber and onion strips on each guest's plate and a small dish of Hoisin sauce. Follow the instructions on the pancake packet to cook the pancakes, whether through quick steaming or microwaving, for a few seconds to warm them. Serve the lamb on each plate or allow guests to help themselves from the lamb in the roasting tin on the grill, which may still be warm.

Serves 2 to 4, Preparation time approx 10 minutes, Cooking time approx 30 minutes

Marinated Lamb Chops

Marinade of choice (or refer to our marinade recipes)	8 to 12 lamb chops	

Place the chops in a resealable plastic bag or large container, coat them with the marinade, and refrigerate for at least 4 hours to allow the marinade to soak in.

Add your preferred pellets to the smoke box, set the Woodfire to GRILL, and press the WOODFIRE FLAVOUR button. Set the temperature to HI, the timer to 15 minutes, and press START/STOP.

When the ADD FOOD message appears, open the lid and place the chops on the grill grate. Flip the chops halfway through cooking. Once they are cooked, remove and serve.

Serves 4 to 6, Preparation time approx 15 mins, Cooking time approx 15 minutes

Middle-Eastern Rack of Lamb

1 rack of lamb (8 bones). If untrimmed, ask the butcher to prepare it or cut off about 5 cm of fat from the tip of the bones and any meat and fat between those 5 cm of bones. Do not cut too much off that you cut into the meatiest part of the rack.		
Middle Eastern lamb rub (page 12), or rub of choice, or use 1/2 tbsp sea salt and 1/2 tbsp ground black pepper		
Butter	60 g	2 oz

Coat the lamb with butter, then apply the rub or sprinkle salt and pepper. Massage the rub or seasoning into all parts of the lamb and leave it to stand.

When you're ready to cook, set the Woodfire dial to GRILL, adjust the temperature to HIGH, set the timer for 10 minutes, and press START/STOP to start preheating. Once the ADD FOOD message appears, raise the lid and keep it open. Place the lamb firmly on the grill grate and sear each meat side for approximately 1 minute. Turn off the Woodfire and remove the lamb from the grill grate to prevent further cooking at this stage.

Set the Woodfire dial to ROAST, adjust the temperature to 190C, set the timer for 30 minutes, and press START/STOP to initiate preheating. After preheating, raise the lid and position the lamb on the grill grate with the rib side down. Close the lid to continue cooking. The meat is done when a meat thermometer inserted into the meat reads an internal temperature between 65 and 70C. Once cooked to your liking, remove the lamb and let it rest for 10 minutes before serving.

Serves 2, Preparation time approx 10 minutes, Cooking time approx 40 minutes

Shawarma Seasoned Lamb Skewers

1 leg or lean shoulder of lamb, excess fat removed and cut into 2.5 cm chunks

1 large onion, peeled, each layer cut into 2.5 cm squares

12 long wooden skewers, soaked in water for 30 minutes before use (or metal)

Lamb Shawarma Seasoning (great for all meats and vegetables)

Ground black pepper	1 tbsp	Dried oregano	1 tsp
Ground allspice	1 tbsp	Sea salt	1 tsp
Garlic powder	1 tbsp	Ground nutmeg	2 tsp
Ground cloves	2 tsp	Ground cardamom	2 tsp
Ground cinnamon	2 tsp	Chilli powder	1 tsp

Combine enough shawarma seasoning to lightly coat the lamb in a large bowl and add the lamb. Mix thoroughly and rest in the refrigerator for at least an hour. Just before cooking, skewer the lamb with a square of onion between each piece.

Add your choice of pellets to the smoke box and set the dial to GRILL, press WOODFIRE FLAVOUR, adjust the temperature to MEDIUM, and the timer for 20 minutes. Press START/STOP to start preheating. When the ADD FOOD message appears, lift the lid and place the skewers across the grill grate. Close the lid to commence cooking.

Flip the skewers halfway through cooking and check their progress often after that. When cooked to your satisfaction, remove them and serve with your favourite sauces or salad or fold them into wraps.

Serves 4 to 6, Preparation time approx 1 1/2 hours, Cooking time approx 20 minutes

Smoked Breast of Lamb

1 whole breast of lamb, from thin end to lamb ribs, cut in half to fit on the Woodfire grill grate. Remove the thin membrane from the surface of the ribs if possible. Score the breast lightly and diagonally but not on the rib side.			
Sea salt	1 tbsp	Ground black pepper	1 tbsp

Chill the lamb in the fridge for approximately an hour before cooking. Firmly rub the pepper and salt onto the lamb, covering the scored areas and other parts holding the seasoning. You can add more seasoning later once the lamb has released some fat for the seasoning to cling to.

Position the lamb on the grill grate with the ribs facing down. Close the lid. Add your preferred pellets to the smoker box. Set the Woodfire dial to SMOKER, adjust the temperature to about 130C, set the timer for 3 hours, and press START/STOP to begin.

After 45 minutes, lift the lid and check on the lamb. The thinner end will cook faster than the thicker lamb ribs end. Check every half an hour to monitor the cooking progress and remove the narrow end when it is cooked to your liking. If needed, this 45-minute mark is also a good time to add more pellets, salt, and pepper. Remove the lamb when it is cooked to your liking.

Serves 2, Preparation time approx 1 hour, Cooking time approx 3 hours

Smoked Lamb Cutlets

| Lamb cutlet chops | 900 g | 2 lb | Sea salt | | 2 tsp |
| Ground black pepper | | 2 tsp | Spray oil | | |

Chill the lamb for about 15 minutes before smoking. Put the lamb in the air fryer basket and position the basket on the grill grate. Close the lid. Add your preferred pellets to the smoke box. Set the dial to SMOKER, adjust the temperature to 120C, and set the timer for 30 minutes. Once the 30 minutes is up, turn off the Woodfire and remove the air fryer basket with the chops.

Set the Woodfire dial to GRILL, adjust the temperature to HI, set the timer for 20 minutes, and press START/STOP to initiate preheating. When the ADD FOOD message appears, lift the lid and place the chops on the grill grate. Keep the lid open and lightly spray the chops with oil. After approximately 5 minutes, flip the chops, lightly spray them with oil, and continue cooking until they are to your liking.

Smoked Leg Of Lamb

1 leg of lamb, boned and tied				
Red wine vinegar	60 ml	1/4 cup	Dried parsley	2 tsp
3 garlic cloves, grated			Dried thyme	2 tsp
Garlic powder		2 tsp	Sea salt	1 tsp
Paprika		2 tsp	Ground black pepper	1/2 tsp
Dried oregano		2 tsp	Juice of 1/2 a lemon	

Combine everything except the lamb in a large bowl. After mixing, place the lamb in the bowl and rub the mixture firmly all over (see our rubs and seasoning recipes for alternatives). Leave the meat marinating for 2 hours or, for added tenderness, cover the bowl containing the lamb and the mixture with cling film and refrigerate overnight.

Place the lamb on the grill grate and close the lid. Load your preferred pellets into the smoke box, set the dial to SMOKER, the temperature to 120C, and the timer for 2 hours. Press START/STOP to begin cooking. Check the lamb after 30 minutes and then every 15 minutes until its internal temperature reaches 65 to 70C using a thermometer, with the exterior appearing dark and well-cooked.

If the timer runs out, add increments of 10 minutes as needed, although you'll unlikely require extra time. The cooking duration may vary depending on how the lamb was rolled and the marinating time. Once cooked, remove the lamb from the woodfire, cover lightly with foil, and let it rest for 15 minutes before slicing.

Serves 4 to 6, Preparation time approx 2 hours, Cooking time approx 2 hours

The Art of Wet Brining

Ah, the art of brining. It's a little secret that both home cooks and professional chefs know can transform your cooking from good to gourmet, especially when it comes to smoking or barbecuing different kinds of meat. Brining may seem like an extra step you can't be bothered with, but it has many benefits that will elevate your Woodfire dishes and leave your guests asking for your secret.

Firstly, let's understand what brining is. Brining involves soaking your chosen cut of meat in a mixture of water, salt, and often a variety of other flavourings and seasonings. This process infuses the meat with these flavours, but the true magic lies in the science of it. The salt in the brine breaks down some of the meat's muscle fibres, making it more tender, and allows the meat to absorb the liquid, which in turn helps it stay juicy and succulent even after hours of smoking and other forms of cooking.

Brining is especially beneficial for leaner cuts of meat, like turkey, chicken, and pork, or lean meats, which tend to dry out more easily during cooking. The process creates a protective moisture barrier so that even as the meat cooks and loses its natural juices, it remains moist and flavourful thanks to the brine.

A wonderful thing about brining is how customisable it is. You can add a variety of herbs, spices, sugars, and even citrus fruits to your brine, creating a unique flavour profile for your meat. This is a great way to add a depth of flavour that rubs and marinades can't achieve, as the brine permeates the meat more deeply.

Another significant advantage is that the meat cooks more evenly. Because the salt modifies the protein structure of the meat, it allows heat to pass through more uniformly, preventing those unfortunate instances where the meat is undercooked in some spots and overcooked in others. Thus, your cooking becomes less stressful and more foolproof.

There's also a remarkable difference in texture. The breakdown of muscle fibres during brining results in a noticeable tenderness in the final product. That tough pork chop? It can be transformed into a tender, juicy cut that melts in your mouth simply by brining it.

Finally, brining also enhances the colour of the meat. That beautiful golden-brown you see on roast turkeys in food magazines? That's a sign the bird was likely brined before it went into the oven.

This general guide on brining various types of meat encourages experimentation with salt, herbs, spices, sugar, and different meat cuts and types. However, be cautious, as over-brining certain meats may produce a mushy texture. While many enthusiasts have unique methods and recipes, consider this guide a starting point.

Pork: Dissolve, by stirring, 50 g sea salt in 1 l water. Submerge pork chops, tenderloin, or other cuts in the brine for 1 to 4 hours (or 30 minutes per 500 g for large cuts). Mix more brine if needed. Pat dry before cooking.
Chicken: Dissolve, by stirring, 40 g sea salt in 1 l water. Submerge chicken pieces or whole chicken in the brine for 1 to 4 hours or up to 8 hours for an xl chicken. Mix more brine if needed. Rinse well, and pat dry before cooking.
Turkey: Dissolve, by stirring, 40 g sea salt in 1 l of water. Mix more brine if needed. Submerge the turkey (thawed if frozen) in the brine for 8 to 24 hours, depending on the size. Rinse well, and pat dry before roasting.
Beef: Dissolve, by stirring, 50 g sea salt in 1 l water. Mix more brine if needed. Submerge beef cuts like steaks or roasts in the brine for 1 to 2 hours. Longer for larger cuts. Rinse well, and pat dry before cooking.
Fish & Seafood: Dissolve, by stirring, 20 g sea salt in 1 l water. Mix more brine if needed. Submerge fish and seafood in the brine for 1 to 2 hours. Rinse well and pat dry.

Always use cold water for brining and refrigerate or store the brining meat in a cool, shaded spot, covered. Partially thawed meat can be brined, provided no solidly frozen parts exist. If you're incorporating sugar or want to dissolve the brine better, boil it while stirring continuously. Then, allow it to cool before refrigerating until cold before adding the meat.

Next Level Brine Recipes

Garlic Lemon Chicken

Cold water	2 l	4 pints	2 sprigs rosemary, chopped		2 tbsp
Sea salt	60 g	2 oz	4 bay leaves, fresh or dried		
2 lemons, quartered			Clear honey	60 ml	1/4 cup
10 sprigs parsley, fresh			6 garlic cloves, crushed		
7 sprigs thyme, fresh			Black peppercorns		1 tbsp

Pour roughly 1 litre of water into a large saucepan, ensuring it can hold the chicken and all the ingredients. Bring the water to a boil, add all the ingredients (excluding the chicken) and reduce the heat to medium. Stir until the salt is fully dissolved. Remove the pan from heat, add the remaining water to expedite cooling, and let it completely cool before placing it in the fridge for about 2 hours.

Once chilled, immerse the chicken or other poultry, ensuring it's positioned breast-side down for 8 to 12 hours. If the chicken floats, exposing part of it, ensure the breast faces down and is submerged. When ready to cook, remove the chicken from the brine, pat it dry, and proceed with your chosen cooking method. If cooking chicken portions, brine for 4 to 8 hours. Optionally, you can use a rub or seasoning of choice before cooking.

Apple Cider Pork Butt (or Shoulder)

Apple cider	1.5 l	3 pints	Worcestershire sauce	125 ml	1/2 cup
Water	1 l	2 pints	Garlic powder		2 tbsp
Apple cider vinegar	500 ml	1 pint	Onion powder		2 tbsp
Sea salt	80 g	1/3 cup	Classic Carolina rub/seasoning (page 9) or a pork rub of choice		2 tbsp
Brown sugar	100 g	1/2 cup			

Combine all the brine ingredients and stir until the salt and sugar have dissolved. Be sure the pork is almost entirely immersed in the brine. Cover with cling film and refrigerate for between 8 and 10 hours. When ready to cook, remove the pork from the brine, pat it dry, and proceed with your chosen cooking method. If cooking pork chops or more minor cuts, brine them for 4 to 6 hours. Optionally, you can also use a rub or seasoning before you cook. If you have a meat injector, you can inject a little of the brine into the meat at multiple places before cooking.

Delicate Herbed Fish

Cold water	1 l	2 pints	Coriander seeds		1 tsp
Sea salt	80 g	1/4 cup	Wakame (optional)		1 tsp
The zest of 1 lime			1 handful of mixed fresh dill, coriander and parsley		
The zest of 1 lemon					

Toast the coriander seeds in a pan large enough for the water over medium heat until they emit a light aroma, taking care not to burn them. Incorporate the water, optional wakame, and salt, then bring the mixture to a boil, stirring until the salt dissolves. Remove from heat and add zests and herbs. Allow the brine to cool in the fridge for 2 hours before use. When ready, immerse the fish fillets (skin on one side or off) in the brine for 30 minutes, then rinse with cold water and pat dry with a kitchen towel. Follow with your selected cooking method.

Traditional Lamb

A few sprigs of fresh rosemary or thyme, or 1 tsp of dried					
Black peppercorns		1 tsp	Sea salt	75 g	1/4 cup
1 stick celery, chopped			Cold water	2 l	4 pints
1 carrot, chopped			1 small onion, chopped		
2 dried bay leaves			2 garlic cloves, crushed		

In a large pan, boil 1 l of water with all ingredients except the lamb, ensuring the salt is dissolved. Let it cool completely. Submerge the lamb leg or shoulder in the brine and refrigerate for 12 to 24 hours. After brining, pat the lamb dry and follow your chosen cooking method. Limit the brining to 4 to 8 hours for minor cuts like chops.

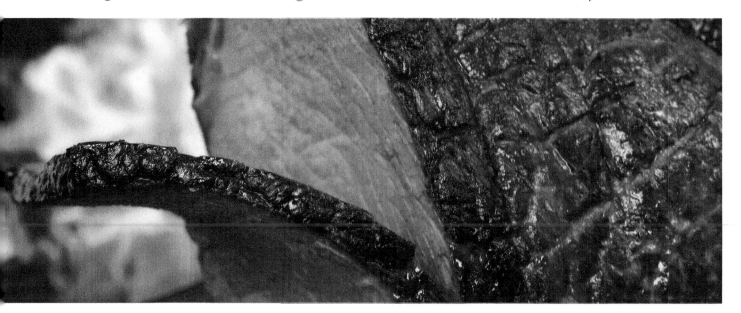

Dark Coffee & French Onion Beef

Warm water	2 l	4 pints	6 garlic cloves, finely grated		
Brewed French roast or dark coffee	1 l	2 pints	Worcestershire sauce	30 ml	2 tbsp
Sea salt	100 g	1/3 cup	Garlic powder		2 tsp
1 packet dry French onion soup mix			Onion powder		2 tsp
1 onion, diced			Ground black pepper		2 tsp

In a large pan over medium heat, stir warm water and all other ingredients until the soup powder and salt dissolve. Let the brine cool completely. Once cooled, immerse the beef in the brine and refrigerate for 8 to 12 hours, flipping occasionally. After brining, pat the beef dry and follow your chosen cooking method. Limit the brining to 2 to 6 hours for smaller cuts like steaks and ribs.

These select brine recipes offer a taste of how to customise them to your liking. The simplest method, using just water and salt, is quite popular. However, for those seeking adventure and curiosity in the kitchen, the possibilities are endless.

Flavours and seasonings: Experiment with different flavours and seasonings to enhance the taste of the meat. However, be cautious with strong or overpowering flavours, as they can mask the natural flavours of the meat.

Meat quality: Choose high-quality meat for brining. Poor-quality or spoiled meat will not improve significantly through the brining process and can pose health risks.

Brining time: Be mindful of the recommended brining time for the specific type and cut of meat you are brining. Brining for too short a time may not impart enough flavour, while brining for too long can lead to an overly salty or mushy texture.

Post-brining rinsing: Many people prefer to rinse all of their meat thoroughly under cold water to remove excess salt from the surface. You can experiment with that too, but the most important factor is to towel dry the meats after brining before seasoning and smoking and cooking.

By paying attention to these factors, you can successfully brine meat and achieve delicious, flavourful results.

MEAT INJECTION

The Woodfire can cook faster than other smokers and barbeques, so adding extra liquid inside the meat can make a huge difference in the texture and flavour. While brine is commonly used to inject meat for flavour and moisture, other liquids or marinades can also be used. Here are a few examples:

Marinades: You can inject the meat with various marinades, such as barbecue sauce, teriyaki sauce, soy sauce, citrus-based marinades, or herb-infused liquids. These can add different flavours and enhance the taste of the meat.

Broths or Stocks: Injecting meat with broth or stock, such as beef, chicken, or vegetable stock, can help add moisture and flavour. It is beneficial for lean cuts of meat that tend to dry out during cooking.

Butter or Fat: Injecting melted butter or other fats, such as olive or flavoured oils, can help keep the meat moist and enrich the flavour.

Rubs or Seasonings: While not liquids, you can inject the meat with dry rubs or powdered seasonings dissolved in a small amount of cold water. This can help infuse the meat with flavour from the inside.

Ensure the consistency is suitable for the injector and can flow easily through the needle. Also, ensure that the ingredients are safe for consumption and compatible with the meat you inject.

Experiment with different flavours and combinations to find what works best for your taste preferences and the meat you cook.

Here's a step-by-step guide on how to use a meat injector. If using brine, see our information on brining and brine recipes for ideas (pages 45-49).

Prepare the meat: Ensure that your meat is clean and free from any excess moisture. Pat it dry with paper towels if necessary. Make sure the meat is at a temperature that is safe for consumption, especially if you plan to marinate it for a while.

Assemble the meat injector: Fill the barrel with the prepared liquid, leaving a small space at the top for the plunger. This could involve taking the injector apart by unscrewing the plunger from the barrel.

Prime the injector: Hold the injector with the needle pointing up and slowly press the plunger until the liquid flows out of the needle. This step removes any air bubbles and ensures a smooth injection process.

Inject the meat: Insert the needle into the meat, targeting the thickest parts. Slowly depress the plunger to inject the liquid into the meat. Pull the needle out slightly and inject in different directions to distribute the liquid evenly. This way, you can target many parts with limited surface puncture holes.

Repeat the process: Continue injecting the liquid at various points throughout the meat, spacing the injections evenly. The number of injections required will depend on the size and type of meat you use.

Allow the liquid to distribute: Once you've completed the injection process, allow the liquid to distribute throughout the meat. You can either proceed with cooking immediately or let the meat marinate in the refrigerator for a few hours or overnight to enhance the flavour further.

Cook the meat: Follow your preferred cooking method for the type of meat you're using. Remember that the injected liquid may affect cooking times, so monitor the meat's internal temperature using a meat thermometer to ensure it reaches the desired level of doneness.

Remember to clean your meat injector thoroughly after each use by disassembling it and washing all the components with warm, soapy water. Rinse well and allow them to air dry, or use a clean towel before storing.

Air-Fried Mongolian Beef

Flank steak (Bavette) or skirt steak, sliced across the grain to about 1/2 cm thick and in small squares or strips of no more than 7.5 cm				450 g	1 lb

Mongolian Sauce

Water	125 ml	1/2 cup	Cornflour	60 g	1/2 cup
Demerara sugar	100 g	1/2 cup	4 garlic cloves, finely grated		
2 spring onions, chopped			Ginger, finely grated		1 tbsp
Toasted sesame seeds (optional)		1 tsp	Low-sodium soy sauce	125 ml	1/2 cup
Olive oil	15 ml	1 tbsp			

Place the sliced steak in a large bowl. Add the cornflour to the steak and toss until coated. Allow the steak to sit in the cornflour for 5 minutes.

Position the air fryer basket inside the Woodfire and close the lid. Set the Woodfire dial to AIR FRY, adjust the temperature to HI, and set the timer for 10 minutes. Press START/STOP to start preheating. When the ADD FOOD message shows, place the sliced steak in the air fryer basket and close the lid to begin cooking. Every few minutes, open the lid to toss the slices, ensuring even cooking and preventing them from sticking together.

Mongolian Sauce

Heat the olive oil in a large frying pan on the hob after the steak is cooked. Add the garlic and ginger, and cook for 30 seconds. Then, add the soy sauce, water, and demerara sugar, and stir to combine. Bring the mixture to a boil and cook for a few minutes, stirring occasionally until the sauce thickens. Add the steak to the sauce and continue cooking for 2 minutes, tossing the beef in the sauce. Serve with a sprinkle of chopped spring onions and sesame seeds (optional).

Serves 2 to 4, Preparation time approx 20 minutes, Cooking time approx 16 minutes

Chilli-Rubbed Skirt Steak

1 skirt steak, approx weight			900 g	2 lb

Chilli Rub

Chilli powder	1 tsp	Sea salt	1 tsp
Ground cumin	1 tsp	Ground black pepper	1/2 tsp
Dried oregano	1 tsp	Cinnamon	1/4 tsp

In a small bowl, mix all the rub ingredients well. Lightly coat the steak with oil and season it with the rub. Let the steak sit at room temperature for 30 minutes before grilling.

When ready, set the Woodfire dial to GRILL, adjust the temperature to HI, and set the timer for 10 minutes. Press START/STOP to begin preheating. Once the ADD FOOD message appears, lift the lid, place the steak on the grill grate, and close the lid to start cooking. Flip the steak halfway through the cooking process and continue to monitor it until it is cooked to your liking. Ideally, aim for an internal temperature between 63 and 70C. Remove the steak from the Woodfire and let it rest for 5 minutes before slicing it across the grain into slim slices.

Serves 2 to 4, Preparation time approx 30 minutes, Cooking time approx 10 minutes

East Asian Kofta Kebabs

Minced beef	450 g	1 lb	Breadcrumbs	30 g	1 oz
2 garlic cloves, grated			Soy sauce	15 ml	1 tbsp
Ginger, finely grated		1 tbsp	Toasted sesame seeds, crushed	15 g	2 tbsp
Gochujang paste	60 ml	1/4 cup	Sea salt		1/4 tsp
Sesame oil	15 ml	1 tbsp	Ground black pepper		1/4 tsp
Olive oil	15 ml	1 tbsp			
2 spring onions, finely chopped, including the green					
6 x approx 30 cm / 12-inch wooden skewers (soaked in water for 30 minutes before use, or use metal)					

Combine beef or lamb, breadcrumbs, garlic, spring onions, ginger, Gochujang paste, sesame oil, soy sauce, 1 tbsp crushed sesame seeds, salt, and pepper, mixing well. Divide the mixture into six equal portions, moulding each around a skewer while exposing ample skewer at both ends. Lightly brush with olive oil.

Add your choice of pellets to the smoke box, ideally sweet-scented ones. Set the dial to GRILL, press WOODFIRE FLAVOUR, adjust the temperature to HI and the timer for 15 minutes and press START/STOP to initiate preheating. Once the preheating finishes and the ADD FOOD message appears, open the lid and place the kebabs on the grill grate, aligning them with the grooves. Close the lid to commence cooking.

Flip the kebabs halfway through cooking and check their progress after 7 minutes. When cooked to your satisfaction, remove the kebabs, sprinkle with the remaining crushed sesame seeds, and serve with your favourite East Asian sauces (or see our sauce recipes)

Serves 2 to 3, Preparation time approx 30 mins, Cooking time approx 10 minutes

Easy Smoked Beef Short Ribs

Beef short ribs	1.5 to 2 kg	3 lb 5 oz to 4 lb 4 oz	Garlic granules		1 tsp
Sea salt		1 tsp	Ground black pepper		2 tsp
Add a dry seasoning instead of sea salt, black pepper, and garlic if desired (or refer to our seasoning recipes)					

Give the ribs a thorough trim to the fat and silver skin layer that won't break down during cooking. To ensure the best results, take your time. Coat the ribs evenly with salt, pepper, and garlic or the seasoning of choice.

Place the ribs on the grill grate. Add your choice of pellets to the smoke box and close the lid. Turn the dial to SMOKER, the temperature to 120C, and the timer for 5 hours ,and press START/STOP to begin cooking.

Check the ribs after 1.5 hours. If some areas appear dry, lightly spray them with water. Close the lid and check the internal temperature after half an hour. Keep cooking until the ribs are at the target internal temperature of 95C and once you are satisfied with the tenderness. Once cooked, wrap them in foil and leave them to rest for 30 minutes before serving.

Serves 2 to 4, Preparation time approx 20 mins, Cooking time up to 5 hours

Fillet & Mushroom Sauce

2 to 4 filet mignon steaks 4 to 5 cm / 1 1/2 to 2 inches thick (the filet mignon is the tenderest end of the beef fillet/tenderloin, so fillet steaks of the same thickness will do too.)					
Sea salt		1 tsp	Ground black pepper		1 tsp
Mushroom Sauce (alternatively, refer to our sauce recipes)					
Unsalted butter	60 g	2 oz	Sea salt		1/4 tsp
6 large white mushrooms, sliced			Ground black pepper		1/4 tsp
1/2 onion, grated			Beef broth or stock	250 ml	1 cup
1 garlic clove, finely grated			Heavy or double cream	125 ml	1/2 cup

While the Woodfire is preheating, set a hob or burner to medium-high heat and add the butter and sliced mushrooms. Cook the mushrooms in the butter until they are tender, then reduce the heat to a simmer and add the remaining ingredients. Time the sauce to coincide with the steaks being cooked. If there's a slight miscalculation, keep the sauce gently simmering on the lowest heat setting and smallest burner or element.

Season the steaks evenly with salt and pepper on all sides. Set the Woodfire to GRILL, adjust the temperature to HI, and set the timer for 10 minutes. Once ready, place the steaks on the grill, close the lid, and turn the steaks over halfway through the cooking time. Ensure the steaks are cooked until their internal temperature reaches a minimum of 50C. Serve with the mushroom sauce on or in a separate dish.

Serves 2 to 4, Preparation time approx 15 mins, Cooking time approx 20 minutes

Glazed Beef Short Ribs

1 skirt steak, approx weight					900 g	2 lb
Ground black pepper		3 tbsp	Sea salt			3 tbsp

Glaze

Apple juice	60 ml	1/4 cup	Clear honey		30 ml	2 tbsp
Golden syrup	30 ml	2 tbsp	Worcestershire sauce		30 ml	2 tbsp
Black treacle	30 ml	2 tbsp	1 beef stock cube			

Trim the ribs to remove excess fat and silver skin that won't break down during cooking. Combine the salt and pepper or use a rub of your choice, sprinkle and pat it all over the meat and leave to stand for 30 minutes. Place the meat on the grill grate and close the lid. Add pellets of choice to the smoke box and set the dial to SMOKER. Set the temperature to 120C, the timer for 5 hours, and press START/STOP to begin cooking.

Add another scoop after the first batch of pellets is close to finishing. If the pellets fail to ignite, press and hold the WOODFIRE FLAVOUR button for approximately 3 seconds until they ignite. If they still fail to ignite, turn off the Woodfire, switch the dial to SMOKER, set the temperature to 120C, the timer for 4 hours, and press START/STOP. While the meat cooks, mix the glaze ingredients well in a bowl.

After approximately 1 1/2 hours of cooking, lift the lid and check on the meat. If it appears too dry, spritz it with water. Close the lid to continue cooking. After three hours, open the lid, transfer the meat to a large shallow baking tray (a lot of the juices will have left drained from the meat at this point) and pour the glaze over it. Close the lid to continue cooking until the meat reaches an internal temperature of around 95C and is done to your liking. Remove the meat and let it rest for 15 minutes before slicing it into ribs and serving.

Serves 2 to 4, Preparation time approx 45 minutes, Cooking time approx 4 hours

Reverse Seared Picanha (Rump Cap)

1 Picanha (Rump Cap), divided into steaks 3 cm thick			
Ground black pepper	1 tbsp	Coarse sea salt	1 tbsp

Leave the steaks in the refrigerator, unwrapped, until you are ready to start smoking. Smoking is best done with cold meats. Dry any moisture from the steaks and rub the salt and pepper over them. Place the meat on the grill grate, close the lid, add your preferred pellets to the smoke box, set the Woodfire dial to SMOKER, adjust the temperature to 120C, and the timer for 1 hour. Press START/STOP to begin.

Aim for an internal meat temperature of approximately 65C for medium-rare using a thermometer. Searing will slightly increase the temperature. Once the desired internal temperature is reached, turn off the Woodfire. If the temperature has not been achieved, continue cooking until it is. Remove the steaks from the Woodfire.

Close the lid, set the Woodfire dial to GRILL, adjust the temperature to HI, and the timer for 15 minutes. Press START/STOP to begin preheating. Once the ADD FOOD message appears, lift the lid and place the steaks on the grill grate, pressing them down. Keep the lid open. Cook for about a minute or two on each side to achieve a nice sear and a slight further cooking.

Serves 4 to 6, Preparation time approx 20 minutes, Cooking time approx 1 hour

Reverse Seared Tomahawks

2 tomahawk steaks, 4 to 7 cm / 1 1/2 to 2 1/2 inches thick, bone-in (this can be done with any ribeye steak the same size and thickness, bone in or out)				
Sea salt		1 tbsp	Ground black pepper	1 tbsp
Olive oil	15 ml	1 tbsp		
2 tbsp rub of choice, optional, or just a little more salt and black pepper will be great (see our rub recipes)				

Firmly rub salt into the steaks and refrigerate uncovered for at least 4 hours, ideally overnight. When ready to grill, remove the steaks from the fridge, press in your chosen rub, or add more sea salt, pepper, and olive oil and place them on the grill plate. Next, load your pellets into the smoke box, and turn the dial to SMOKER. Set the temperature to 120C, the timer for 45 minutes, and press START/STOP to begin cooking.

Monitor their internal temperature with a thermometer, aiming for 50C. Once this temperature is reached, remove the steaks and place them on kitchen paper to absorb excess moisture. Next, press START/STOP to stop the Woodfire, turn the dial to GRILL, set the temperature to HI, and the timer for 10 minutes—though it won't be needed that long—then press START/STOP to begin cooking.

When the ADD FOOD message appears, lift the lid and return the steaks to the grill grate. Press the steaks down for 1 minute until a nice browned exterior on each side with the lid open. Finally, remove the steaks from the grill and serve.

Serves 4 to 8, Preparation time approx 4 hours , Cooking time approx 45 minutes

Rib Roast & Jacket Potatoes

Rib roast, boneless (aka standing rib roast)				2 to 2.5 kg	4 lb 4 oz to 5 lb 8 oz
Sea salt		1 tbsp	Ground black pepper		1 tbsp
Garlic powder		1 tbsp	Dried rosemary		1 tbsp
3 to 4 medium-sized Russet, Idaho, or King Edwards potatoes					
Olive oil	15 ml	1 tbsp	Extra salt, if desired		

In a bowl, combine 1 tbsp each of salt, pepper, garlic powder, and rosemary. Place the roast on a plate or dish, rub in the salt mixture, and refrigerate uncovered for at least 4 hours, or ideally, overnight. Remove the roast from the fridge one hour before cooking to reach room temperature.

Meanwhile, wash and dry the potatoes, then coat them with olive oil and a pinch of sea salt. Place the roast and the potatoes on the grill grate and close the lid. Load your choice of pellets into the smoke box and set the dial to SMOKER, the temperature to 120C, and the timer for 3 hours and press START/STOP to begin cooking. Using a thermometer, cook until the meat's internal temperature reaches 55 to 65C. Place the potatoes alongside the roast. Check the meat after the first hour, then every half-hour afterwards. It might take less time than 3 hours, depending on the meat.

Once cooking is finished, remove the roast and potatoes. You can choose to cover the roast with foil and let it rest for 15 minutes. Make slits in the potatoes, open them up, and add butter and sea salt. After the roast has rested, slice it into 2 cm thick slices across the grain, not with it, and serve with the jacket potatoes.

Serves 4 to 6, Preparation time approx 4.5 hours, Cooking time approx 3 hours

Small Brisket

Spray water for occasional spritzing

Rub of choise	3 tbsp	Brisket, approx weight	1.5 kg	3lb 5 oz

Trim excess fat from the brisket, but leave a thin layer and remove any silver skin. Season the brisket with your chosen rub, applying a little pressure as you do, and leave it to rest in the fridge for an hour before cooking. Fill the smoke box with pellets of choice, and place the brisket on the grill grate. Close the lid. Set the grill to SMOKER at 120C and timer for 4 hours. Press START/STOP to begin.

Cook the brisket until it reaches a probe-tender consistency, between 90 and 96C internal temperature, which may vary. Cooking time may vary depending on the cut and quality of the meat, so check on it hourly and give it a little spritzing, but don't drench it. Depending on your preferred level of smokiness, add more pellets once the others have burned down, but use at most two lots in total. Once the brisket has finished smoking, wrap it in foil or butcher paper and let it rest for an hour. You could place it in a cool box or a cool and shady part of the kitchen. You could also wrap a towel around the foil to help keep more heat in.

Serves 4 to 6, Preparation time approx 90 minutes, Cooking time approx 4 hours

Smoked Beef Burgers

Minced beef	900 g	2 lb	Sea salt		1/4 tsp
Ground black pepper		1/4 tsp	Dried mixed herbs of choice		1 tsp
Garlic powder		1/2 tsp	Onion powder		1/2 tsp
2 egg yolks					

Add your preferred pellets to the smoke box and select GRILL, followed by WOODFIRE FLAVOUR. Set the temperature to HI and the timer to 10 minutes. Next, press START/STOP to initiate preheating. While preheating, combine the mince, herbs, egg yolks, garlic, and onion powder in a large bowl.

Divide the mixture into 8 equal portions and shape them into burgers, about 2 cm thick. Use your thumb or fingers to create a 1 cm indent in the centre of each burger to help them retain their shape during cooking. Season with salt and pepper.

When the ADD FOOD message appears, open the lid and place the burgers on the grill grate, pressing them firmly down. Close the lid to start cooking. Flip the burgers halfway through and close the lid again to continue cooking. Once the cooking is complete, remove the burgers and serve them however you wish.

Serves 4 to 6, Preparation time approx 20 mins, Cooking time approx 10 minutes

Smoked Brisket

Rub of choice (or refer to our rub recipes)	80 g	1/2 cup
Brisket	3 to 3.5 kg	6 lb 9 oz to 7 lb 9 oz
Water or mix of apple cider vinegar and water for spritzing		

Trim excess fat from the brisket but leave about .5 cm thickness. Season the brisket with your chosen rub. Fill the smoke box with pellets and place the brisket on the Woodfire grill grate. Set the grill to SMOKER at 120C and timer for 8 hours. Depending on your preferred level of smokiness, add more pellets once the others have burned down, but use at most two lots in total.

Cook the brisket until it reaches a probe-tender consistency, between 90 and 95C internal temperature. Once the brisket has finished smoking to your liking, remove it from the Woodfire, wrap it in foil or butcher paper and let it rest for an hour. Cooking time may vary depending on the cut and quality of the meat, so check on it hourly. If the brisket is looking too dry at times, give it a slight spritzing with water.

Serves 8+, Preparation time approx 15 mins, Cooking time up to 8 hours

Smoked Sirloin Steak

2 to 4 sirloin steaks, 2.5 to 3.5 cm / 1 to 1 1/2 inch thick				
Sea salt and ground black pepper for seasoning (or refer to our seasoning recipes)				1 tbsp
Olive oil	30 ml	2 tbsp		

Add pellets of choice into the smoke box, set the dial to SMOKER at 120C and the timer for 40 minutes, and press START/STOP to begin. Season the steaks with salt, pepper, or your preferred seasoning. When the ADD FOOD message appears, place the steaks on the grill grate and close the lid.

Periodically check their internal temperature using a thermometer, removing them at 55 to 60C. Press START/STOP to end the process, regardless of the remaining time.

Set the dial to GRILL, temperature to HI, and timer for 10 minutes. Once heated, coat the steaks with avocado or olive oil using a spray or brush. With the lid open, sear each side and edge of the steaks for 30 seconds. Remove the steaks and let them rest for 5 minutes before serving.

Serves 2 to 4, Preparation time approx 10 mins, Cooking time approx 40 minutes

Smoked Pot Roast

Brisket, topside, or silverside roasting joint, fat and skin trimmed off	1.2 to 1.5 kg	2 lb 9 oz to 3 lb 5 oz
Seasoning of choice (or refer to our seasoning recipes)		1 tbsp
Beef stock or broth (the volume depends on the size of the roasting dish and contents)		
Vegetables of choice (potatoes, carrots, onions, celery, mushrooms, cabbage, etc.). Refer to the recipe instructions for more information		
3 garlic cloves, finely grated	Fresh rosemary, chopped	1 tbsp

After trimming excess fat and skin from the beef, season it generously with your chosen seasoning, patting it on. Allow the joint to rest for 20 to 30 minutes at room temperature. Chop and peel enough vegetables to serve 4 people as a side dish. Prepare sufficient beef stock to cover the vegetables when combined later, depending on the size of your roasting dish.

Place the joint on the grill grate and close the lid. Load your preferred pellets into the smoke box, set the dial to SMOKER, the temperature to 150C, and the timer for 1 hour. Press START/STOP to begin. Check the joint after 30 minutes and then every 10 minutes until its internal temperature reaches 70 to 75C using a thermometer.

Once the desired temperature is achieved, press START/STOP to turn off the Woodfire and remove the beef. Arrange a single layer of chopped vegetables in the roasting dish, place the joint on top so that it doesn't rise above the edge of the dish, and surround it with more vegetables, finely grated garlic, and rosemary. Pour in the beef stock, just covering the vegetables. Lightly cover the dish with foil and place it on the grill grate.

Turn the dial to ROAST, set the temperature to 150C, and the timer for 2 hours. Close the lid and press START/STOP to start cooking. After 1 hour, check if the vegetables are tender, and continue checking every 15 minutes until they reach your desired tenderness and the meat is tender. Remove from the grill and serve.

Serves 4, Preparation time approx 30 mins, Cooking time approx 3 hours

Smoked Ribeye & Peppercorn Sauce

2 to 4 ribeye steaks, about 2.5 cm thick			Coarse sea salt		1 tbsp
Olive oil	15 ml	1 tbsp	Ground black pepper		1 tbsp

Jamie Oliver Style Peppercorn Sauce

Black peppercorns		1 tbsp	Sea salt		1/4 tsp
Unsalted butter		1 tbsp	Beef stock or broth	180 ml	3/4 cup
Olive oil	15 ml	1 tbsp	Worcestershire sauce	15 ml	1 tbsp
2 shallots, peeled, finely chopped			Double cream	125 ml	1/2 cup

Season the steaks with olive oil, salt, and pepper. Add pellets of choice to the smoke box, turn the dial to GRILL, and press the WOODFIRE FLAVOUR button. Set the temperature to HI and the timer for 10 minutes. Press START/STOP to start preheating. Once the ADD FOOD message appears, place the steaks on the grill grate and close the lid to begin cooking. After 5 minutes, turn the steaks over and close the lid to continue cooking until they reach an internal temperature of around 65C or until they are cooked to your liking.

Peppercorn Sauce

While the grill is preheating and cooking, coarsely crush 3 tsp of the peppercorns, avoiding over-crushing, and set them aside. Melt butter and oil in a frying pan over medium heat. Add shallots, salt, and crushed and whole peppercorns, cooking until the shallots soften slightly, about 3 to 4 minutes. Add stock and Worcestershire sauce and briefly boil, then simmer until reduced by up to half. Stir in the cream and return to a simmer, then remove from heat and serve.

Serves 2 to 4, Preparation time approx 15 minutes, Cooking time approx 10 minutes

Smoked Roast Beef

Top round or topside beef, approx weight				900 g	2 lb
1 tsp plain flour	1 tsp	1/4 tsp sea salt			1/2 tsp
1 tsp mustard powder	1 tsp	1/4 tsp ground black pepper			1/2 tsp

Combine the flour, mustard powder, salt, and pepper, and coat the mixture on the beef.

Add your preferred pellets to the smoke box, set the Woodfire dial to ROAST, press the WOODFIRE FLAVOUR button, adjust the temperature to 160C, set the timer for 1 hour, and press the START/STOP button to initiate preheating.

When the ADD FOOD message appears, lift the lid, place the beef on the grill grate, and close the lid to begin cooking. A suitable internal temperature for the meat is around 60C. Once the desired temperature is reached, remove the beef and let it rest for 20 minutes before slicing.

Serves 4, Preparation time approx 10 minutes, Cooking time approx 1 hour

Smoked T-Bone Steaks & Garlic Butter

2 large t-bone steaks or porterhouse steaks, large enough to fit next to each other on the grill grate				
Ground black pepper (instead of the salt and pepper, try one of our rub or seasoning recipes or one of your choice)				1 tsp
Sea salt	1 tsp			
Garlic Butter				
Unsalted butter, slightly softened	120 g	4 oz	Ground black pepper	1/4 tsp
3 garlic cloves, finely grated			Sea salt	1/4 tsp
Worcestershire Sauce	5 ml	1 tsp	Fresh parsley, finely chopped	1 tbsp

Garlic Butter

In a bowl, combine the ingredients for the garlic butter. Mix thoroughly using a fork. Transfer the mixture onto a sheet of cling film. Shape the butter into a log, approximately 4 cm thick using the cling film. Seal the ends tightly by twisting the cling film. Roll the wrapped butter back and forth to create an even log shape. Refrigerate until firm. When ready to use, unwrap the butter and cut slices according to your preference. Place a slice or two on the still-warm or hot steaks when serving.

Steaks

Season the steaks firmly with salt and pepper or your choice of rub. Add your preferred pellets to the smoke box, set the Woodfire dial to GRILL, press the WOODFIRE FLAVOUR button, adjust the temperature to HI, set the timer for 10 minutes, and press START/STOP to begin preheating. Once the ADD FOOD message appears, lift the lid and place the steaks on the grill grate. Close the lid to start cooking. Flip the steaks after 5 minutes and periodically check their internal temperature with a meat thermometer until they reach 63 to 70C or cook to your liking.

Serves 2, Preparation time approx 15 minutes, Cooking time approx 10 minutes

Smoked Rump Tail (Tri-Tip)

1 rump tail (tri-tip), excess fat and silver skin removed			
Ground black pepper	2 tbsp	Sea salt	2 tbsp
(Alternatively, try the extra ingredients from the Texas Style rub (page 8) instead of the black pepper and sea salt. No more than 4 tbsp)			

Coat the trimmed rump tail with the seasoning. If you're having trouble sticking the seasoning, use the smallest olive oil as a binder, rub it all over the meat, and pat it on the seasoning.

Place the meat on the grill grate and close the lid. Add pellets of choice to the smoke box, turn the Woodfire dial to SMOKER, set the temperature to 120C, and set the timer for 2 hours. Press START/STOP to begin cooking.

Check on the meat after about 30 minutes and check the temperature. Once the temperature hits about 55C, it is done. But if not done to your liking, you could continue to run out the clock, making sure not to overcook. Remove from the Woodfire, wrap in foil, and rest for 20 minutes or leave in the Woodfire for 10 minutes in the residual heat after switching Woodfire off.

Serves 4 to 8, Preparation time approx 30 minutes, Cooking time approx 2 hours

Smoky Bacon Burgers

Minced beef		900 g	2 lb	2 egg yolks		
Sea salt			1/4 tsp	Ground black pepper		1/2 tsp
Mixed dried herbs of choice			1 tsp	Garlic powder		1/2 tsp
Onion powder			1/2 tsp	8 burger buns		
4 rashers of bacon diced						
Fillings						
Iceberg lettuce				2 large tomatoes, sliced		
1 onion, peeled, sliced				Pickle slices		
Tomato ketchup/mustard (or refer to our sauce recipes), 8 slices of cheese of choice, long toothpicks or short skewers						

Place bacon rashers on the grill grate and close the lid. Add your chosen pellets to the smoke box, select GRILL, press WOODFIRE FLAVOUR, set the temperature to HI and the timer for 10 minutes, then press START/STOP to preheat.

Combine mince, egg yolks, sea salt, pepper, dried herbs, garlic powder, and onion powder in a large bowl during preheating. Divide the mixture into eight equal balls and shape them into beef burgers slightly smaller than the buns. Create an indent in each beef burger's centre, roughly half the depth.

Once the ADD FOOD message appears, position the beef burgers on the grill grate beside the preheating bacon and close the lid. Flip beef burgers and bacon midway through cooking. When done, assemble the burgers with fillings, ensuring the cheese slice is between the beef and bacon to melt slightly. Assemble the smoky bacon burger to your preference, using a long toothpick or skewer to hold it together if needed.

Serves 4 to 8, Preparation time 30 mins, Cooking time approx 10 minutes

Smoky Beef Jerky

Beef silverside/top round, sliced at about 5 mm / 1/5 inch thick across the grain (aka: against the grain)	450 g	1 lb
Marinade of choice (or refer to our jerky marinade recipes)		

Place the marinade and beef strips in a large resealable plastic bag, massaging the bag to ensure the marinade evenly coats the beef. Refrigerate for 8 hours. Afterwards, remove the beef from the marinade, discarding excess liquid. Arrange the beef in a single layer in the air fryer basket, grill grate, or wire rack, and close the lid.

Add your chosen pellets to the smoke box. Set the mode to DEHYDRATE, temperature to 65C, and timer for 6 hours. Press WOODFIRE FLAVOUR and START/STOP to begin cooking.

Check the beef jerky after 4 hours, and continue cooking if a crisper texture is desired. Once done, open the lid and remove the beef jerky. Store in an airtight container for up to 2 weeks at room temperature.

Serves 2 to 4, Preparation time approx 20 mins, Cooking time approx 4 hours

Smoky Meatloaf

Minced beef	900 g	2 lb	Panko or coarse breadcrumbs	50 g	1/2 cup
4 garlic cloves, grated			Sea salt		1/4 tsp
1 medium onion, diced			Ground black pepper		1/4 tsp
2 large eggs			Paprika		1 tsp
Fresh parsley, finely chopped		1 tbsp	Parmesan cheese, grated/shredded	20 g	2 tbsp
BBQ sauce or tomato ketchup (or refer to our sauce recipes)				80 ml	1/3 cup

In a large bowl, combine all ingredients and mix well. Divide the mixture evenly into two portions and shape each into a loaf. Position the loaves in the air fryer basket, place the basket on the grill grate, and close the lid. Add your chosen pellets to the smoke box. Turn the dial to SMOKER, set the temperature to 150C, and the timer for 45 minutes. Press START/STOP to start cooking.

Check the loaves from time to time with a thermometer. The ideal internal temperature should reach between 65 and 70C, so remove the loaves once this is achieved and before they burn. Once cooking is finished, remove the air fryer basket and let the meatloaves rest for 5 minutes before slicing. If preferred, brush on some BBQ or tomato sauce before serving.

Serves 4 to 6, Preparation time approx 15 mins, Cooking time approx 45 minutes

Steak & Asparagus Spears

| Olive oil | 30 ml | 2 tbsp | Ground black pepper | | 1/2 tsp |
| Sea salt | | 1/4 tsp | Asparagus spears | 450 g | 1 lb |

4 to 6 steaks of choice, 200 to 300 g / 7 to 10 oz each about 2.5 cm / 1 inch thick

Add your choice of pellets to the smoke box and close the lid. Turn the dial to GRILL and press WOODFIRE FLAVOUR. Set the temperature to HI and the timer for 10 minutes. Press START/STOP. Preheating will begin.

While the grill preheats, add the oil, salt, and pepper to a large bowl and toss the steaks in the mixture. Remove them and toss the asparagus spears in the remaining mixture.

Once the preheating is complete and ADD FOOD appears, place the steaks on the grill grate, pressing them down firmly to create nice dark lines. Add the asparagus to any available space around the steaks. Close the lid to begin cooking. After 5 minutes, turn over the steaks and asparagus, and close the lid until cooked.

Serves 4 to 6, Preparation time approx 10 mins, Cooking time approx 10 minutes

Is That Blood On The Plate?

Is that blood on your plate? Is the liquid seeping out, blood? You might think so, especially with a rare steak still sporting a red, almost blood-like colour. But the answer, surprisingly enough, is no, it isn't blood. The moment cattle are butchered, all the blood is drained from their bodies. So, when you get your hands on a raw steak at your local butcher's or supermarket, there's virtually no blood left. So, what's the red stuff?

It's something called myoglobin. Myoglobin is a protein that resides in the muscle tissue of many animals, including our bovine friends that provide our beloved steaks. This protein's job is to carry and store oxygen in muscle cells. The protein can bind oxygen and keep it ready when the muscle needs to act. The myoglobin in the steak is a deep purple colour when raw. But you know how the steak goes from red to pink to brown as you cook it? That's the myoglobin reacting to the heat. Heat changes the myoglobin's structure when the steak hits your grill. This structural change also causes a colour change, and that's why your steak changes colour as it cooks.

When you see juices seeping out of the steak as it cooks, you see mostly water. As the myoglobin changes colour, some dissolves in the water inside the steak. This combination of water and myoglobin forms the juices that seep out as the steak cooks. It's not blood but water and myoglobin. You might also find some of the juices from your steak are a bit fatty. As the steak cooks, any fat within it begins to melt. Some melted fat can escape and mix with myoglobin-filled water, making the juices more flavoursome. This mix of fat, water, and myoglobin gives your steak its aroma and flavour.

Interestingly, the amount of juice that comes out of your steak and the colour of those juices can vary depending on how you cook your steak. You might have noticed that a well-done steak doesn't have as much juice as a medium or rare steak. That's because the longer you cook a steak, the more the proteins, including myoglobin, squeeze out water. When you cook a steak too well done, almost all of the myoglobin has changed colour, and much of the water has been squeezed out. This is why well-done steak is drier and doesn't have as much of a red or pink colour.

On the other hand, if you cook a steak to rare, you're only heating it enough to start the myoglobin denaturing process but not enough to finish it. This leaves plenty of myoglobin in its original state, giving the steak that deep red, rare colour. Plus, because you're not cooking the steak for as long, you're not squeezing out as much water, leaving the steak juicier.

The Benefits Of Woodfire's AIR FRY

Air frying enables you to prepare tasty and healthier versions of your favourite fried foods quickly and easily. Instead of immersing the food in oil, air frying employs hot air to cook the food. The large Woodfire air fryer basket allows air to circulate above, below, and on all sides. This method results in a crispy and crunchy texture without the need for excess fat and calories. Furthermore, air frying usually consumes less energy than other methods, making it an efficient and cost-effective option.

SAFE TO USE: Air frying utilises a convection mechanism, circulating hot air around the food to create a crispy exterior while keeping the inside tender. Ideal for those seeking a healthier alternative to traditional frying, air frying can recreate the texture of deep-fried food with minimal oil use.

REDUCED HARMFUL COMPOUNDS: When foods are cooked at high temperatures using any cooking method, they can produce harmful compounds such as acrylamide, heterocyclic amines, and polycyclic aromatic hydrocarbons. Consumption of these compounds can pose a health risk to humans. Therefore, it is worth noting that cooking any food at high temperatures using any cooking method can form these harmful compounds. While meat is a significant contributor, other foods cooked at high heat can also create these compounds. According to research, air frying has been found to potentially decrease the level of acrylamide by as much as 90%. Studies have indicated that air frying can reduce the presence of potentially cancer-causing compounds like heterocyclic amines.

WEIGHT LOSS: Air frying utilises hot air for cooking food, and air frying is often marketed as a healthier alternative to traditional deep frying due to the lower requirement of cooking oil. As a result, the calorie and fat content of air-fried food may be reduced. Bear in mind that the health benefits of air frying may depend on the ingredients and cooking techniques employed. For example, cooking processed frozen foods containing high levels of salt, sugar, and artificial additives may not result in a healthy outcome, unlike using the air fryer mode for cooking fresh vegetables.

FOOD ROTATION: When using all Woodfire modes, we can usually rely on the timer or internal food temperatures to indicate when the food is ready. However, when air frying, it's crucial to periodically check and flip the food during cooking to ensure even hot air circulation. This will help achieve evenly cooked results.

Woodfire Desserts

BBQ desserts play a significant role in rounding off a great barbecue experience. Here's why:

Completes the Meal: Like any other meal, a dessert can provide a satisfying conclusion, leaving guests with a lasting impression of the overall experience.

Balances the Flavours: BBQ dishes often have strong, savoury flavours. A sweet dessert can provide a perfect contrast, balancing out the palate.

Adds Variety: Offering desserts provides more options for guests. This is particularly beneficial for those who prefer something lighter after a heavy meal or those with a sweet tooth.

Creates a Full BBQ Experience: A BBQ is as much about the ambience and experience as the food. Serving dessert can extend the enjoyment of the BBQ and emphasise the theme.

Cater to Everyone: Desserts ensure everyone's preferences are catered to, mainly when a variety is provided.

Remember, the best BBQ desserts are often simple and easy to eat, reflecting the casual and relaxed nature of wood-fired cooking.

Caramel sauce, saving a little for drizzling, or use the below ingredients and recipe					80 ml	1/3 cup
4 to 6 apples			Chopped walnuts or pecans		30 g	1 oz
Sultanas or chocolate chips	80 g	3 oz	Ground cinnamon			1/2 tsp
Quick oatmeal	30 g	1 oz	Butter, softened		30 g	1 oz
Sugar	10 g	1 tbsp				

Caramel Sauce

Swiftly caramelising sugar is essential to avoid burning. Use a large, heavy-bottomed saucepan over medium heat, stirring vigorously as the sugar melts. As it melts, reduce the heat and continue stirring until fully liquified. Stop stirring once it's melted, then add the butter, continuing to whisk until it's melted. Remove the pan from the heat, wait a few seconds, then gradually add cream while whisking. The mixture may foam up. Keep whisking until smooth, then let the caramel cool until needed.

Baked Apples

Set the Woodfire dial to BAKE, the temperature to 180C and the timer for 20 minutes. Press START/STOP start preheating. Meanwhile, core the apples, leaving a half-inch at the bottom, and prepare a cavity for the filling about an inch wide. Mix all ingredients except the apples and some of the caramel sauce, and stuff the apples. Encase each apple loosely in foil, ensuring a tight seal.

When the ADD FOOD message appears, place the foil-wrapped stuffed apples on the grill grate and close the lid to cook. After around 15 minutes, check an apple for tenderness, continuing to monitor the apples until they are cooked to your preference. Serve the cooked apples with the remaining caramel sauce.

Serves 2 to 6, Preparation time approx 20 minutes, Cooking time approx 20 minutes

Caramel Bananas & Ice Cream

2 to 4 bananas, unpeeled			Ground cinnamon		1/2 tsp
Caramel sauce, shop-bought (or a topping dessert sauce of your choice)				125 ml	1/2 cup
Walnuts, chopped (or another dessert extra, such as crushed chocolate)				60 g	2 oz
Ice cream of choice					

Place the air fryer basket in the Woodfire. Add your choice of pellets to the smoke box, turn the dial to AIR FRY, and press the WOODFIRE FLAVOUR button. Set the temperature to 190C and the timer for 10 minutes—press START/STOP to start the preheating.

Peel the bananas and slice them lengthwise. Lightly sprinkle sweet cinnamon over the bananas.

When the ADD FOOD message appears, open the lid and place the bananas in the air fryer basket cut side up. Close the lid to begin cooking.

Once the bananas are cooked, remove them from the basket and transfer them to plates or bowls. Add scoops of ice cream, chopped nuts, and a drizzle of caramel sauce.

Serves 2 to 4, Preparation time approx 10 mins, Cooking time approx 10 minutes

Doughnuts

Lukewarm milk	250 ml	1 cup	1 egg		
Active dry yeast or instant yeast		1 tbsp	Unsalted butter, melted		
Sugar (plus 1 tsp for shaking)		1 tbsp	Plain flour	380 g	3 1/4 cup
Sea salt		1/2 tsp	Olive oil or coconut spray		

Combine lukewarm milk, 1 tsp of sugar, and the yeast in a bowl. Allow it to sit for 10 minutes until foamy. If there's no foaming, it could be due to incorrect milk temperature or issues with the yeast. In such cases, use properly heated milk and fresh, usable yeast. Add salt, egg, melted butter, and 250 g of flour to the milk mixture. Mix until well combined, then add the remaining flour until the dough becomes firm and non-sticky. Knead the dough for 5 minutes until it is elastic and smooth.

Cover the dough in a clean, lightly greased bowl with cling film. Allow the dough to rise in a warm place until it doubles in size. To check if the dough is ready, make a dent and see if it holds its shape. Transfer the dough onto a floured surface and gently roll it out to a thickness of approximately 1.2 cm. Use a 7 cm round cutter to cut out 10 to 12 doughnuts and a 2.5 cm round cutter to remove the centres. Place the doughnuts and doughnut holes on lightly floured parchment paper, cover loosely with more parchment paper, and let them rest for about 30 minutes.

To begin cooking, position the air fryer basket on the grill grate and close the lid. Set the Woodfire dial to AIR FRY, the temperature to 180C, the timer for 10 minutes, and press START/STOP to initiate preheating. Once the ADD FOOD message appears, open the lid, lightly spray the air fryer basket with oil, and arrange the doughnuts in a single layer. Give the doughnuts a light oil spray and close the lid to commence cooking. Check on them after 5 minutes and periodically after that until they become golden brown. Repeat the process with the remaining doughnuts or doughnut holes. Once cooked, allow them to cool slightly before sprinkling them with sugar or placing them in a bag and shaking sugar onto them.

Serves 4 to 6, Preparation time approx 1 hour, Cooking time approx 10 minutes

Grilled Fruit Skewers

Prepare enough sliced, chopped, and whole fruits to fit on 8 to 10 skewers. Choosing firm fruits, not soft or overripe ones, is best for grilling. Your options are nearly limitless: melons, pears, apples, avocados, peaches, pineapple, bananas, figs, and strawberries, among many others, and pretty much any that can maintain their shape during grilling

8 to 10 wooden skewers, soaked in water for 20 minutes before use					
Olive oil	30 ml	2 tbsp	Sea salt		1 tsp
Clear honey	30 ml	2 tbsp			

Set the Woodfire to GRILL, adjust the temperature to high, set the timer for 15 minutes, and then press START/STOP to preheat. Load the skewers with the fruits, brush them with olive oil and sprinkle lightly with some salt.

Once the ADD FOOD message appears, place the skewers on the grill grate and close the lid to start cooking. Check and rotate the skewers every 5 minutes. Once the fruits are grilled to your preference, transfer them to a dish, drizzle with honey, and serve.

Serves 2 to 4, Preparation time approx 20 minutes, Cooking time approx 15 minutes

Grilled Pineapple

1 large pineapple, skin removed, sliced lengthways				
1/3 cup brown sugar	60 g	1/3 cup	Ground cinnamon	1 tsp
1/2 cup butter, melted				

To grill pineapple on the Woodfire, turn the dial to GRILL, set the temperature to HI, and the timer for 10 minutes. Press START/STOP to begin preheating. While the Woodfire is preheating, whisk together the butter, brown sugar, and cinnamon. If the mixture is too thick, microwave it for a few seconds. Coat the pineapple slices evenly in the mix.

Once the ADD FOOD message appears, place the pineapple onto the grill grate, close the lid, and press START/STOP to start cooking. Flip the pineapple after 5 minutes and continue cooking until it reaches your desired level of doneness.

Serves 2 to 4, Preparation time approx 30 mins, Cooking time approx 10 minutes

Meringue Cookies

Egg whites			Sugar		200 g	1 cup
1 pinch of sea salt						

In a mixing bowl, combine the egg whites and salt. Beat them using an electric handheld whisk, by hand, or in a food processor until frothy. Whilst whisking, gradually add the sugar. Continue whisking until the mixture stiffens and you can form upright peaks.

Set the Woodfire dial to AIR FRY, temperature to 150C, timer for 30 minutes, and press START/STOP to begin preheating. When the ADD FOOD message is displayed, open the lid and place a sheet of baking paper or grill mat on the grill grate, avoiding burning yourself. Use a spoon, piping bag, or a plastic bag with a small hole in the corner to quickly place the mixture in biscuit-sized shapes on the paper or mat.

Close the lid to start cooking. Monitor the meringue every 5 minutes until they are cooked to your liking, ensuring they do not brown on the surface. Opening the lid frequently may cause cracks in the meringue, resembling a "biscuit-like" effect. Once cooked to your liking, remove the meringue biscuits to cool and firm up.

Serves 4 to 6, Preparation time approx 20 minutes, Cooking time approx 30 minutes

Roasted Whole Pineapple & Cinnamon

1 fresh pineapple, skin removed			Zest of one small orange or one small orange		
1 tsp cinnamon powder		1 tsp	Ginger, finely grated		1 tsp
Anis, or Sambuca	30 ml	2 tbsp	Clear honey	15 ml	1 tbsp

Turn the Woodfire dial to ROAST, set the temperature to 180C and the timer for 20 minutes, then press START/STOP to preheat. In the meantime, mix all ingredients, except the pineapple, in a large shallow bowl. Then coat the pineapple thoroughly by rolling it in the mixture and rubbing it firmly by hand or applying with a brush.

Once the ADD FOOD message appears, place the whole pineapple on the grill grate and close the lid. After 10 minutes, turn the pineapple, checking and rotating every 5 minutes until it is golden brown, tender, but firm when poked with a knife. Once done, remove from the Woodfire and serve.

Serves 2 to 4, Preparation time approx 10 minutes, Cooking time approx 20 minutes

FISH - SHELLFISH - CRUSTACEANS

63C

POULTRY

74C

BEEF

50C

LAMB

50C

PORK

75C

BEEF STEAKS

BLUE/BLEU	55C
RARE	60C
MEDIUM RARE	63C
MEDIUM	71C
WELL DONE	77C

Top chefs press steaks with their fingers to gauge doneness instead of puncturing the meat with a thermometer. However, mastering this technique requires practice.

The recommended temperatures listed serve as minimum guidelines to eliminate harmful bacteria and reduce the risk of foodborne illnesses during cooking. However, as these are minimum temperatures, practice is essential to achieve the perfect results tailored to your taste preferences.

DEHYDRATE - Lid Closed - DEHYDRATE Mode

These charts guide cooking various foods. However, it is essential to note that individual preferences may not align with the settings suggested in the charts, as some people may favour their food rare, medium-rare, well-done, and so forth. Therefore, we have added blank charts for you to customise as you'd like and lined pages for recording notes, which might include changing cooking times and temperatures.

INGREDIENT	PREPARATION	DEHYDRATE TEMP	DEHYDRATE TIME
FRUITS & VEGETABLES - dehydrate			
Apples	Cut into 5 mm slices, remove core, rinse in lemon water, pat dry	55C	6 to 8 hours
Asparagus	Cut in 2.5 cm pieces, blanch	55C	6 to 8 hours
Bananas	Peel, cut into 1 cm slices	55C	6 to 8 hours
Beetroots	Peel, cut into 5 mm slices	55C	6 to 8 hours
Aubergine	Peel, cut into 6 mm slices, blanch	55C	6 to 8 hours
Fresh Herbs	Rinse, pat dry, remove stems	55C	4 hours
Ginger Root	Cut into 1 cm slices	55C	6 hours
Mangoes	Peel, cut into 1 cm slices, remove seed	55C	6 to 8 hours
Mushrooms	Clean with soft brush (do not wash)	55C	6 to 8 hours
Pineapple	Peel, cut into 1 cm slices, remove core	55C	6 to 8 hours
Strawberries	Cut in half or in 1.3 cm slices	55C	6 to 8 hours
Tomatoes	Cut into 1 cm slices; blanch if planning to rehydrate	55C	6 to 8 hours
MEAT, POULTRY, FISH - dehydrate			
Beef Jerky	Cut into 5 mm slices, marinate overnight	65C	4 to 6 hours
Chicken Jerky	Cut into 5 mm slices, marinate overnight	65C	4 to 6 hours
Turkey Jerky	Cut into 5 mm slices, marinate overnight	65C	4 to 6 hours
Salmon Jerky	Cut into 5 mm slices, marinate overnight	65C	4 to 6 hours

Grill Chart - Lid Closed - GRILL Mode

POULTRY - grill					
Chicken Breast (boneless)	2 to 4	Marinate or season as desired	HI	15 to 25 mins	Flip halfway
Chicken Breast (bone-in)	2 to 4	Marinate or season as desired	HI	25 to 30 mins	Flip halfway
Chicken Leg With Thigh (bone-in)	2 to 4	Marinate or season as desired	HI	20 to 30 mins	Flip halfway
Chicken Sausage	10 to 16	Marinate or season as desired	HI	10 to 20 mins	Flip halfway
Chicken Tenderloins	8 to 12	Marinate or season as desired	HI	10 to 15 mins	Flip halfway
Chicken Thighs (boneless)	8 to 10	Marinate or season as desired	HI	15 to 20 mins	Flip halfway
Chicken Thighs (bone-in)	8 to 10	Marinate or season as desired	HI	15 to 25 mins	Flip halfway
Chicken Wings	15 to 25	Marinate or season as desired	HI	15 to 25 mins	Flip halfway
Turkey or Chicken Burgers	6 to 8	Season with salt and pepper	HI	8 to 15 mins	Flip halfway

BEEF - grill					
Beef Burgers (thick)	4 to 6	Season with salt and pepper	HI	8 to 15 mins	Flip halfway
Fillet Steak	4 to 6 3 to 5 cm thick	Marinate or season as desired	HI	10 to 25 mins	Flip halfway
Flank Steak (Bavette)	1 to 2 450 to 650 g 2.5 cm thick	Marinate or season as desired	HI	12 to 25 mins	Flip halfway

BEEF - grill - continued					
Hot Dog Sausages	8 to 12		HI	8 to 12 mins	Flip halfway
Sirloin Steak	2 to 4 2.5 to 3 cm thick	Marinate or season as desired	HI	8 to 15 mins	Flip halfway
Ribeye Steak	2 to 4 2.5 to 3 cm thick	Marinate or season as desired	HI	8 to 15 mins	Flip halfway
Skirt Steak	2 to 4 2 to 3 cm thick	Marinate or season as desired	MED	8 to 15 mins	Flip halfway
Rump Steak	2 to 4 2 to 3 cm thick	Marinate or season as desired	MED	8 to 15 mins	Flip halfway

PORK & LAMB - grill					
Baby Back Ribs	1 to 2 racks divided in half	Marinate or season as desired	MED	1 hour+	Flip frequently
Bacon (thick cut)	6 to 12 rashers		MED	8 to 10 mins	Flip halfway
Rack of Lamb	1 full rack or about 8 bones		HI	15 to 25 mins	Flip halfway
Pork or Lamb Steaks	4 to 8	Marinate or season as desired	HI	10 to 15 mins	Flip halfway
Pork or Lamb Chops	4 to 8	Marinate or season as desired	HI	12 to 18 mins	Flip halfway
Pork Tenderloins (fillets)	1 to 2 around 500 g each	Marinate or season as desired	MED	20 to 30 mins	Flip halfway
Sausages	8 to 12		MED	12 to 20 mins	Flip halfway

171

		SEAFOOD - grill			
Cod (other white fish fillets)	4 to 6 120 to 170 g each	Coat lightly with oil of choice, season as desired	HI	4 to 8 mins	Flip halfway
Halibut (fillets)	4 to 6 120 to 170 g each	Coat lightly with oil of choice, season as desired	HI	6 to 10 mins	Flip halfway
Salmon (fillets)	4 to 6 120 to 170 g each	Coat lightly with oil of choice, season as desired	HI	6 to 12 mins	Flip halfway
Scallops	8 to 12	Coat lightly with oil of choice, season as desired	HI	4 to 8 mins	Flip halfway
Prawns (large whole)	10 to 20	Coat lightly with oil of choice, season as desired	HI	5 to 10 mins	Flip halfway
Swordfish (steaks)	2 to 4 250 to 350 g each	Coat lightly with oil of choice, season as desired	HI	8 to 10 mins	Flip halfway
Tuna (steaks)	4 to 6 120 to 180 g each	Coat lightly with oil of choice, season as desired	HI	6 to 10 mins	Flip halfway

		VEGETABLES - grill			
Asparagus (spears)	10 to 16	Trim, coat lightly with oil of choice, season as desired	HI	8 to 12 mins	Toss Basket frequently
Peppers (bell peppers)	4 to 6	Trim, coat lightly with oil of choice, season as desired	HI	8 to 12 mins	Toss Basket frequently

		VEGETABLES - grill - continued			
Pak Choi	4 to 6	Coat lightly with oil of choice, season as desired	HI	8 to 14 mins	Toss frequently
Broccoli	2 heads	Cut into 2.5 cm pieces, coat lightly with oil of choice, season as desired	HI	10 to 18 mins	Toss frequently
Brussels Sprouts	800 g to 1 kg	Halved, trimmed, coat lightly with oil of choice, season as desired	HI	12 to 18 mins	Toss frequently
Corn on the Cob	4 to 6	Coat lightly with oil of choice, season as desired	HI	10 to 16 mins	Flip halfway
Aubergine (egg plant)	2 to 4	Sliced, coat lightly with oil of choice, season as desired	HI	8 to 12 mins	Flip halfway
Onions (white or red)	6 to 10 cut into halves	Peeled, cut in half, coat lightly with oil of choice, season as desired	HI	8 to 16 mins	Flip halfway
Portobello Mushrooms	6 to 10	Cleaned, coat lightly with oil of choice, season as desired	HI	8 to 12 mins	Flip halfway
Courgettes	2 to 4	Cut in quarters lengthwise, coat lightly with oil of choice, season as desired	HI	8 to 12 mins	Flip halfway

		FRUIT - grill			
Avocados	6 to 8	Cut in half, remove pits, coat grill with spray oil	HI	4 to 8 mins	Flipping not necessary
Bananas	4 to 6	Peel, cut in half lengthwise, coat grill with spray oil	HI	4 to 6 mins	Flip halfway
Lemons & Limes	2 to 4	Cut in half lengthwise	HI	4 to 5 mins	Flip halfway
Mangos	4 to 6	Cut in half, remove skins and pits, coat grill with spray oil	HI	6 to 10 mins	Flip halfway
Melon (triangles or slices)	6 to 8	Cut into triangles or slices 2 to 3 cm thick	HI	4 to 6 mins	Flip halfway
Pineapple	6 to 8	Cut into lengthways slices or circular slices 2 to 3 cm thick	HI	6 to 8 mins	Flip halfway
Stone Fruit (plums, apricots, peaches, etc)	6 to 8	Cut in half, remove pits, press cut-side down on grill grate	HI	6 to 8 mins	Flipping not necessary

		BREAD & CHEESE - grill			
Bread (bread roll, baguette, etc)	1 to 4 1 cm to 2 cm slices or lightly pressed halves	Brush or spray with oil of choice	HI	4 to 6 mins	Flip halfway
Halloumi Cheese	400 to 600 g	Cut in 1 to 2 cm thick slices	HI	4 to 6 mins	Flip halfway

FROZEN - Lid Closed - GRILL Mode

FROZEN POULTRY - frozen - grill					
Chicken Breasts (boneless)	4 to 6	Marinate or season as desired	MED	15 to 25 mins	Flip halfway
Chicken Thighs (bone-in)	4 to 8	Marinate or season as desired	MED	20 to 25 mins	Flip halfway
Burgers (all meats, veg and nut)	4 to 6	Season with salt and pepper	MED	8 to 12 mins	Flip halfway

FROZEN BEEF - frozen - grill					
Rump Steak	4 to 6	Season with salt and pepper	MED	18 to 25 mins	Flip halfway
Fillet Steak	4 to 6	Marinate or season as desired	MED	16 to 20 mins	Flip halfway
Sirloin Steak	4 to 6	Marinate or season as desired	MED	18 to 25 mins	Flip halfway
Ribeye Steak	4 to 6	Marinate or season as desired	MED	18 to 25 mins	Flip halfway

FROZEN SEAFOOD - frozen - grill					
Cod (other white flaky fish fillets)	4 to 6	Coat lightly with oil of choice	HI	14 to 18 mins	Flip halfway
Salmon	4 to 6		HI	14 to 18 mins	Flip halfway
Prawns (large whole)	10 to 20		HI	8 to 10 mins	Flip halfway

BBQ SMOKER - Lid Closed - SMOKER Mode

Do not add oil to the meat when smoking, or use very little.
Add pellets of choice to the smoke box before choosing SMOKER, TEMP, TIME,
then START/STOP to continue.

BEEF - smoker					
Joint (shoulder/silverside/topside/braising)	1.4 to 1.8 kg joint	Season as desired	120C	3 to 4 hours	Internal Temp 85C
Brisket	2 to 4 kg joint	Season as desired	120C	4 to 6 hours	Internal Temp 85C
Bone-In Short Ribs (Jacob's Ladder)	6 to 9 ribs 170 to 225 g each rib	Season as desired	135C	3 to 4 hours	Internal Temp 85C
Boneless Short Ribs (Jacob's Ladder)	6 to 9 ribs 170 to 225 g each rib	Season as desired	135C	2 to 3 hours	Internal Temp 85C

LAMB - smoker					
Shanks	2 to 4	Season as desired	120C	3 to 4 hours	Internal Temp 85C
Whole Leg	1.4 to 2.4 kg	Season as desired	120C	4 to 6 hours	Internal Temp 85C
Shoulder	1.6 to 2.4 kg	Season as desired	120C	4 to 6 hours	Internal Temp 85C

POULTRY - smoker					
Chicken (whole)	1.5 to 2.5 kg	Season as desired	190C	45 to 75 mins	Internal Temp 74C
Chicken (thighs)	6 to 8	Season as desired	190C	20 to 25 mins	Internal Temp 74C
Turkey (breasts)	1 to 1.5 kg	Season as desired	160C	25 to 40 mins	Internal Temp 74C Flip Halfway
Turkey (legs)	4 to 6	Season as desired	180C	45 to 60 mins	Internal Temp 74C
Duck (breasts)	4 to 6	Season as desired	180C	15 to 30 mins	Internal Temp 60C
Duck (legs)	4 to 6	Season as desired	190F	30 to 45 mins	Internal Temp 74C
Chicken (wings or drumsticks)	20 to 30 wings 8 to 16 drumsticks	Season as desired	190F	25 to 45 mins	Internal Temp 74C

PORK - smoker					
Shoulder	1.8 to 2.4 kg	Season as desired	120C	4 to 6 hours	Internal Temp 85C
Tenderloin (fillet)	2 to 4	Season as desired	150C	35 to 45 mins	Internal Temp 85C
Loin	1 to 1.5 kg	Season as desired	120C	3 to 4 hours	Internal Temp 85C
Baby Back Ribs	1 or 2 racks, cut in half	Season as desired	120C	60 to 75 mins	Internal Temp 85C
Spare Ribs	1 or 2 racks, cut in half	Season as desired	120C	2 to 3 hours	Internal Temp 85C

AIR FRYER - Lid Closed - AIR FRY Mode

FROZEN FOODS - air fry					
Chicken Cutlets (sliced breaded breast)	4 to 6		190C	14 to 16 mins	Flip halfway
Chicken Nuggets	12 to 24		190C	12 to 20 mins	Shake basket frequently
Vegan Nuggets	12 to 24		190C	10 to 18 mins	Shake basket frequently
Potato Wedges	500 to 800 g		190C	12 to 20 mins	Shake basket frequently
Chips (thick cut)	1 kg		190C	25 to 30 mins	Shake basket frequently
French Fries (thin cut	1 kg		190C	18 to 25 mins	Shake basket frequently
Chicken Dippers	15 to 30		190C	10 to 15 mins	Shake basket frequently
Chicken Kiev	4 to 6		190C	18 to 25 mins	Flip halfway
Battered Fish Fillets	4 to 6		190C	12 to 18 mins	Flip halfway
Fish Fingers	8 to 12		190C	10 to 15 mins	Flip halfway
Onion Rings	400 to 600 g		190C	10 to 12 mins	Shake basket frequently
Roast Potatoes	500 to 800 g		190C	20 to 25 mins	Shake basket frequently

UNFROZEN - PORK, LAMB, & BEEF - air fry					
Pork and Lamb Steaks	4 to 6	Coat lightly with oil of choice, season as desired	190C	15 to 20 mins	Flip halfway
Pork and Lamb Chops	4 to 6	Coat lightly with oil of choice, season as desired	190C	20 to 25 mins	Flip halfway
Pork Tenderloins (fillets)	1 to 2 500 to 700 g each	Coat lightly with oil of choice, season as desired	190C	20 to 25 mins	Flip halfway
Bacon	6 to 12 rashers		190C	10 to 12 mins	Flip halfway
Pork and Beef Sausages	6 to 12	Coat lightly with oil of choice, season as desired	190C	10 to 20 mins	Flip frequently

UNFROZEN - POULTRY - air fry					
Chicken Breast (boneless)	4 to 6	Coat lightly with oil of choice, season as desired	190C	10 to 15 mins	Flip halfway
Chicken (boneless thighs)	4 to 6	Coat lightly with oil of choice, season as desired	190C	18 to 25 mins	Flip halfway
Chicken (bone-in thighs)	4 to 6	Coat lightly with oil of choice, season as desired	190C	20 to 30 mins	Flip halfway
Chicken (wings or drumsticks)	15 to 25 wings 8 to 12 drumsticks	Coat lightly with oil of choice, season as desired	190C	30 to 45 mins	Flip halfway

179

UNFROZEN - VEGETABLES - air fry					
Asparagus (spears)	10 to 16	Coat lightly with oil of choice, season as desired	190C	8 to 12 mins	Flip halfway
Beetroots	4 to 6	Coat lightly with oil of choice, season as desired	190C	25 to 35 mins	Flip halfway
Capsicums (bell peppers/pep pers)	4 to 6	Coat lightly with oil of choice, season as desired	190C	8 to 14 mins	Flip halfway
Broccoli	2 heads	Coat lightly with oil of choice, season as desired	190C	10 to 15 mins	Shake basket frequently
Brussels Sprouts	800 g to 1 kg	Coat lightly with oil of choice, season as desired	190C	20 to 30 mins	Shake basket frequently
Carrots	1 kg	Coat lightly with oil of choice, season as desired	190C	20 to 25 mins	Shake basket frequently
Cauliflower	2 heads	Coat lightly with oil of choice, season as desired	190C	20 to 30 mins	Flip halfway
Corn on the Cob	4 to 6	Coat lightly with oil of choice, season as desired	190C	10 to 16 mins	Flip halfway
Kale (for chips)	250 to 400 g	Coat lightly with oil of choice, season as desired	190C	10 to 14 mins	Flip halfway
Green Beans	500 to 700 g	Coat lightly with oil of choice, season as desired	190C	15 to 20 mins	Shake basket frequently

UNFROZEN - VEGETABLES - air fry					
Mushrooms	500 g to 1 kg	Halved or Sliced coat lightly with oil of choice, season as desired	195C	10 to 15 mins	Flip halfway
Potatoes (Russet or other of choice)	1 kg	Wedges Cut in 2.5 cm wedges, toss lightly with oil of choice, season as desired	195C	25 to 35 mins	Shake basket frequently
	1 kg	Fries - Thin Cut toss lightly with oil of choice, season as desired	195C	20 to 25 mins	Shake basket frequently
	1 kg	Chips - Thick Cut toss lightly with oil of choice, season as desired	195C	25 to 30 mins	Shake basket frequently
	6 to 8 whole	Pierce with a fork	195C	45 to 50 mins	Flip halfway

*Oil of choice could be olive oil, vegetable, or any other, ideally, healthy cooking oil.
Shake the basket and flip as desired if not prompted by Woodfire.*

These charts are designed to provide information on preparing, cooking times, temperatures, and methods for various popular dishes. However, we appreciate that you may want to cook other meals not featured in these charts. To find the appropriate settings and methods, compare the dishes you'd like to cook with those in the charts and identify a suitable match. The following pages are dedicated to helping you record details of your chosen dishes. You can complete the chart rows accordingly. Then, as you experiment or tweak settings for the foods we've mentioned.

We have inserted olive oil throughout, but you might want to choose your preferred oil, such as vegetable oil or any healthy cooking oil. If the Woodfire doesn't prompt you, shake the basket and flip your ingredients as needed.

MY FOODS					
FOOD ITEM	WEIGHT/SIZE /NUMBER	FOOD PREPARATION	TEMP	TIME	METHOD

MY FOODS					
FOOD ITEM	WEIGHT/SIZE /NUMBER	FOOD PREPARATION	TEMP	TIME	METHOD

NOTES

NOTES

homechefbooks.com

Printed in Great Britain
by Amazon

41735045R00106